Christianity from the Ground Up

Christianity from the Ground Up

*How the Human Experience Reconciles
Christianity, Logic, and Science*

Ian Dodkins

FOREWORD BY
Kerry Walters

RESOURCE *Publications* · Eugene, Oregon

CHRISTIANITY FROM THE GROUND UP
How the Human Experience Reconciles Christianity, Logic, and Science

Copyright © 2024 Ian Dodkins. All rights reserved. Except for brief quotations in critical publications or reviews, no part of this book may be reproduced in any manner without prior written permission from the publisher. Write: Permissions, Wipf and Stock Publishers, 199 W. 8th Ave., Suite 3, Eugene, OR 97401.

Resource Publications
An Imprint of Wipf and Stock Publishers
199 W. 8th Ave., Suite 3
Eugene, OR 97401

www.wipfandstock.com

PAPERBACK ISBN: 978-1-6667-8182-3
HARDCOVER ISBN: 978-1-6667-8183-0
EBOOK ISBN: 978-1-6667-8184-7

VERSION NUMBER 01/16/24

All Scripture quotations, unless otherwise indicated, are taken from the Holy Bible, New International Version®, NIV®. Copyright ©1973, 1978, 1984, 2011 by Biblica, Inc.™ Used by permission of Zondervan. All rights reserved worldwide. www.zondervan.com The "NIV" and "New International Version" are trademarks registered in the United States Patent and Trademark Office by Biblica, Inc.™

Scripture quotations marked NASB® are taken from the New American Standard Bible®, Copyright ©2020 by The Lockman Foundation. Used by permission. All rights reserved. lockman.org

Scripture quotations marked NKJV are taken from the New King James Version®. Copyright © 1982 by Thomas Nelson. Used by permission. All rights reserved.

This book is dedicated to the people I have lost in my life:

To my brother Andrew; you had such a naturally kind heart.

To Vijay, my friend in Capoeira, you danced and moved so beautifully and kept us all happy despite having so much pain inside your heart—I am sorry we could not save you, but you saved us, and kept us together in our love for you.

To my father, who I'd hoped would be able to read this book, but you died on the day I finalized the draft. You were a great role model, a caring father and a dedicated, but thankfully not overly vocal, Christian.

And finally to my daughter Luena. I know you have my heart and mind, and with the hope that God gives me, I know one day we will be reunited. I pray that you will live life with a light heart, and joy in everything you do.

"One of the great agonies of life is that we are constantly trying to finish that which is unfinishable. Like David, we find ourselves having to face the fact that our dreams are not fulfilled. Life is a continual story of shattered dreams.

Mahatma Gandhi labored for years for the independence of his people. But Gandhi was assassinated, and died with a broken heart, because that nation that he wanted to unite ended up being divided between India and Pakistan as a result of the conflict between Hindus and Muslims. Woodrow Wilson dreamed a dream of a League of Nations, but he died before the promise was delivered.

The Apostle Paul talked about wanting to go to Spain. It was Paul's greatest dream to go to Spain, to carry the gospel there. Paul never got to Spain. He ended up in a prison cell in Rome. This is the story of life.

Our forebears used to sing about freedom. They dreamed of the day that they would be able to get out of the bosom of slavery, the long night of injustice. They thought about a better day as they dreamed their dream. They would say, 'I'm so glad the trouble don't last always. By and by, by and by, I'm going to lay down my heavy load.' So many died without having the dream fulfilled.

Each of you in some way is building a kind of temple. The struggle is always there. It gets discouraging sometimes. Some of us are trying to build a temple of peace. We speak out against war, we protest, but it seems that your head is going against a concrete wall. It seems to mean nothing. And so often, as you set out to build the temple of peace, you are left lonesome; you are left discouraged; you are left bewildered. Well, that is the story of life.

The thing that makes me happy is that I can hear a voice crying through the vista of time, saying: 'It may not come today or it may not come tomorrow, but it is well that it is within your heart. It's well that you are trying.' You may not see it. The dream may not be fulfilled, but it's good that you have a desire to bring it into reality. It's well that it's in your heart."

Adapted from Martin Luther King Jr.'s final address at Bishop Charles J. Mason Temple in Memphis, the day before his assassination, 3 April 1968[1]

---

1. Clayborne, *Autobiography Martin Luther King*, 340–41

Contents

Foreword by Kerry Walters | ix
Acknowledgements | xi
Introduction | xiii

1. Reproduction and Colonization | 1
2. The Benefits of Optimism | 21
3. Forgiveness | 35
4. The Crucifixion | 44
5. Happiness and Suffering | 62
6. Gratitude and Humility | 73
7. Knowledge, Love and Jealousy | 97
8. Do what is Possible | 107
9. Going to Church | 129
10. Fasting | 154
11. A Religious Experience | 167

Bibliography | 187

Foreword

THERE ARE MOMENTS IN a person's life in which all one's frustratingly loose ends come together, or at least show signs of beginning to do so. That moment came for Dr. Ian Dodkins as he sat nursing a coffee in a Portuguese café. His years of searching for meaning in life brought him to the revelatory point in which three truths, which undoubtedly had been slowly coalescing in his mind for some time, became clear: that logic has its limits, that a loving God exists, and that each human possesses a destiny.

It's commonplace to say that we live in an increasingly post-Christian culture. But the fact that traditional Christianity has lost a good deal of its currency doesn't mean that people no longer hunger for transcendent depth. Loss of faith in centuries old dogma and doctrine can be disconcerting, but it can also offer a liberating opportunity for fresh exploration and insight.

Dr. Dodkins' story is a spiritual odyssey in search of a new paradigm—one which led him to a Christianity stripped down, as he says, to the "fundamentals of [its] functional truth"—that I think speaks to the longing of many people. Part autobiography, part philosophical analysis, and part theological reflection, *Christianity from the Ground Up* is bound to provoke some controversy. But at the same time—and probably for many of the same reasons—it offers a sorely needed fresh perspective.

Prof. Kerry Walters

> BA, MA, PhD, Professor emeritus of Philosophy at Gettysburg College, Pennsylvania, USA.

> Author of Revolutionary Deists[1], Giving up god . . . to find God[2]. and many other award winning books, as well as the popular YouTube channel: Holy Spirit Moments, with Fr. Kerry Walters.

> 1. Walters, *Revolutionary Deists*
> 2. Walters, *Giving up god*

Acknowledgements

I THANK GOD EVERY day for life, for having enough food to live, and to be able to act and make a difference in this world. Most of all I thank God for loving me without inhibition. I am grateful you have given me the opportunity to write this book.

Thanks also go out to my dear friends in Malawi, Portugal, Northern Ireland, Wales and England for loving and encouraging me: just because I don't write to you doesn't mean I don't think about you and miss you. An especial thanks to my beautiful wife Eliza James. Eliza—you have huge strength, an enormous heart, are an intuitive Christian, and an inspirational singer. Also I would like to thank Malawi and the Malawian people for welcoming me into their arms and providing me a home. I would like to thank my sister Fiona Lay, who has cared for both my parents, while I've been neglecting my family responsibilities during my work and global travels.

In my life I have read extensively on philosophy and Christian history, and have been a scientist and scientific researcher. I am indebted to all those who have done sincere and diligent studies in these fields. Christian scholars and scientists have more in common than most realize, especially in the tireless work they do out of love, rather than money.

Introduction

I'M NOT YOUR TYPICAL Christian. I don't believe Jesus was the son of God, and a universal religion to me shouldn't be based on the mythology and beliefs of just one culture, albeit the diverse and rich culture emanating from Israel. I have worked in research science for many years, and hold a degree, Masters, and PhD. I have studied and fully support most of the modern theories of evolution. I believe the Earth is 4.5 billion years old, not 4,000 years old. I have seen dinosaur fossils and indeed studied evolution through fossils; I have seen the vestigial leg bones in whales that show how they had been land mammals which later returned to the oceans. I have seen pastors who promise miracles, yet have failed to produce them, and pastors who have shown miracles, only to be later proven as frauds. There are parts of the Bible I don't believe are literally true. There are parts of the Bible I find distasteful or even wrong. I know that many religions operated and still operate as a pervasive system of control and power, and have historically persecuted other religions. Yet, I am a Christian—and I know why I am a Christian.

I see no conflict between my values and the core values of Christianity. I see no conflict between science and Christianity; which many Christians and Scientists would both contest. For me, from my experiences in life, there are certain characteristics that a true spiritual religion would have. I believe this truth can be found within all of us. But why Christianity? It is a religion that fulfills the fundamental needs of us as both humans, and as individuals crying out for spiritual understanding and fulfillment. There are 2.6 billion Christians in the world today, out of a population of 8 billion. It's the most popular religion in the world. While it is cultural in many countries, enforcement of Christianity as a religion is extremely rare, so they must be finding something in Christianity. Am I a Christian because it's trendy, because I was brought up a Christian or because it benefits me?—No. While I can and will logically explain why I am a Christian, the real reason goes back to the effects of a religious experience I had many years ago, which overturned everything I thought I knew, and which I shall describe at the end of this book.

Christianity is far beyond just being a tool for living; even beyond the way to define our purpose. It contains some fundamental truth that can be difficult to see when we investigate it just academically or intellectually; though being a scientist I'll be giving many intellectual opinions. It doesn't matter to me where it comes from, or the minutia of this or that text. The underlying message of Christianity is very clear. We can know and understand that just serving our material bodies is neither our purpose nor is it ultimately fulfilling. I hope you enjoy this book, and get some value and enjoyment from this journey you are about to embark on with me. Even when you disagree with parts, which I fully expect you to do, I hope it stimulates you and will help you on your own personal journey. Maybe it will give you renewed strength in your life, deeper knowledge, or even just pause for reflection.

For non-christian readers, I want to assure you that I'm not writing as a christian apologist, nor is this book an attempt at conversion. What guided me in writing this book is that I have a strong background in science and critical thinking, and a strong interest in diverse religions and philosophy. Despite thinking deeply about religion and questioning a variety of different philosophical and religious beliefs, I was brought to Christianity through actual feelings and reflections on my own life as a whole, as well as a unique religious experience I had while an agnostic. My position on Christianity is probably not the Christianity that most Christians would ascribe to, but it contains the solid bedrock of perspectives, principles and values detailed by Jesus and St. Paul; principles that not only guide me, but which I now see to be self-evident in life. It's a Christianity that makes complete sense to me both intellectually and spiritually. I hope also for those Christians that are questioning their faith either due to terrible events in their life, because of questions over the Bible, or because of some Christian beliefs or Christian teachings they are wrangling with, that they can now feel content that they are raising questions; that they too are on a path of discovery and understanding. Ultimately what we need to arrive at is the truth that satisfies our doubts, brings confidence in our values, and brings us a resilience and long-lasting contentment in life.

I struggled determining which biblical version to use. For use of language and because I'm very familiar with the version, I have predominantly used the New International Version of the bible. Occasionally I have used the New King James Version (NKJV) or the New American Standard Bible (NASB) due to wording I felt was better in the context, or because the NIV does not contain the passage. At such times it is recorded in the footnotes.

Dr Ian Dodkins

1. Reproduction and Colonization

IN THIS FIRST CHAPTER I ask you to bear with me; the start of this book may seem a little science heavy. I do not see a conflict between science and Christianity. For you to understand why, and for those of you with a non-scientific background, I ask that you patiently let me discuss science. Conversely, for those who are not religious, I ask that you are patient while I detail the psycho-social and spiritual aspects of Christianity. Without at least gaining some insight into both science and religion, the purpose of this book will be wasted: which is to explain both logically and intuitively/experimentally, why I am a Christian and not specifically an atheist, agnostic, Hindu, Muslim, Jew, Stoic or indeed Taoist (though I can sympathize strongly and see value in all these beliefs). While most of this book is about Christianity, this initial chapter approaches from the other direction i.e. why not atheism or other religions.

The Purpose of Life

What is the purpose of life? This is a different question from what is the purpose of *your* life, which you feel may be specific to you. Here I'm asking, what is the purpose of the human species or indeed all living things? As a biologist the answer is quite simple. Life has no final goal, it is a process. Almost all living organisms have DNA (deoxyribonucleic acid). An exception are viruses, which use what's considered a more primitive molecule similar to DNA, called RNA (ribonucleic acid), and also 'prions' which are proteins that can reproduce themselves, though we don't yet know if we should classify prions as life. DNA is referred to as having a double-helix structure; two strands of molecules twirling around each other like a plait. The molecules, which are composed of nucleic acids, are strung along the DNA and code for different proteins in our body. A gene is a length of this DNA which can be used as a blueprint for making a protein which in turn is used to make our bodies cells, or components of those cells. Thus, features such as our hair colour, eye colour, height, that you have arms and ears, and your whole physical form, are all coded by genes. Environmental factors also have an influence, for example you may be shorter if you are malnourished as a child, but the base plan of your body and mind is determined by genes.

While Richard Dawkins popularized how genes work in the book The Selfish Gene[1], he also authored a parallel book but with a more scientific approach, called The Blind Watchmaker[2]. The former title unfortunately misrepresents evolution but the title was important not because of the word *Selfish* but because of the word *Gene*. The point being, that when we talk of *survival of the fittest* in evolution, we don't mean survival of the fittest individual, we mean survival of the fittest gene. A population of humans, or any species, is a mixture of genes, with many genes being similar or identical within the population. For example, you share genes with your mother and father, but you also share genes with your friend, or a random person in New Zealand, because you're human. Animals with hair will share similar genes; those genes that code for hair production. Some genes may vary because of mutations what have been passed on down that family line. For example, a grey squirrel has genes that code for gray fur, but a red squirrel genes which code for ginger fur. If this mutated gene is not detrimental to the survival and reproduction of that individual, and especially if it confers a survival or reproductive advantage for the individual, that gene will be passed on to your children and thus continue in the population. Thus the concept of the 'gene pool' and 'genetic diversity'. When we have sexual reproduction and produce a child, it is a mixture of the genes from the two parents.

Why do many organisms have two parents? Because animals are constantly fighting for survival against disease causing bacteria. Bacteria have very short life spans and they can adapt and evolve very quickly. Two people are attracted to each other for various reasons, but one of them is a compatible (i.e. different) immune systems. Immune systems are complex, and by two parents combining their genes they can produce children with an immune system where the child may have

---

1. Dawkins, *The Selfish Gene*
2. Dawkins, *The Blind Watchmaker*

increased resistance to a wide range of diseases. With several children there is more chance that some of them will fight off bacteria and thus survive to reproduce themselves, continuing the genes for this immune system, as well as preserving other genes carried by those individuals. While disease tends to be the main pressure on survival of larger organisms such as humans, other environmental pressures affect which genes survive and which don't, such as lack of food resources, necessity to run faster to out compete others in hunting food, genes for social interactions, and intelligence to outwit others.

What we call 'success' in biology is simply being able to reproduce i.e. for those genes to survive to another generation. For that we need to have survived all the hazards of the environment as we develop to sexual maturity, as well as attracting a mate such that we can produce young that will themselves survive. These two processes of survival and reproductions form the two types of evolution: natural selection and sexual selection. If your genes don't allow you to develop a functioning nervous system, it's unlikely you'll find food. You will thus be a victim of natural selection and die long before reproductive age. If you reach reproductive age, but all the females (or males) don't want to mate with you because you have tiny hands or a strange face, or any characteristics that may be considered less attractive than those around you, then you probably won't reproduce. In both cases, the genes that code for these characteristics are likely to die out and be removed from the gene pool.

There are some basic trends in evolution: for example evolution to be multicellular is believed to have occurred at least 52 times, and it is currently believed to be because multicellularity provides a more efficient method of removing waste metabolites (products) from cells. Life on Earth has passed through five major global extinction events, and from an atmosphere of zero oxygen, rapidly increasing when photosynthesizers evolved (probably as a competitive strategy to create a toxic oxygen environment), to around 30 percent oxygen at the time of the dinosaurs, then down to 21 percent oxygen in our current time. During this period, there has been a tendency for increasing complexity in individual organisms i.e. single celled bacteria becoming colonial groups of cells, then forming multicellular organisms with specialized cells making up organs within the animal's body. Complexity in the physiology of larger plants and animals, as well as in the internal structure of bacteria, occurred because there has been evolutionary time to develop that complexity. Indeed, because evolution is produced by alterations to genes through mutation (as well as viruses sometimes mixing up our genes) the progression of evolution is usually dependent on *pre-adaptation* i.e. similar structures that with a small change or mutation can serve a different function. For example, for humans to be able to evolve speech they required good breath control, and it has been suggested that this may have arisen due to a previous adaptation to swimming in water[3]. Why do we have a hard skull close to the surface, yet internal bones in the body? Because our skeleton developed from the skeletons of early fish-like chordates that had similar structure. Although evolution may seem slow, sudden or harsh changes in environment can produce strong selective pressures, as occurred with the major extinctions. Also, although mutations are believed to gradually occur at random, even the mutation of a single gene can lead to dramatic changes in body plan. For example the Hox gene, which determines the body plan, can make an insect grow another pair of legs.

Ecological complexity also increased with time. For example, when plants evolve and a forest develops, plants can attract insects with nectar for pollination, but then birds can feed off the insects, and snakes may then feed off the bird eggs: the more that new species evolve, the more ecological structure develops, the more opportunities there are for species to adapt and evolve to the new food sources and the new physical habitat structure.

Despite evolution depending on a species' evolutionary history, and there being some basic trends toward multicellularity and increased complexity, the second major misconception about evolution, is that it has direction[4]. Evolution is simply an adaption to the current environment; that is the weather, food resources, competition for resources, our social environment etc. Our gene pool changes in response to these environmental pressures, but the environment is not stable, so this is an ongoing process. If there is geographic separation between members of a species and they are under different environmental conditions, the evolutionary divergence can be large enough that, over time, they cannot reproduce with each other, and become separate species. Indeed the simple definition of a species is "individuals that can reproduce with each other and produce fertile young". When there is speculation of how humans will evolve in the next 1 million years, it is simply for amusement than

3. Morgan, *Aquatic Ape Hypothesis*
4. Ridley, *The Red Queen*

for any scientific understanding. Unless you can accurately predict the environment over that time, the ways we will adapt to that environment, how human populations will interbreed, potential geographical isolation, social developments over that period, and the fluctuation in all these factors, such speculation is pointless. With humans having such a rapidly changing and complex political and social environment, such changes are impossible to know.

Thus, as the environment changes, so do the creatures that survive in that environment, and so do the genes of that population; and sexual selection also factors in to some aspects of the genes which survive. Natural selection has been shown consistently in various studies, one of the most famous being with bird species in the Galapagos islands. On these isolated islands in the pacific ocean, the microclimate for each island affects the plants which grow on each of the islands. While the sparrows in these islands are all the same species, the islands are sufficiently isolated from each other that the bird populations for each island don't reproduce with those of other islands. Because of the lack of interbreeding between the populations, and because of the different microclimates, the shape of the beak of the different populations varies. Some have short broad beaks for cracking harder seeds that predominate on their islands, others have narrow pointy beaks that are useful for accessing smaller softer seeds. This is determined by the microclimate, that effects the predominant food source, which confers a survival advantage on certain beak types.

It is not just environmental pressures which act like a sieve, filtering out genes that are detrimental to survival and reproduction, the quirks of sexual selection also have an effect. Some of our physical or behavioral traits can be considered attractive to potential mates because they are an indicator that we have genes beneficial for survival or for bringing up our young; if due to these characteristics they choose to reproduce with us, this is sexual selection. For example, symmetry in organisms tends to indicate that we are resistant to disease or injury, since disease and injury often affects one side of the body more than the other. Thus symmetry is a typical trait that is considered visually attractive in many species (internally we are not at all symmetrical, with our liver on our right, and out heart and stomach left of centre). Also, large muscles may indicate a greater capacity to protect young from a physical threat, kindness may indicate that we will care for our young or that we can work well in a social group. However, in selecting mates these are just indicative features: they don't operate like natural selection whereby an organism dies and thus logically cannot later reproduce, they only suggest to a mate that there may be a benefit. If the environment changes, a famine results, and the large muscly man starves to death because he has insufficient food, that benefit does not get realized.

I said quirks of sexual selection, because some selected traits can have more socially agreed value and indeed may even inhibit survival success. In some cases, it could be a demonstration that the individual is strong enough to survive despite an inhibition of success, a form of showing off or 'peacocking', or just a developed convention of what is attractive and gains social status. The term 'peacocking' comes from the large colourful but otherwise useless tail of the male peacock. It is saying, "I can get more resources than just those for my survival; I can grow and maintain this unwieldy tail and also fight off attackers despite this hindrance". For sexual selection to produce a genetic trait ubiquitous within the species, such as a peacock tail, this sexual preference would have to develop over many generations until it becomes a characteristic. Early sexual selection in humans is considered to have effected our development of facial hair (beards in men), penis size (which are relatively large in relation to body size compared to other primates), and breasts (which are flat when not breastfeeding, in other primates). In modern human society such peacocking can also involve not just our bodily features, but social activities that entail a cost, such as buying an unnecessarily expensive car or watch, piercing your tongue, or giving a very visual display of a donation to charity.

This book wasn't written to justify evolutionary theory; there are plenty of books which address this specifically, and biology as a science backs up evolutionary theory. For most evolutionary scientists, they have no interest in arguing about evolution or the age of the Earth with people outside their own study because such critics are generally uneducated in the real scientific basis of evolutionary theory, and are unwilling to change their views because of religiously held convictions. A discussion based on logic is not going to change the mind of someone who does not accept logic. However, while the theory of evolution has been repeatedly tested, has a solid logical basis, and encompasses a gigantic amount of supporting evidence, sometimes there are justified criticisms of specific processes of evolution. Pre-adaptation of certain features leading to others can be questioned and intermediate examples between related species are often not available in the fossil record. Indeed, progress in DNA analysis is revealing that some of our assumptions about relationships between physically similar species is not quite right, and helping us greatly improve our understanding of these evolutionary changes, which previously was guessed at mostly through physical, anatomical and fossil analysis. Thus, it is important as scientists to recognize that just because a certain evolutionary development makes sense, does not mean it happened in that way, and we need to clearly distinguish what makes a good story from what we have direct evidence for. For those critical of evolution, it is also important to realize that not having all transitional species, nor sufficient causal links between some pre-adaptation and resultant mutations, in no way suggests evolution is a flawed theory. As with all science, we learn more as we test and investigate, and what we know about evolution is far in advance of what Charles Darwin originally suggested in his ground-breaking book On the Origin of Species[5]. Selective breeding of animals and plants has been on-going for more than 10,000 years, and the physical and anatomical relationships between species and generations of a single species was widely recognized even in 1859 when On the Origin of Species was written. However, it took until 1953 for Watson, Crick and Franklin to discover that DNA was the mechanism by which evolution occurred, greatly supporting the theory of evolution and leading to modern molecular studies in genetics and evolution.

A third misconception about evolution is that genetic 'success' means anything beyond a narrowly scientific and simplistic definition. Genetic success has no intrinsic value. Evolution is valueless, and is simply a logical conclusion: The more able a gene is to survive and reproduce, the more of that gene there will be in the gene pool. The less able a gene is to survive and reproduce, the more it will decrease within the gene pool. There is no inferred purpose, meaning, or implied benefit behind this process. Indeed, a population cannot evolve and adapt to a new or changing environment if some genes, those that are detrimental to survival, don't decrease in frequency and die out. As a population we are not in this genetic battle; evolution operates at a mechanistic level beyond our human interpretation of 'what is good' or 'what is bad'. It is simply a direct physical (as in physics) response. A comparison I like to make is that calling a gene 'selfish' is very similar to when we burn charcoal, and the carbon in the charcoal binds with oxygen, releasing energy. Do we call the carbon 'selfish' because it has grabbed hold of the oxygen? Evolution is simply a process, and it neither has purpose nor in most cases, direction. It's more akin to a series of environmental

5. Darwin and Leonard, *Origin of Species*

'sieves'. If those genes (or combination of genes) mean that individual will not survive to reproduce, those genes will decrease in frequency in the population, being sieved out by the environmental or competitive pressures, and may even die out. Maybe the environment may change, and those few genes may then make a come back and begin to increase again. Indeed, we know the environment isn't stable, and this is what actually happens. For example, human height has tended to increase in recent human history, probably due to sexual selection, with women often preferring taller men. Height is a good indicator of strength, and that the the male has a good ability to obtain resources. However, during periods of famine, these tall men cannot support that larger structure and smaller men are actually more likely to survive, as they need less food. An example of this genetic selection can be found with human pygmy tribes, that are inevitably found as the native humans in the interior of continents; there being fewer food resources than in coastal areas.

Whether we're a bacterium, a lion, or a human, there is a natural biological tendency: reproduction and colonization. Reproduction, because organisms that enjoy sex and who's young get to reproductive age have genes that contributed to the gene pool. Colonization, because organisms reproduce at a rate such that they will completely fill the local environment to the point it can no longer sustain them. Thus, organisms at this stage are pushed to either out-compete others for the limited resources or must colonize new territories to get resources.

Studies of evolution have been associated with eugenics. However, it's important to understand that science is value-free. Science doesn't tell us what we should or should not do, it just tells us what is. Unfortunately politicians get hold of science and because of a personal opinion or belief, apply their own values to it, and convince others of what they should or should not do. The Nazis in second world war Germany and their eugenic experiments and belief in 'purifying' a race is a prime example. Under this political theory, blonde haired white skinned people were a superior race of humans, and other races should be eliminated if we are to have a strong human race. Nazis in Germany rounded up and executed Jews, black people, mentally and physically disabled people, Jehovah's Witnesses, Gypsys, and homosexuals during the 'holocaust' (1933–1945). A knowledgeable scientist would point out that we cannot judge what are *good genes* or *bad genes*; evolution is a process which occurs relative to a varied environment. More importantly, reducing the genes in the human gene pool is a problem for future adaptations to a changing environment, and thus for survival of any species. Genetic diversity in a population is a definite advantage for long term survival of a species. For example, it was noticed that in some parts of sub-Saharan Africa a trait of getting curved instead of fully disk shaped red blood cells became prevalent in some human populations. This was detrimental to the transport of oxygen in the blood and could lead to sickle cell anaemia. The reason for the high numbers of people in these areas with sickle cell anaemia at first puzzled scientists, but then they discovered this trait had a selective advantage in protecting against the fatal disease of Malaria. The Black Death plague killed about a third of the population in Europe between 1347 and 1353, but this created such a strong selective pressure on the population, post Black Death, health and disease resistance increased. From a biological and scientific perspective, there is no intrinsic or moral value associated with the survival or removal of genes—it is a process. If, as humans, we are to consider the survival of the human race to be of value, we would do well to maintain genetic diversity.

Religion

All human civilizations have developed religion. A pre-agricultural hunter gatherer society built the first known temple at Göbekli Tepe in Turkey 12,000 years ago. At the time all humans were living as hunter-gatherers, taking another 2,000 years before developing settled agriculture.

Some historians and researchers believe religion developed as a social tool, serving the purpose of organizing humans at a scale larger than the village. If people have similar values and conform, they can operate better and cooperate as a unit, overcoming more disorganized local tribes. By having a fictional deity or deities, we don't have to support the personal politics of a leader, who others in the group will become jealous of and try to dispose. Instead the fictional deity is someone outside the tribe, who everyone can revere, and who requires us to uphold a set of fixed shared values. Of course, leaders will still try and manipulate the concept or values of that deity to fit in with their own plans, or pretend a unique link or voice from the deity so that they can have more leadership and control over others. This human manipulation of religion or personal interpretation of a deity's desire has happened in many religions, in the past and today, including in Christianity.

Religion may also function as part of the biological imperative for reproduction. Many religions promote large families, prohibit the use of contraception, and have social pressure for marrying. Some religions also encourage colonization, dominance over neighbouring tribes, and conversion of neighbouring tribes. A God who promises land, and justifies the subjugation of their neighbors, has a clear role in the biological imperative of colonization. Restriction of marriage outside the group also serves a biological purpose, both through reducing the chances of other genes 'diluting' the tribe, and through preventing descent within the tribe due to outside religious ideas disturbing the structure of authority or causing ideological clashes. Even today resentment between religions over ideological differences (such as eating restricted foods, polygamy, ownership of holy sites, or interpretations of history) can be a source of conflict between religious groups.

Religion can thus be used as a biological tool to improve our genetic survival at the cost of others, to dominate and subdue others, to gain status in our social network, and to unify people in a single objective, even if that objective is unethical. Religious wars in history aren't just occasional, they are common place. Having lived in Northern Ireland, I understand that what is considered a religious war is usually a fight over resources between two groups, identifying themselves through religion to help clearly separate their tribe from the enemy tribe; based on ideology, territorial origin, or a politicized version of their history. Undoubtedly much of religion is simply a mechanism for the animal imperative of reproduction and colonization, driven by genes that have evolved through being successful at reproduction and colonization. Even the apparently virtuous behaviour of an individual can be considered a visible signal to the group that you are a good individual and thus the group should support you, since it is to their benefit. These virtuous behaviors can be helping members of your own group, or can be slander, murder, and theft directed toward the enemy of the group.

Personally, I cannot accept any part of a religion or religious practice that clearly establishes a separate in-group (the religion or community) and out-group (enemy of the religion or other community), that seeks to persecute individuals, or that focuses on reproduction and colonization as a religious goal. These are all biological imperatives dressed up as spirituality. I believe a true religion must have a spiritual requirement that goes beyond our biological needs and desires: beyond wars for resources, beyond reproduction, beyond money, beyond food. I also believe most people don't want a religion who's purpose is to serve their animal needs, or to make them feel safe and accepted in their tribal in-group, but are seeking something further, beyond their biological nature, to something profound and of spiritual value; something that takes them away from these base needs, something greater than their community or tribe, and a perspective on life that gives them spiritual fulfillment.

But isn't Christianity just serving the biological needs of reproduction and colonization? Doesn't it have it's own in-group and out-group, with church communities prioritizing themselves and demonizing others? The Old Testament has considerable material where God asks the Jews to persecute neighbouring peoples and tribes:

> When the Lord your God brings you into the land you are entering to possess and drives out before you many nations—the Hittites, Girgashites, Amorites, Canaanites, Perizzites, Hivites and Jebusites, seven nations larger and stronger than you, and when the Lord your God has delivered them over to you and you have defeated them, then you must destroy them totally. Make no treaty with them, and show them no mercy.[6]

> However, in the cities of the nations the Lord your God is giving you as an inheritance, do not leave alive anything that breathes. Completely destroy them—the Hittites, Amorites, Canaanites, Perizzites, Hivites and Jebusites—as the Lord your God has commanded you. Otherwise, they will teach you to follow all the detestable things they do in worshiping their gods, and you will sin against the Lord your God.[7]

Early on in the Old Testament, in God's covenant with Abraham, God says "Then I will make my covenant between me and you and will greatly increase your numbers."[8], and "I will make you very fruitful. I will make nations of you, and kings will come from you. I will establish my covenant as an everlasting covenant between me and you and your descendants after you for the generations to come, to be your God and the God of your descendants after you. The whole land of Canaan, where you now reside as a foreigner, I will give you and your descendants after you, and I will be their God."[9] and "I will make your descendants numerous as the stars in the sky and will give them all these lands, and through your

---

6. Deut 7:1–2
7. Deut: 20:16–18
8. Gen 17:2
9. Gen 17:6–8

offspring all nations on earth will be blessed."[10] God promised Moses land that would be taken by force "I will establish your borders from the Red Sea to the Mediterranean Sea, and from the desert to the Euphrates River. I will give into your hands the people who live in the land, and you will drive them out before you."[11]

In Islam, between 622 to 632 the Prophet Muhammad led several military attacks, initially and primarily against his own tribe in Mecca, to force conversion, and then against three Jewish tribes in Medina, Banu Qaynuqa, and Banu Nadir, then finally the Jewish fortress at Khaybar. He also sent his military forces to attack pagan tribes in the Byzantine Empire and Ghassanids in Northern Arabia. Most of the Arabian peninsula became subjugated under Islam. After Prophet Muhammad's death imperial Islamic expansion continued through war for over 1,000 years, through the establishment of Caliphates (a government under an Islamic steward) all across: North Africa, Iberia (Spain and Portugal), the Arabian Peninsula, Turkey, other areas in the Middle East, India, South East Asia, and East Africa. Within Islam war is justified when fighting in self-defence, in defense of one's faith, or if fighting on behalf of those whose rights have been violated.

While Christianity has a commandment against killing, between 1095 and 1291 both common people and Knights embarked on the Crusades to take back the Holy lands of Jerusalem from the Muslims—or at least they justified the Crusades under this guise: the Crusades started with Pope Urban II encouraging military support for the Byzantine Empire (the remains of the Roman Empire), but cascaded into a much broader campaign. There was an initial holy "People's Crusade" of peasants, initiated by Peter the Hermit, which ended in their own slaughter, but then there were hugely successful knights campaigns in which the knights were mostly interested in pillaging and grabbing land, and slaughtering men, women and children as they conquered; although some had religious motivations having been told that joining the Crusades would mean their sins were forgiven. Lasting around 200 years the Crusades were disparate, including the liberation of the Iberian peninsula in 1147. Jerusalem was surrendered by Muslim al-Kamil (barring some Islamic holy sites) in the Treaty of Jaffa on 18 February 1229, after the 6th and final crusade led by Fredrich II (Italian born,

10. Gen 26:4
11. Exod 23:31

but titled at various times King of Germany, Italy, Sicily and then finally King of Jerusalem).

Europeans are also no stranger to the inter-denominational religious war. Between 1524 and 1648 Catholic and Protestant countries fought political battles, throughout Europe. The Thirty Years War (1618–1648) resulted in one third of the protestant population in Germany being slaughtered—a casualty rate twice that of World War One. The remnants of the Protestant and Catholic conflict even continued as far as the Irish Republican Army (Catholic) and Ulster Defense Force (Protestant) terrorism during *The Troubles* in Northern Ireland (1960–1998).

We can clearly see that religion is used as a tool to unify nations and groups in war against others. Some apologists would say that it wasn't religion, but instead politicians and political power that was using religion as a cover. However, there is no doubt that established religious institutions have instigated, funded and led conflicts throughout the world. There is strong evidence that religion is a tribal tool for war; but this isn't the whole story.

If reproduction and colonization is the purpose of religion, why does celibacy appear as a practice in Hinduism, Jainism, Buddhism and Christianity? Why don't Catholic priests marry; and by implication don't have sex or children? Judaism and Islam on the whole denounce celibacy, with a notable exception of the Jewish Essenes who practiced it. Christian monks and nuns also practice celibacy, with them being wholly devoted to God. Celibacy serves as an active statement that spirituality is more important than the biological desires of the body, and that the mind and spirit should have authority above basic animal needs.

St. Paul writes "It is good for a man not to have sexual relations with a woman. But since sexual immorality is occurring, each man should have sexual relations with his own wife, and each woman with her own husband. The husband should fulfill his marital duty to his wife, and likewise the wife to her husband. The wife does not have authority over her own body but yields it to her husband. In the same way, the husband does not have authority over his own body but yields it to his wife. Do not deprive each other except by mutual consent and for a time, so that you may devote yourself in prayer. Then come together again so that Satan will not tempt you because of your lack of self control. I say this as a concession, not as a command."[12]

12. 1 Cor 7:1

From this we can clearly see that the ideal is not to have sex, but if you have the desire for sex you should marry, and sex isn't something you indulge in, but is a gift to your husband or wife; a gift you are expected to provide as part of the marriage contract. In the Bible Adam and Eve are commanded by God to fill the Earth, and God promised land to both Abraham and Moses. Many Bible scholars point out that this command and those promises are not to us all; but only to Adam and Eve, Abraham, and Moses, respectively, and at a specific time. Paul also states "Now to the unmarried and the widows I [Paul] say: It is good for them to stay unmarried, as I do."[13] So clearly it is not for Christians to simply be reproducing.

Within the New Testament we are asked to treat foreigners well, and offer hospitality, as well as to look after those worse off than ourselves: "You shall treat the stranger who sojourns with you as the native among you, and you shall love him as yourself."[14] Unlike Islam, where the wife is expected to take the religion of the husband (which often results in Muslim parents restricting the marriage of a daughter to a non-Muslim), Christians are not prohibited from marrying those of other faiths: "If any brother has a wife who is not a believer and she is willing to live with him, he must not divorce her. And if a woman has a husband who is not a believer and he is willing to live with her, she must not divorce him. For the unbelieving husband has been sanctified through his wife and the unbelieving wife has been sanctified through the believing husband. Otherwise your children would be unclean, but as it is, they are holy. But if the unbeliever leaves, let it be so."[15] This clearly is not an attempt to create an isolated in-group or tribe for competitive advantage, that would see other religions as an out-group. Instead it shows a confidence in the religion itself to 'sanctify' or influence others without force, allowing those of other faiths to determine their own fate regarding their own religious beliefs.

Thus, while there can be some indications in the Bible, particularly in the Old Testament, that the Jewish and Christian God is there to benefit the tribe that follows him, through benefiting their reproduction and colonization, overwhelmingly Jesus as found in the New Testament calls for us to renounce such material desires: "So therefore, any one of you

---

13. 1 Cor 7:8
14. Lev 19:34
15. 1 Cor 7:1–16

who does not renounce all that he has cannot be my disciple"[16]; "And he said to all "If anyone would come after me, let him deny himself and take up his cross daily and follow me"[17]; "Sell your possessions and give to the needy. Provide yourself with moneybags that do not grow old, with a treasure in heaven that does not fail, where no thief approaches and no moth destroys."[18] Paul wrote to the Galatians a very clear statement of self-denial and renouncement of all worldly ideas of gain: "I have been crucified with Christ. It is no longer I who live, but Christ who lives in me. And the life I now live in the flesh I live by faith in the Son of God, who loved me and gave himself for me."[19] and Jesus makes clear statements about not focusing on worldly wealth nor putting your family (genes) before spirituality: "No one can serve two masters, for either he will hate the one and love the other, or he will be devoted to the one and despise the other. You cannot serve God and Money."[20]; "If anyone comes to me and does not hate his own father and mother and wife and children and brothers and sisters, and yes, even his own life, he cannot be my disciple."[21] Now this may seem to be extreme and even contradict other parts of the Bible, for example honoring your mother and father (in the Ten Commandments), but in the context in which it is written, it is simply an emphasis that God and spirituality come before all worldly (biological) needs and desires.

Through celibacy, turning the other cheek[22], not focusing on material wealth, forgiving others, welcoming strangers, and allowing intermarriage, we can see that Christianity in the Bible, whether or not in practice, is not about reproduction and colonization i.e. not about furthering our genetic heritage. Even when religion may be considered as virtue signaling to our in-group, to be seen as a good person such that the group will protect or reward us, Jesus instead says "When you give to someone in need, don't do as the hypocrites do—blowing trumpets in the synagogues and streets to call attention to their acts of charity! I tell you the truth, they have received all the reward they will ever get. But when you give to the needy, do not let your left hand know what your right

16. Luke 14:33
17. Luke 9:23
18. Luke 12:33
19. Gal 2:20
20. Matt 6:12
21. Luke 14: 26
22. Luke 6:29

hand is doing, so that your giving may be in secret. Then your Father, who sees what is done in secret, will reward you."[23]

Christianity, especially through the words of Jesus and St. Paul, resolutely denounces that we search for material gain and social status. We need not directly condemn money or worldly things as evil, but instead clearly understand that this is not our focus and we should not serve them i.e. your actions should not be for material gain, but should for the service of God. We have bodies and can use money as tools to achieve God's work, but they are not an end in themselves. The theologian and philosopher Søren Kierkegaard emphasized the apparently unethical but very important Old Testament story where Abraham is called by God to sacrifice his own son: "Then God said, 'Take your son, your only son, whom you love—Isaac—and go to the region of Moriah. Sacrifice him there as a burnt offering on a mountain I will show you.'"[24] It was clear to Kierkegaard[25] that Christianity is not a religion which is there to fulfill our needs and desires, nor a tool for our material benefit (what he termed the *aesthetic*), nor even a set of ethical guidelines, but instead something spiritual for which our material wants and needs must drop away, such that we serve God. Truly we are aiming for something beyond the mundane; beyond the material; beyond human desires; beyond reproduction and colonization. We are aiming for something profound and complete, and resting entirely within God.

Before leaving this chapter, I wanted to make a brief comparison of Stoicism and Christianity. This is because they undoubtedly influenced each other[26, 27] and I personally feel a strong admiration and affinity to it. Thus I feel I must justify why I am principally a Christian and not a Stoic.

Stoicism's start, around 300 BC, is credited to the Ancient Greek, Zeno. Notable figures shortly after also contributed significantly to Stoicism, such as the Greek slave Epictetus (50–135 AD), the Roman Seneca the Younger (4 BC– 65 AD) and the Roman Emperor Marcus Aurelius (121–180 AD). There are three basic principles of Stoicism. The first is to focus your energy and thoughts on what you can control, and not waste time on what you cannot control; thus being more efficient in your use of time and not being anxious about things you cannot change (such as

23. Mat 6:2–4
24. Gen 22:2
25. Kierkegaard, Fear and Trembling
26. Rasimus et al., Stoicism in Early Christianity
27. Engberg-Pedersen, Paul and the Stoics

the past, or other people's behaviour). The second is to live with *Arete*. Arete is an ancient Greek term meaning excellence, and in Stoicism it implies that you should live with virtue i.e. to achieve the ideal virtuous person that you can be, positively contributing to society, regardless of your role in society, be that Emperor or slave. Health, wealth and pleasure are neither good nor bad, and can be enjoyed but are not an end in themselves. Instead the pursuit of virtue and aiming for the model ideal of your ideal self is the objective, and will bring happiness. The third principle is personal responsibility. We often blame outside events for our unhappiness or dissatisfaction, but Stoicism states that it is our judgement of these events that make us unhappy. When someone insults us, we can feel offended, but maybe instead we should see that those words don't really change who we are unless we let them. Instead we can understand that the insult reflects more on the character of the person who gave the insult than on us, and we do not have to be manipulated by these external factors. Instead, we can understand that only our own virtue will make us happy or sad. Another comparison may be a sports game: it should not make us less happy because we lost, because the crowd booed us, or because our captain has decided to throw us off the team. What should determine our happiness is only that which is under our control: whether we tried our best. We have personal responsibility to live up to our virtuous ideals, and we should not blame others for things that we have control over: we cannot blame others for making us angry (that is our emotional response), or not giving us the job because they judged us inadequate for the role (whether they were right or wrong, we only have control over our response, not their decision).

With Jesus and Paul being around when Seneca was alive, they were both undoubtedly aware of this popular Roman philosophy. Stoicism believes in the *logos*, which is a fundamental principal of reason in the universe, pervading and animating the universe. In Greek it means *word*, and is the same term used to describe Jesus "In the beginning was the Word [logos], and the Word was with God, and the Word was God. He was with God in the beginning."[28] Paul even directly preached to Stoics when he went to Athens in Greece:

> "A group of Epicurean and Stoic philosophers began to debate with him [Paul]. Some of them asked, 'What is this babbler trying to say?' Others remarked, 'He seems to be advocating

28. John 1:1-2

foreign gods.' They said this because Paul was preaching the good news about Jesus and the resurrection. Then they took him and brought him to a meeting of the Areopagus, where they said to him, 'May we know what this new teaching is that you are presenting? You are bringing some strange ideas to our ears, and we would like to know what they mean.'"[29]

Shortly afterwards in the Bible, Paul also references the Stoic poet, Aratus, who was a student of the Stoic Zeno.

Similarities between Stoicism and Christianity include not having a focus on worldly wealth and status, not being flamboyant with worship or one's own presentation, and the importance of pursuing virtuous behaviour. Indeed St. Paul's life is a paragon of Stoicism in his asceticism, not complaining about his personal conditions, and in facing difficulties, such as his imprisonment, with fortitude and even contentment.

Many believe Stoicism is atheistic, and indeed many modern Stoics are atheist, however Zeno believed that God was the reasoning universe itself, and both Epictetus and Seneca believed in the Roman God (Zeus) as creator and ruler of the universe. In general early Stoics believed in a single creator God, but not that this God was omnipotent, but more a part of nature, or even subject to the laws of nature, as well as subject to human-like emotional states. The Christian God is omnipotent and undoubtedly more personal, having a personal relationship with each of us. Christianity accepts despair and desperation as part of the human condition much more readily, and requests us to comfort each other and trust in God, whereas Stoicism would primarily make an appeal to logic. Possibly Stoicism is more suitable to the intellectually inclined, that can logically reflect on situations in order to reduce their suffering; though this didn't help with the Stoic called Dionysius the Renegade, a student of Zeno. Later in life, when he suffered great eye pain, he abandoned Stoicism and instead became a Hedonist.

Christianity rarely asks us to only apply logic to a situation, but instead to trust in God. Indeed the bible regularly illustrates that faith is more important then logic. For example, Moses parting the Red Sea: "Then Moses stretched out his hand over the sea, and all that night the Lord drove the sea back with a strong east wind and turned it into dry land. The waters were divided, and the Israelites went through the sea on dry ground, with a wall of water on their right and on their left."[30];

29. Acts 17: 18-20
30. Exod 14:21-29

and when Elijah outruns a chariot: "So Elijah said, 'Go and tell Ahab, 'Hitch up your chariot and go down before the rain stops you." The power of the Lord came on Elijah and, tucking his cloak into his belt, he ran ahead of Ahab all the way to Jezreel."[31]

While Stoics do believe they are serving God in line with a natural pattern, Stoic concepts of ethics tend to be self determined or socially determined. This can be appealing for a modern audience, with relativistic moral values. Instead, Christianity focuses on service to God, and a more clearly defined ethical code. For example, the King Leonidas I of Sparta (a city state of Greece) believed the young Spartans training for war could be inspired to virtue, service and glory through teaching Stoic philosophy. Conversely Christianity condemns violence, and while recognizing that some professions such as soldiers, prostitutes and tax collectors may not be honourable, forgiveness of sins would be an important part of dealing with this rather than accepting it and trying simply to be as virtuous as possible in such a profession (as a Stoic would). In the modern age of social media, it is easy to get sucked in by political arguments and shifting social opinions that persuade us one way or another, and before we know it we are subverting God's command to love one another, or the Christian requirement to treat each other equally. If we do not carefully reflect on the values we follow, the society in which we live is likely to choose those values for us.

Within Stoicism, the concept of determining what is under our control and what isn't produces an acceptance of reality as it is, which can bring comfort. In Christianity instead we accept that we will suffer if we make a stand against an unjust society. While Stoics are known for being able to resist persecution with fortitude, such as when the master of Epictetus broke Epictetus' leg for amusement, it is not common for Stoics to martyr themselves for their beliefs. The Stoic view point is more likely to be *I cannot change society on my own, and since it is out of my control, I should simply do what is within my control*. However, often there is friction between what is sensible and what is just; in Christianity a deep faith can carry you through that. Stoics were materialists, and believed logic should be applied rather than trusting in supernatural intervention. Maybe this is true, but maybe it produces a degree of passivity and acceptance that Christianity (rightly or wrongly) defies. The illogical and non-materialist declaration of faith through martyrdom

---

31. 1 Kgs 18:45–46

is not characteristic of Stoicism, but is certainly characteristic of early Christianity. Indeed Christian martyrdom probably had profound effects on Saul, himself a persecutor of Christians, who was later transformed in faith to become the most influential Christian in history after Jesus. The strong faith required for martyrdom can seem like a hopeless and pointless sacrifice at the time, but that faith can transform later people and societies. It may even have affected the Roman Emperor Constantine, who stopped Christian persecution in Rome when he himself became a Christian. This issued in the widespread adoption of Christianity throughout the Roman Empire.

A difficulty in Stoicism can also be in determining what is in your control and what is not in your control. With a faith, you believe that God will find a way and you trust that he loves you. For example, if you had an incurable disease, would you believe it is out of your control? Yet, David Fajgenbaum was a medical student who was diagnosed with the rare Castleman disease in 2010, and then by raising his own funding and experimenting on himself, eventually found a cure (though this resilience was not attributed to his faith in God). Possibly it depends on how the specific religion or philosophy affects us personally, and certainly I see that people of different religions and philosophies can often have more in common in their ethics, virtue and fortitude, than individuals within the same religion or philosophy. That's also why I don't want you to read this book as prescriptive religious advice or a one-sided opinion, but simply as my own personal analysis, views and experiences which may help you reflect on your own views.

2. The Benefits of Optimism

WEATHER IS DIFFICULT TO predict. In surfing and sailing you'll only seriously consider the weather forecast over the next 3 days. Small perturbations in temperature, wind direction and air pressure can cascade into much larger perturbations, with each passing day increasing the difference from the original prediction. That's a little like life. We have an idea what will happen tomorrow, but even then small events can result in drastic changes. Imagine the times that you could have left the house for work a little earlier, and a truck didn't see you on the street and ran into you. But thankfully you're still alive and here reading this.

Patricia, a pretty young woman with long wavy raven dark hair, was on a ferry to the USA, to meet her husband and children she had not seen for over 4 months. The ferry was crossing the large stretch of the Atlantic Ocean, between Lisbon and Staten Island: 3,390 miles. This journey by ferry takes 11 days, with an overnight stop-off right in the middle of the Atlantic Ocean, at the isolated islands of the Açores. This is a beautiful string of volcanic islands, unique for their flora and fauna which is a mix of species from the Americas and Europe, as well as having some species unique to these islands. I once visited these islands to do an ecological survey. I remember taking aquatic plant samples from a tiny inflatable boat, on the 'Flores' (Flowers) island; dragging aquatic plants up on a hook and string from the bottom of a dark mist covered lake. The lake was in the centre of a volcano's mouth, at the centre of a small isolated island, in the centre of the Atlantic Ocean; 1,400 miles from the nearest major land mass (Portugal). It was exquisitely lonely.

Anyway, Patricia's trip to the Açores was understandably idyllic, and on her approach to the main São Miguel island, dolphins were diving in and out the water while riding the bow wave of the boat. Quaint houses lined the main street of the capital, Ponte del Garda. The passengers had time to disembark and visit a friendly cafe. They then visited a building that had previously been a synagogue disguised as a church.

In 1492 and 1502 Catholic decrees in Castille had ordered all Jews and Muslims in Iberia (Spain and Portugal) to convert to Catholicism or be tortured and expelled—the Spanish Inquisition. Jews were often rooted out by the notable absence of pork sausages which were typically hung from the rafters to provide food over the winter months; though in a Jewish community in the small Portuguese town of Mirandela to divert suspicion Jews developed a famous chicken and bread Alheira sausage, identical to the u-shaped pork sausages Catholics were hanging. This church Patricia was visiting was built in the 1830s, long after the Spanish Inquisition, and while the period was not as severe in its persecution of non-Catholics, Jews were still being expelled from Iberia and also Morocco. The Jews fleeing to the Açores were welcomed; though they knew they would have to hide their religious beliefs. This church, while having the shape and immediate appearance of a Catholic church, was one such place that fleeing Jews had established in the Açores to enable them to continue their faith: looking carefully you could see protruding from the eaves symbols of the Star of David, the seven branched candelabrum, known as the menorah, and Noah's ark.

After leaving the Açores Patricia's Ferry headed to New York—you may have noticed, sailors never say where they are going, only where they are heading. This is because the weather can easily change, a storm comes down, and the boat is forced to sail to an unknown port. On this particular evening the wind did begin to get stronger. Within a couple of hours waves were beating heavily at the bow. Feeling sea-sick Patricia left her cabin and walked to the stern of the boat, watching the remaining sun sparkle on the lifting sea spray, and breathing in the crisp air. Suddenly the boat jerked. She had a hand on the wet rail, but Patricia's body lurched over and her hand slid smoothly off. She plopped heavily in the water, with another swell suddenly engulfing her. No-one noticed.

The sea was neither flat, nor was it daytime; even on a flat day, you can see only about 12 miles across the sea surface. The slight curvature of the Earth prevents you seeing small boats much further than this. Higher up from the sea surface you can see further, but with ocean waves of only a meter height, you'll be lucky to see someone from a boat even if only 20 meters away. On this day, with stormy weather, eight meter waves, outside major shipping lanes, and nighttime creeping upon her, the chances of

Patricia's survival were close to zero. With such a dire situation, is it even worth the effort of struggling to keep afloat? Why would she fight against the inevitable? These were the thoughts going through Patricia's mind, and sadness knowing that she would never see her family again. She could see the Ferry lights disappearing toward the horizon as she made her last tired and pointless splashes against the undulating sea.

Probabilities; we work with them every day. You apply for a job and there are 300 applicants. What is the probability of getting the job? 1 in 300. You toss a coin, what is the probability that it will land on heads? 1 in 2. But is this really true? Each of the 300 applicants for the job are assumed to have equal probabilities of 1 in 300, but we know each individual is different in their ability and experience, and we know that one of them will get that job. With hindsight, once we know who got it, the probability of them having the job is 100 percent. Why did they get that job? Better qualifications? More experience? So they didn't have 1 in 300 chance of getting the job in the first place, they had a much higher probability. Maybe the person had worked with the recruiters before and was well known to them.

Probabilities are not real. They are predictions based on past behaviour, and calculated with limited knowledge of the facts. Is the world exactly the same as it was 1,000 years ago? Is it exactly the same as it was 10 years ago, or even 5 minutes ago? Not only do things change, but more factors come into play than we can possibly calculate or predict. I worked in ecology, which looks at communities of species and all their complex interactions with each other and the environment. Indeed the complexity is so high that ecologists understand that perfect predictions are impossible; we can only draw broad conclusions. Any greater understanding requires so much more information, which is too expensive or impractical to obtain, and even then, like the weather, small perturbations can cause large changes in the final outcome; an effect known as 'chaos' in science. Think of the toss of a coin; if we knew the forces acting on the coin when it was thrown into the air, we could calculate its rotational velocity, the distance from the ground, and with measurement of the tiny air currents, we could give a much higher probability of whether the coin would land on heads or tails. Probability is simply a mathematical trick to substitute for a lack of knowledge or information. Indeed, as with the interview case: we know that if we prepare for the interview, if we apply for an appropriate job, if we have the qualifications necessary for the job, all these will increase our chances. Of course, we usually don't know the other candidates, and thus lack information to calculate an accurate probability, but with some effort we can make improvements in our chances. Even so, we never really know the outcome. Something either will or will not happen, but inevitably we cannot determine this and probability calculations are just a tool to be able to make a guess. The problem of assuming we can predict what will happen based on previous conditions is illustrated by the Taoist philosopher Lieh Yukou in the fifth century BC, in the text known colloquially as the Book of Lieh Tzu:

> "There was a Confucian scholar who was journeying from his hometown to the capital. While he was passing through a quiet and untraveled area, a group of bandits robbed him of his money, his horse, and his carriage. The scholar continued his journey on foot as if nothing had happened. The robbers were surprised that their victim showed no signs of disappointment or grief, so they caught up with him and asked,
>
> 'Most people are alarmed when they lose their belongings but you are not. Why?'
>
> The scholar said, 'A virtuous man is not attached to his possessions. Moreover he won't satisfy his needs by taking things that are not his own.'
>
> The bandits looked at one another and said, 'Sounds like words from a wise man.'
>
> Later, when the robbers had time to think it over, they said among themselves,
>
> 'Such a wise man will rise in power in the government and he'll send the police after us. We had better kill him before he gets to the capital.' So they ran after the scholar and killed him.
>
> When the news of the scholar's death reached the capital, a family elder told his clan members, 'When you run into bandits, don't act like that stupid scholar.'
>
> Not long afterwards, one of the younger members of this clan went to the remote areas of the country on business and came upon some bandits. Remembering what the family elder had said, the young man argued with the robbers and defended his possessions. When the bandits went off with his belongings, the man still did not give up. He ran after the robbers and begged them to return his goods. The bandits looked at the young man and said, 'We spared your life and you didn't appreciate it. You

are a fool and a nuisance, and your footprints are going to lead the police to us.' So the bandits killed the man on the spot."[1]

So what happened to Patricia? Well, I missed out an important aspect of the story. Patricia was a Christian. She believed God would save her. She ignored probabilities and rather than rationalization that it was pointless attempting to swim, she made a plan. First she allowed herself to sink into the water so she could pull off her shoes, pants and jacket. She pushed back to the surface, and then a large swell lifted her high into the air and then back down, and this repeated every few seconds. Unperturbed, she gradually calmed her breathing, closed her mouth and teeth slightly to control water and spray going into it, and with controlled movements within the turbulant ocean, kept herself as vertical as possible. Very slowly and conserving energy, she kicked her legs while paddling her hands in a circular motion. She tried not to panic, and in her mind she prayed.

The ferry was gone. It was dark. She could not see the swells which buffeted her around, but it started to feel rhythmic. She realized that her dress was synthetic and would not let air pass through it. Awkwardly she removed it, and once again allowing herself to be temporarily submerged, used her hands to feel the material such that she could tie knots in the sleeves and at the very bottom. Going back to the surface blackness, she lifted the knotted dress from the water and pulled it back to fill it with air. This gave her a little respite, helping her to float and occasionally rest. It was not the best, and occasionally she had to refill it, but it gave her occasional respite. She paddled, filled the dress with air, and rested for a time over a full six hours in the broad, deep, cold ocean.

Eventually her skin became numb. She couldn't feel her limbs at all, but somehow they were still jerkily and autonomously paddling to keep her afloat. After a time the light of dawn started to peak above the horizon, reflecting beautifully across the wide expanse. The swell had died down but she maybe had only two hours of energy left. Despite this, it was a glorious morning, and if she had to die now, this huge sky and golden ocean was the most beautiful casket she could imagine. The air felt like the cleanest most enjoyable breaths she had ever taken in her life, and the warming sun like gold showering on her exhausted body. She felt grateful for every last moment of life she had.

---

1. Wong, Lieh Tzu

The truth was, she couldn't remember much more as she began to sink below the ocean's surface. While her arms were flailing randomly but slowly, their utility waned and her head submerged, her hair trailing from the surface.

The fishermen had seen the object from a distance. Was it trash, or maybe a buoy they could collect and reuse? On approaching, the submerged shape revealed the outline of a person. One man rushed for the life ring. He jumped in to the calm sea with the life ring, and holding on to the rope, dived down and then raised the body to the surface. The other fishermen rapidly pulled the flotation device toward the boat and hauled them both in. She was still alive. What were the chances? Zero percent or one-hundred percent? Neither—things either happen or they don't, but we only know after the fact. Probability is just a psychological trick.

This story with Patricia was fictional. It comes from a mind experiment I created a long time ago to illustrate that optimism often has benefits in improving our chances of a positive outcome. If she had considered that the chances of survival were zero, and thus had given up, it's very unlikely she would have made it. If you believe that its not worth applying for the job because 1 in 300 is too unlikely, then you won't get the job. If you believe that you can't make a difference to others in your life, your chances of doing so are small. In our example, Patricia had nothing to lose, whereas applying for jobs requires an investment of time, so that's why it is better to be selective and make judgments about where it is best to invest your time. However, it is always better to do something rather than nothing. Great things come from commitment and devotion.

While being fictional, a similar event to Patricia's did occur on 24 November 2022 when a man fell from the cruise ship 'Carnival Valor' in the Gulf of Mexico. He was in the water for 15 hours before being found alive by air-sea rescue. At the time this was referred to as 'The Thanksgiving Miracle'. In a personal example of how faith can provide you with more opportunities, let me retell an episode in my life. I was catching a flight to Amsterdam, where I needed to attend a meeting which would lead to a job in Malawi. Because of traffic I was terribly late for the plane, and I arrived at the airport in London 30 minutes after the plane should have left the ground! It seemed impossible that the plane would still be there. I rang a friend to tell them that I had missed the plane, and he told me "just have faith in God". This spurred me to continue to rush to the check-in desk at the airport. Amazingly they told me the plane had been delayed because of the weather conditions on the incoming flight. I only had hand luggage, and though they rushed me through security, they told me it was unlikely I'd be let on the plane. When I arrived at the entry gate, sure enough, it was completely empty, and the entry gate was locked. Still believing there could be a way, I ran down the corridor and found an attendant. This attendant said they would ring to see if they would open the doors so I could board. It worked. They unlocked the doors, and I entered a plane full of disgruntled passengers who had been waiting almost an hour for take off. Without even time to put my luggage away or put on my belt, as soon as I sat down, the plane began taxiing down the runway.

I used to surf with a French friend, called Guillaume. He once told me that his father was in the French Navy and one of his main jobs was recovering ships and submarines that had sunk. When they recovered and accounted for the bodies, what was interesting was the married men had a much higher survival rate than single men. This was unusual, as you'd expect single men tend to be younger and fitter. The French Navy's opinion was that married men knew they had to survive for their families; there was a reason outside themselves that drove them to fight to stay alive.

Victor Frankl, was a Polish Jew and a psychologist as World War Two started. When Poland was invaded by Germany, along with many other Jews, he was taken to a Nazi concentration camp. While suffering the terrible conditions and abuse in this camp, he continued with his psychological analyses, studying why it was some people gave up and some persevered. His conclusion was that those who survived had found meaning in their lives. It didn't have to be something big; it could be coming back to a family member, an unfinished task in life, supporting another in the camp, or even a menial daily task to which they were dedicated. From these experiences he wrote and published the famous book Man's Search For Meaning[2].

Looking at these examples we can see that it is useful in our lives to have some meaning, some desire to achieve something outside ourselves, something important to us, whether or not it is to others. Also, we can achieve more than we can at first even believe, if we have faith and perseverance. In Christianity, this sense of meaning usually comes

2. Frankl, *Man's Search for Meaning*

through serving God. This service, while underlined by Christian principles, tends to be unique and personal. Optimism, not in the sense of being unrealistic or cheery, but in believing that if we work in God's service everything will work out as it needs to, provides this solid rock on which Christians can lean in times of stress and doubt. It simultaneously provides some flexibility in our final goal. While we may choose to persevere to become the fastest 100 meter sprinter, but then lose our legs in a horrific accident, our faith in God helps us to adapt and feel that we still have an important destiny even if it isn't that which we may have first thought was important. Looking back at stressful events in my past, now I can see that I should have shown greater faith. Not because everything I wanted occurred. Often events developed in ways I could not have at all predicted, and I suffered great change and loss. However, looking back things appear to have worked out in the way they needed to, and ultimately to a deeper, more interesting and productive life.

I titled this chapter *The Benefits of Optimism* only to avoid talking about faith from the start, because it wasn't the faith in the Resurrection of Jesus or a spiritual faith I wanted to discuss, but instead the faith that despite great suffering and confusion, we should understand that it all works out for the best. Indeed, if we believe that God is omnipotent and that he loves us completely, a belief in God is analogous to having faith that everything will work out for the best. St. Paul wrote to the Corinthians: "Now we see but a poor reflection as in a mirror; then we shall see face to face. Now I know in part; then I shall know fully, even as a I am fully known. And now these three remain: faith, hope and love. But the greatest of these is love."[3] Thus, while love is the most important aspect of Christianity, faith and hope are also fundamental. The Bible consistently requests that humans trust in God. When the storm fell on the Sea of Galilee (known as Lake Kinneret in Israel) and the apostles cowered down with a lack of faith, Jesus reprimanded them, calming the waters and walking across its surface[4]. Throughout the Bible we are given illustrations how faith overcomes the odds, such as the battle between David and Goliath[5]. To pull through difficult times or struggles we must have some form of faith; whether in ourselves, our destiny, or God. Thus, when I refer to the benefits of optimism, it is more this type of faith that everything in the end will work out for the best despite the trials and

3. 1 Cor 13:12–13
4. Matt 8:23–27
5. 1 Sam 17:4–50

difficulties, not the type of blind optimism that comes from deceiving ourselves or closing our eyes to reality. Indeed Viktor Frankl said those in the concentration camp with blind optimism did not fare well, because when their optimism was later found to be misplaced, their psychological state would sink much lower and they would suffer greatly. Thus it is the dual tasks of having meaning in our life that pushes us forward, and having faith that in some way it will all work out for the best, while modestly understanding that we may not know exactly how and humbly accepting that it may still be a path that includes great suffering.

We should not confuse the long term faith in God and that everything ultimately works for the best, with our own short term conveniences in life, or even in the perspective of our own short life. We can blindfold ourselves and drive a vehicle saying "I have faith God will protect me". In Africa I have seen pastors bringing poisonous snakes into the church and declaring "I know God will protect me". In most cases the blindfolded driver crashes and the snake-handler pastor gets bitten. They may even be surprised at the outcome. Faith does not operate like this; it is not magic, nor is it a demonstration or show. Faith operates from diligent and dedicated focus on the cause or the objective. If you are dedicated to the objective of driving safely, you will not blindfold yourself. If you are dedicated to the objective of teaching your congregation about God, you will not bring snakes into the church. Of course if you are dedicated to the objective of creating a magic show, maybe you will bring a snake into church.

Some studies have shown that in career success, determination and consistency were more important than intelligence and hard work. You fail, you learn, you try again. You fail, you learn, you try again. Indeed there is a Russian saying "Persistence is a second chance." What we learn from books is knowledge from the past, from a different time under different conditions, with different people. While books can guide us, what we learn from trying and failing, then adapting and trying again, is what gives us true wisdom. Applying this to life we can consistently move forward and adapt, even if it feels that for long periods (often many years) we are not doing so.

So faith isn't a passive "God will do everything for me" but an active "God will support me in fulfilling my service and duty to God". Reverend Martin Luther King famously wrote in reference to the 1960s American civil rights movement: "If you can't fly then run, if you can't run then walk, if you can't walk then crawl, but whatever you do, you have to keep moving forward." Despite all the difficulties we are called to face, and these can be horrifically challenging, we are still called to trust in God and that he will ease our burdens.

Philippians states "Do not be anxious about anything, but in everything by prayer and supplication with thanksgiving [gratitude] let your requests be known to God."[6] and in Psalms, "Cast your burden on the Lord, and he will sustain you, he will never permit the righteous to be moved."[7] Thus it is not a desperate struggle, but a strength and confidence gained from faith that God has ultimate power and whatever the outcome, it is part of God's overall plan; that we are simply servants working for God, and that we can have faith, and joy, that everything will be as it should. Before becoming a Christian I wondered whether faith was simply a useful psychological method of improving one's personal performance. In intellectual and sporting activities science has shown that people with low or high stress perform poorly. Low stress usually occurs when someone doesn't care about the outcome, so they don't try. High stress occurs with high levels of anxiety and expectation, with adrenalin being released into the body to the point where it impedes our thought and coordination processes. The *fight or flight* response evolved when we were in life threatening physical situations, such as facing a sabertooth tiger; yes, both humans and saber-tooth tigers did co-exist around 300,000 years ago. The adrenalin dump produces improved strength, and takes blood away from the skin and deeper into the body to prevent wounds causing severe blood loss. However, adrenalin also reduces fine motor control such that coordinated action can be impeded. Chuang Tzu (369–286 BC), a prominent Taoist philosopher noted: "When an Archer is shooting for nothing, he has all his skill. If he shoots for a brass buckle, he is already nervous. If he shoots for a prize of gold, he goes blind or sees two targets. He is out of his mind! His skill has not changed but the prize divides him. He cares. He thinks more of winning than of shooting; and the need to win drains him of power."[8]

Much of martial arts (from boxing, to mixed martial arts, to Japanese sword fighting) relies on breath control such that you breath slower and deeper. This helps control adrenalin release and helps retain rational thought and motor skills. There are many studies showing the pronounced effect of religious faith on improving sporting

6. Phil 2:4
7. Ps 55:22
8. Merton, *Way of Chuang Tzu*, 107.

achievement, as well as other 'Coping Self-Efficacy' (CSE) methods. Fundamentally, faith that provides a moderate level of stress, where you want to achieve your objective, but are not overly fearful, confused by too many alternatives, or excessively concerned about failure, is extremely useful in achievement. Such a tool as faith is especially useful in a modern, socially complex and intellectually demanding society which as a human species we haven't fully adapted to. Thus, the resort to faith for Christians not only provides us with greater chances of success, but like the resort to logic for the Stoics, can be a tool for avoiding excessive stress. So logically, faith in God, yourself or faith in a positive long term destiny, can help. Of course it isn't for logical reasons that I am a Christian, but I'll explain more about that later.

Hope is related to faith. If you have faith that an omnipotent God exists, and that the final outcome that God desires is for the best, then logically overall you can have hope that everything will eventually turn out as it should, or indeed must. It would also thus be likely that, if you also want things to turn out for the best, that your hope would be aligned with fulfilling God's wishes. So you may hope to be the best chess player in the world, and that will guide your focus. But even if you aren't you can have faith that despite all these struggles it is for a reason, and you won't be constantly stressed that you're not there yet—you will keep working consistently on the path. As many say, life is a marathon, not a sprint. If you refer back to the quote from Martin Luther King Jr. at the start of this book, you can see that he is emphasizing the purpose in your heart, regardless of the trials, regardless of the failures. Similarly to Stoicism, it isn't even that you achieve your goals that is important, but that you vigorously apply yourself to doing the best you can do; though in Christianity there is the additional faith that despite some failures, or even complete failure, you can believe that in some way in the future, your positive actions can lead to a final positive outcome, even if beyond your own lifetime.

Christianity tells us that in the large picture of the operation of the universe, God does things for a final good outcome, but also that each of us has a reason as an individual to exist. Even the most seemingly humble of roles is an important task in fulfilling our service to God. So what if you make sausage rolls? Is it not important to feed people? Can world leaders, church pastors, and those helping the needy, live without food? For much of our life we may not know what we are called to do, but much of that is preparation for when we do know what we are called to do. I worked most of my life as a researcher in environmental science, then changed and started working on a different continent for an aid agency. For me it was a huge change, but my background, both professionally, and personally (going through depression, separating from my partner and losing my daughter) created a background that helped me empathize with people, matured me, and helped me orientate myself toward work that I felt was of practical benefit. When making this change I explained to the Zimbabwean pastor who's church I was attending in London, that I had felt I had climbed high up on a ladder, only to realize I'd put my ladder against the wrong building. And this is true, sometimes our paths take us completely different directions from what we originally intended, but having faith in God can provide us a much more interesting future than we would have expected just by following our own limited perspective. I am sure even now, that my path will again reorient in the future, but these experiences will not be lost and I shall continue to refine my tasks to fulfill the duties which I must fulfill at that time.

For most of our life we don't have a clear idea of where we are heading, let alone where we are going to end up. In the past, during a feudal period in our history, people would tend to adopt the profession of their father or mother, or in some tribes they would be born into a clan that would be healers, or warriors. From a young age you expect to be taught that trade, maybe as a carpenter, home-maker, hunter, or politican, and then follow that through and live that life-style. In modern society we are told we can be anything, but really many of these choices are illusory. You cannot try every profession, and if you try, you won't reach any great skill in a specific area if you lack time and focus. I have often advised friends "you can do anything, but you can't do everything". While not denying our desires to define ourselves through our personal choices, we should not feel dissatisfied that our role in life does not have high status; we are part of a larger plan. Christianity also advises us that we have a specific role in our service to God:

> "What, after all, is Apollos? And what is Paul? Only servants, through whom you came to believe—as the Lord has assigned to each his task. I planted the seed, Apollos watered it, but God has been making it grow. So neither the one who plants nor the one who waters is anything, but only God, who makes things grow. The one who plants and the one who waters have one purpose, and they will each be rewarded according to their

own labor. For we are co-workers in God's service; you are God's field, God's building."[9]

From this then, we can see that it is extremely beneficial to find meaning in our life, even if that may shift. To fulfill that meaning it is useful to have focus, to have faith, and to have hope, and not to be disparaged if we feel our part is small, as long as we are being effective in what we are achieving. While we are still struggling to find purpose in life, we are gaining experience which will help to guide future decisions; most of what we learn practically in life is through trial and error: we know when we like something, and when we don't, only when we're doing it, regardless of preconceptions. But while we're gaining that experience it is useful to have small goals, and to work to achieve them. This may be being the fastest runner at school, getting a poem published, psychologically supporting your terminally ill father, or some social contribution to your society or wider community. A quote going back to nineteenth century France (and which Oscar Wilde later adapted) states "The smallest deed is better than the grandest intention". We may plan to be global leaders or national heroes, but these outcomes can be through inheritance, luck, or a series of many small actions. As long as we are moving in the right direction, and have our ladder on the right building, each small step is a step in the right direction. Our conditions and destination my change, but still we are building something cohesive and positive of benefit. Fundamentally what we need is a good heart, and the the actions we need to fulfill our destiny will often arise from our current situation.

We may have a nice specific objective that gives us meaning in life, and a plan exists in our mind, but reality is inevitably different from our expectation. The plan soon gets beaten, as a dull sword on an anvil, continually being shaped, altered, sharpened, by hard reality. The intention is the first stage. We can't know what we don't know unless we just step forward and make our ideas reality; gaining knowledge through practical experience. Advice from people and books is beneficial, but the most useful and most specific learning is through experience. For Christians, we need to trust in God and live in faith. Several people that knew Martin Luther King said that, despite him being a great leader, he was not afraid to speak of his uncertainty and fears. But he also asserted that we live not by sight but by faith (he was referring to 2 Cor:5–6). King is quoted as saying "Take the first step in faith. You don't have to

9. 1 Cor 3:5–9

see the whole staircase to take the first step," sometimes adding "and God will find footing for the next". So in conclusion, knowing that many readers will be wondering what path they should take, I would say to follow God, keep a good heart, and in faith just take a step forward and the staircase of your life and destiny will begin to reveal itself. For these reasons, it is vital for us to live with faith in God, in our ability to deal with the unexpected future with the tools we have, and in our place in the world and a greater plan for human-kind.

3. Forgiveness

ONE OF THE MOST criticized aspects of Christianity is that of forgiveness. It just doesn't seem natural. Humans will go to quite extreme lengths to punish those who have done wrong, even to their own detriment. Think of when you're driving and someone pulls out; you bib your horn, maybe even shake your fist, to someone you are never likely to meet again. There is an evolutionary reason for this. It's a function of your behaviour as a social animal: you're reprimanding someone for the benefit of the wider society. Even as individuals we support giving people multiple life sentences in prison for crimes they have committed, even though we don't know them or their victims. We want to regulate people and create a society where people comply to certain standards and behaviors.

While forgiveness in Christianity is a heavily criticized aspect of the religion, I believe it is absolutely fundamental to living a healthy human life. Does forgiveness mean that Christians are free to commit crime, immoral acts, or to *sin*, knowing that we will be forgiven? Most Christians affirm that Jesus died as a sacrifice, cleansing humanity of sin. We reach God not through good acts or being moral, but only through God's grace. God loves us and decided we are worthy of this love despite our sins. So then, why be moral? In this chapter I want to show you why moral flexibility isn't how forgiveness functions, and also why forgiveness is absolutely fundamental in society.

Inspiration from the radio isn't the most dramatic method of having your eyes opened, but here it goes . . . One cool autumn I was laying on my bed. It was a lazy Sunday, and I was listening to BBC Radio 4. In my travels this radio station has often been a fine companion. The second Gulf War had finished just over a year before, so it must have been 2012. The aftermath of the US led coalition entering Iraq saw accusations of rendition, water-boarding, and torture by electric shock, by the US military toward Iraqi captives; totally contravening the Geneva convention which emphatically prohibits torture. The Geneva convention is a legal agreement signed by 196 countries, including all United Nations member states and the UK. It is composed of four treaties and three protocols which address the treatment of non-combatants, and prisoners of war. All military personnel in these signatory nations are taught the rules of the Geneva convention, since they are expected to abide by them. I know this because I was myself when I was in the military. However, in the Abu Ghraib detention centre in Iraq (as well as elsewhere) these legally binding rules were ignored. As well as torture, men were forced to be naked in front of female military personnel and otherwise humiliated and ridiculed. Initially the military denied this, but photos were leaked and witnesses came forward. The radio programme I was casually listening to comprised an interview with one of the military personnel who had been involved in the abuse and torture of the prisoners at Abu Ghraib detention centre.

The interviewee explained how he had personally been involved in the heinous acts. He explained that it wasn't personal anger in the aftermath of war, nor a vendetta, nor sadism, that lead to these abuses. It was part of structured systematic torture with orders coming from senior members of staff. While it was intended to break the prisoner's morale and provide intelligence, it was already well known that intelligence gathered through torture is usually incorrect since tortured prisoners will say anything to make the torture stop. The interviewed sergeant expressed his deep regret at what he had done, and admitted to the interviewer that, despite getting orders to torture the prisoners, he knew that it was against the laws of the Geneva convention and that ultimately he had personal responsibility for his own actions. Indeed, the middle-aged soldier, on returning to civilian life, had felt such enormous guilt that he had attempted suicide twice. The interview process seemed like a cathartic release for the sergeant, though at times he would give a prolonged pause as he fought his internal emotion, such that he could present a clear, careful and factual record of events. It was a powerful interview. It had me gripped, and occasionally shedding a tear. The real impact was at the end. After wrapping up, the presenter stated that four weeks following recording, the soldier had made a third, and this time successful, suicide attempt.

Like most mature adults, I've had my fair share of prolonged suffering; a type of suffering where repeated weeping becomes a tiresome act. Instead you show no emotion, save maybe an involuntary tear down a stone cold face, simply continuing with whatever activities you have to do at the time. I felt sorry for the torture victims, but I realized my empathy laid more with the soldier's pain. He'd tortured people, he had killed himself leaving behind a wife and children. What he had done was morally reprehensible. But still, it was clear this was an upstanding man. A good man who had done terrible things.

An excellent method of conflict resolution developed by Marshall Rosenberg in the 1970s is "Non Violent Communication" (NVC). The method has four simple principles: 1. observation: say what the problem is; 2. feelings: explain how that made you feel; 3. needs: explain what your needs are in relation to this problem; 4. requests: make specific requests about what you want to happen. It has been used globally in high level conflict resolutions. I have also used it myself regularly and very effectively. NVC avoids coercion, manipulation and rhetoric, while also preventing us giving excuses but instead being transparent and honest about our failures, feelings, position and needs; it gives people the breathing room to empathize with our position. It opens us up emotionally and presents a point without threat or emotional black-mail. An important aspect of NVC is expressing our feelings about the situation without being accusatory. Rather than "you made me angry because you took my car without permission" it would be "You took the car, but I needed the car to go shopping. I couldn't go shopping, so I felt angry. Next time could you ask before taking the car?" It is taking away direct blame and critique of the person's character, and separating the action from the actor. You're not upset with the person, but what they did. This gives space for the other person to maintain their dignity, doesn't force them to defend their character, and instead allows them to either justify the action, or to apologize and agree to change their actions in future, or to come to some mutually agreeable solution. I guess, after several months of analyzing why I felt sympathy for the soldier rather than his victims, it was because I had separated the actions from the actor. He seemed such a good man, but he had done bad things.

What is the most difficult thing we can experience in our lives? When I was younger I went through a survivalist phase. I would travel around, living outside, and finding my own food in nature. I even went to Israel and tried to live (unsuccessfully) off my own wits in the barren Negev desert. All I found were scorpions. No water, no vegetation, just scorpions. This was challenging but it wasn't stressful. I've been homeless, which was tough and mildly depressing. I suffered the loss of my mother from cancer. My brother died suddenly when his aorta detached from his heart. I've had a separation from a fiancé. I've had a four year court process with the government to get my legal rights recognized. I've been physically abused and attacked with a knife by my ex-wife who was suffering severe depression and psychosis, only then to have social services take my children away from me when I finally got the courage to report it. Despite pain, hunger, loss of loved ones, and injustices, I still think there is something much worse than all of these: doing something that we hate ourself for. I still sometimes feel bitter about past injustices in my life, and though sometimes I worry for the safety and health of my children, I can still manage to put this past behind me. What I believe really destroys us though, is hatred of ourselves. It can insidiously destroy us from the inside. So this was the realization from the radio programme, with these thoughts swimming around my head for months. I wasn't a Christian at this time, so I didn't see it through the lens of Christianity, but I realized that this soldier was in desperate need of forgiveness, both from himself and from others.

What I know from previous experience, is that our first reaction when we do something wrong, is to justify it. Why did you steal that bread? Because I was hungry. Why did you have an affair? Because my wife wasn't showing me love. Why did you punch that person? Because they insulted me. We create a justification for the bad things we did, hoping our actions will be socially unacceptable. Indeed, some psychologists argue that many of our decisions are made at a subconscious level, and then our conscious brain then creates reasons to justify the decision. I think most of us are not open enough, or psychotic enough, to simply explain a socially unacceptable action by saying "because I wanted to".

We aren't only using these excuses to justify the bad action to our society, we also want to justify that action to ourselves. I had heard a burglar once saying she wasn't to blame for burgling houses; it was the fault of the tenants for having insufficient security. Rarely do we consider ourselves to be bad people. The thief, the abuser, the genocidal dictator, all feel they are doing it for a justified reason. Sometimes they believe they have a moral obligation to do acts which create immense suffering. Adolf Hitler was purifying the German race and reclaiming German territories, but in the process exterminated over 6 million civilians including Jews, Gypsys, homosexuals and Jehovah's witnesses. Pol Pot and the Khmer Rouge wanted a Communist revolution in Cambodia such that they could develop a peaceful agrarian society without immoral Western influence; in the process murdering between 1.5 and 3 million civilians. Joseph Stalin wanted rapid industrialization and collectivist agriculture under Communism, and in an effort to achieve that executed around 23 million citizens. Mao Zedong in China killed between 40 and 70 million in an effort to remove foreign, capitalist and traditional influences in society and enforce Communism. Undoubtedly the soldier on the radio programme wanted to valiantly serve his country. Moral intentions without thought to the individual can create horrific results.

The above examples are extreme. They felt the ends justified the means, and were serving an overarching ideology that they forcibly imposed on others. I have seen interviews with Pol Pot justifying his actions. But even ourselves, on a personal level, when we do something wrong, even if we know it was wrong, we have a natural first line of defence of immediately justifying these actions to ourself and to those around us. "I did it because . . . " This may be an attempt to reduce a reprimand from our fellow humans—we defend our negative actions in court, to friends, to family, and to colleagues, regularly. In some cases this attempt to justify our actions is valid, because we perceived it to be the best solution for everyone at the time e.g. driving up on to a kerb to allow an ambulance to pass, lying to an armed home invader to protect your children, physically defending a person who is being assaulted. However, regularly we justify our wrong doing because we need to maintain our image or status socially. Even in relationships people who don't love their partner will break up, but still find a list of reasons to blame their partner and also to justify that action to themselves. The truth is often because they just don't love them, and if it had been someone they did love, they would have worked around those problems. We regularly blame others or circumstances for something which is fundamentally just our decision.

Justifications aren't only about maintaining our social image, but also about maintaining our internal image of who we are. This self-definition of what is acceptable can depend on our internal values. For a soldier, they may feel that their obligation to defend their country justifies the killing of an enemy soldier. A pacifist may believe killing any human is not justified. A financier may see their over-riding obligation to their investors, rather than to the environment or public health. A vegetarian may see that eating meat is bad, whereas a meat eater would generally believe it's natural and healthy. We gradually build this sense of self and then our decisions and actions play into this sense of self.

This can be difficult to see on the surface, but evidence suggests that when we are trying to make a difficult decision, it's important not just to think of the options, but to think of whether that choice reinforces our sense of who we are. How we would ideally act. Decisions that fulfill our own view of self generally lead to more satisfaction. Will I have the steak or the vegetarian lasagne? If you're a vegetarian you will probably choose the vegetarian lasagne; it reinforces that sense of self and your personal values. What happens if there is no vegetarian option? The vegetarian may eat some meat, and justify it to themselves. What if the steak smells so good, and they choose that instead, consciously contradicting their values? Possibly regret.

When we commit actions that go against your own inner sense of self, as we struggle with regret, our ego rises to the surface, desperately trying to preserve that sense of self. Why did you steal? You're not a thief, but you had no other way of finding food, so you stole. You may determine that society has given you nothing, so you have no obligation to give back to society; it was against the Geneva convention, but you had a direct order and you had to obey the chain of command. When we do something that is behaviour outside our sense of who we are, the first impulse is to justify it to ourselves (and others).

What we probably realize, is that in the end, regardless of all society's rules, trends and conditions, ultimately it is ourselves that makes that decision. We may be under pressure, or responding with trained behaviour, such as during a fire-fight in a war, or driving away from a hit-and-run through fear. When you are back to normal everyday life, and are still alive, this regret can seep into you. Even then we have the ability to make the best decision. We can blame others, we can blame pressures, we can blame many factors; but when we look back on our life, fundamentally despite all these factors, the decisions we make are ours.

So let's summarize. When we do a socially unacceptable act, we usually justify that to those around us, to ensure we maintain social acceptance. We justify it to ourselves, to preserve the positive image of ourself, to ourself. While often this blame gets directed at others, or the pressure of the situation, our decisions are fundamentally ours to make.

The problem occurs when we continue to justify negative actions. When we justify our theft because of hunger, we start to establish a pattern. Next time we are hungry we have already justified this action, and we don't need to think before stealing again. Stealing when you are hungry becomes a justified action. If you burgled a house because of poverty, you can justify that it was poorly protected, and then after two or three more houses, it doesn't necessarily matter if you are poor, you have become a burglar. These justifications can build the groundwork of establishing a new pattern.

In western culture the concept of Karma has got a comical reputation. For example, if you trip up a friend, then later you will fall down; it's *karma*. However, we know that retribution doesn't happen in this way. Poor people are not poor because of previous sins, nor are rich people rich because they are moral. Bad things happen to good people and good things happen to bad people. Jesus talking about God says "He makes his sun rise on the evil and on the good, and sends rain on the just and the unjust."[1] There is a more realistic and logical concept of karma in Buddhism than this cartoonish *instant retribution*: when we do negative actions we are reinforcing a behaviour in the mind, and the more we do it, the more it is reinforced. Eventually it becomes second nature. Being negative actions, it affects the people around us, and they in turn begin to act negatively toward us because of who we have become, or penalize us for those negative actions. It's easier to explain with an example: If you hit your partner for a perceived misdemeanor, you may at first shock yourself. You feel guilty, but justify it to yourself. Then second time, it feels somehow that you are indeed justified in taking that action. When you get to beating your partner the third time, it seems the logical thing to do. After ten or eleven times, you see that it is having negative repercussions both for your relationship, your family and your life, but the problem is that the ego wants to justify the behaviour to maintain the sense of self, and each time you do it, it seems increasingly normal. In this way, the ego can prevent us from reforming ourselves.

How do we fight against our own self-justifying ego? If we follow our ego and justify our actions, we can continue a downward spiral and develop a highly negative personality. If we realize we have done wrong, our self-identity is damaged and we can feel paralyzed or even suicidal with guilt? What possible remedy is their to allow us to recognize the terrible things we have done, yet not be dragged into the pit of despair through guilt. What could help us reinvent ourself and become once again who we want to be. Forgiveness.

The power of forgiveness is immense and necessary. Primarily we have to forgive ourselves. Why? Because it's a recognition that what we

---

1. Matt 5:45

did was wrong. Through humility, we disempower the ego. We say no—I accept I did something wrong, and I don't want to do it again. I'm not justifying the act. Given the same situation I shall not repeat that action. Forgiveness of the self is the gateway to changing yourself for the better.

What about forgiving others? Some say forgiving others is important to prevent ourselves being bitter our whole lives. I read an article about a Rwandan woman meeting the man who had hacked her children to death with a machete during the Hutu genocide of the Tutsi. Just two years after the event she met him and told him she forgave him; something I could not have done. However, I accept that, with time, it is important to forgive others so we can get on with our lives and move forwards without wasting energy dwelling each moment on hatred. However, forgiveness is far deeper than just trying to make your life run easier by not harboring grudges. To really be effective it has to come from a place where we accept we're all human and fallible. We are all capable of doing stupid, hateful and terrible things, but we have to know that these actions aren't the whole of who we are and don't define us. There is more to each of us than just one action. I'm sure at the time the genocidal Hutu people somehow felt justified in their anger or envy of the Tutsi minority. Most had their own families. They felt wronged, or that they were justified in taking from those who had more than them, and with those emotions felt that killing Tutsi would solve the problem. Did the man that killed this woman's children feel regret? I would hope so. Hopefully this mother's forgiveness also allowed him to forgive himself and become a better person in his life.

When Jesus asked how we should pray, he gave us the Lord's prayer, one of the central activities of many Christian Communions:

> "Our father in heaven, hallowed be your name, your kingdom come, your will be done, on Earth as it is in heaven. Give us today our daily bread. And forgive us our trespasses as we forgive those who trespass against us. And lead us not into temptation, but deliver us from evil."[2]

This prayer first tells us that God is holy, and then asks that we may reach God's kingdom: a place where we have peace, love, and joy. While some believe this talks about an afterlife, I and many other Christians believe God's Kingdom is something we can find here on Earth, either in our state of being, or when we reach a certain time in our future:

---

2. Matt 6:9–13

"Once, on being asked by the Pharisees when the kingdom of God would come, Jesus replied, 'The coming of the kingdom of God is not something that can be observed, nor will people say, 'Here it is,' or 'There it is,' because the kingdom of God is in your midst.'"[3]

The Lord's Prayer then illustrates that God wills something, and this has a purpose for existence, and shows that as Christians we should want that to be fulfilled. Also, that the will of God is fulfilled in heaven, and he wants he wants his will also to be fulfilled on Earth. We ask for sustenance, not for our whole life, but in each day as it comes. Then importantly, we ask to be forgiven, in the same way that we forgive others. Finally we ask that we are not tempted to do negative or bad things. This request for forgiveness as we forgive others is a declaration of humility, and acceptance that we are just like everyone else. We are simply human and no better or worse than a thief, murderer or rapist.

Of course, there are people who do terrible things because of psychological problems, and no matter how much they forgive themselves or are forgiven they will continue unless they can find treatment. There are also people that will continue to commit terrible acts, and though we can forgive them in the longer scheme of their life, we need to work to prevent these happening. However, the purpose of forgiving ourself is our personal transformation, and the purpose of forgiving others, is both assisting their transformation, and for ourselves in achieving humility and acceptance that we are all together and part of this bundle of human life.

3. Luke 17:20–21

4. The Crucifixion

THE MOST SIGNIFICANT EVENT in the New Testament is undoubtedly the crucifixion of Jesus. Within Christianity there is great symbolism in this event. Traditional Jewish practice required the sacrifice of a lamb on the eve of Passover festival, with the lamb symbolically absorbing the sins, and thus its sacrifice cleansing the people. Jesus symbolizes and replaces this sacrificial lamb, and himself bares the sins of the world, and through the sacrifice of his own life, cleansed the world of sin. By doing this he permitted God's complete forgiveness of humans. Thus, we are not spiritually saved through doing good acts, or obeying the commandments:

> "For by grace you have been saved through faith, and this is not of your own doing; it is the gift of God, not of works, lest anyone should boast"[1]

> "Yet we know that a person is not justified by works of the law but through faith in Jesus Christ, so we also have believed in Christ Jesus, in order to be justified by faith in Christ and not be works of the law, because by works of the law no one will be justified."[2]

Therefore, it is God that brings us to faith, and through this faith we are spiritually cleansed and can become one with God. This does not mean that we do not do good works, but that the good works come from us walking with God, and indeed that we were created for this specific purpose of doing these works.

---

1. Eph 2:8–9
2. Gal 2:16

"For we are his workmanship, created in Jesus Christ for good works, which God prepared beforehand, that we should walk in them."[3]

Previously I stated that I don't believe Jesus was the son of God, nor in a heaven which we reach after we die. This is not controversial; Unitarians and some other Christian sects also don't believe in the divinity of Jesus. Unitarian Christianity developed independently in Poland, Jamaica, Japan, India, England, Wales and the US during the sixteenth-century, and later merged as a church. Early Unitarians were often educated scientists, writers and artists. Isaac Newton, Erasmus Darwin, Florence Nightingale, Frances Harper, Linus Pauling were all Unitarians, as well as US presidents John Adams, John Quincy Adams, Millard Fillmore and William Howard Taft.

Unitarians consider Jesus to be a human inspired by God, and as such, is still our saviour. Burton Mack, historian and author of the popular The Lost Gospel[4], suggested that early Christians did not think Jesus was the son of God, nor that he was resurrected, but instead borrowed the resurrection myth from the local and well known Egyptian rebirth myths, to keep the religion alive following Jesus' crucifixion. Unitarians thus also believe they are restoring an earlier and purer form of Christianity.

Unitarians also do not believe in original sin i.e. the sin of Adam and Eve eating the forbidden fruit from the tree of knowledge being carried down and borne through all generations of humans. Original sin is characteristic of Catholicism, in that everyone has to be baptized to cleanse them of sin, even babies, because somehow this sin is transferred from Adam and Eve to the rest of humanity. Most other Christians believe that no one is without sin, but this sin is simply from our own personal thoughts and acts. This lays much more comfortably with most of us, because there is a sinister side to blaming individuals for things they haven't done. For example, some Evangelical Christians in Houston USA blamed the 2017 Hurricane Harvey on the society's permissive views toward homosexuality. This suggests both that people are hurt by God for other people's sins, and also that there is a direct relationship between sinning and punishment by God. I believe in neither. The pernicious belief that unfortunate events in life is due to their or their ancestors sins also acts as an excuse not to assist those in need,

3. Eph 2:10
4. Mack, *The Lost Gospel*

but the bible states: "He makes his sun rise on the evil and on the good, and sends rain on the just and the unjust."[5]

For many Christians, Adam and Eve eating the forbidden fruit in the garden of Eden is a metaphor. Some have associated it with knowledge of sex, though this seems unlikely given that sex within marriage is not sinful within Christianity.

> "When the woman saw that the fruit of the tree was good for food and pleasing to the eye, and also desirable for gaining wisdom, she took some and ate it. She also gave some to her husband, who was with her, and he ate it. Then the eyes of both of them were opened, and they realized they were naked; so they sewed fig leaves together and made coverings for themselves ... [Then the Lord God said to Adam] 'Because you listened to your wife and ate fruit from the tree about which I commanded you, 'You must not eat from it,' Cursed is the ground because of you; through painful toil you will eat food from it all the days of your life. It will produce thorns and thistles for you, and you will eat the plants of the field. By the sweat of your brow you will eat your food until you return to the ground, since from it you were taken; for dust you are and to dust you will return.' ... And the Lord God said, 'The man has now become like one of us, knowing good and evil.'"[6]

More logically this symbolism represents the transition from a hunter-gatherer human existence to settled agriculture. Eve took the forbidden fruit from the tree of knowledge i.e. not from the food that nature was providing. From simple and immediate foraging, hunting meat and gathering fruit as and when we needed, instead we began to use knowledge to plan ahead; clearing forests and planting grains for a later harvest. We worked on the land, we watered, we bred varieties more suitable to digestion. As more densely populated and complex societies developed, we had to develop more complex ethical laws to differentiate what was good and bad behaviour. A cat kills mice, and male lions fight for dominance of a female harem, but neither we would consider bad behaviour; yet in a settled society of closely cooperating humans we needed to create rules to regulate each other. The stress between immediate personal interest and social benefit increased. With an increased understanding of how to increase food production, through livestock

5. Matt 5:45
6. Gen 3:6–22

breeding and planting cereals and grains, we could get more calories and thus feed more young. We were no longer constrained by our hunter-gather territory and small food supply. Whereas hunter-gathering is a response to hunger, farming requires forethought and planned labour. Hunter gatherer societies may have fewer calories, but they also tend to have more spare time.[7] However, history has shown that when a hunter-gatherer society meets a settled agricultural society, the agricultural society inevitably out-competes them because the population grows faster and can sustain more people for the same territorial area. Out-breeding the competition probably happened when Homo Sapiens from Africa met, fought and inter-bred with the Neanderthals of Europe. It also happened far later, when agricultural Koreans travelled to the hunter-gather society living in early Japan around 300 BC. Interbreeding was such that modern Japanese are 91 percent similar to Koreans, although a small enclave of around 25,000 native Japanese people called the Ainu (which tend to be hairier than the mainland mix of Japanese and Koreans) still reside in the northern islands of Hokkaido, Kuril and Sakhalin.

But why not believe in heaven? I think an afterlife has been invented for one of three reasons: (i) to cope with grief when a loved one dies; (ii) to cope with fear when we ourselves face death; and (iii) to cope with anger at injustice, such that we can see ourselves finally being victorious and those that persecuted us being punished; or alternatively if that injustice is due to a hard life, to see relief and payback for all that we have struggled with. This retributional concept of heaven suggests that God works for us but not for our enemies. It sees God as our personal assistant, rather than caring holistically for the human race as a whole. That conflicts with a view of God as a universal human saviour.

Since in this book I discuss practical and psychological benefits of Christianity, surely then I would also accept that the belief in heaven is useful and valuable? Well—I also feel that if we try to avoid the truth, in the end it is detrimental. Heaven has never made sense to me and I have never intuitively felt heaven existed, but please allow me explain in more logical terms. Similar to many modern physicists, I consider that our human perception of time is illusory, and it is simply an evolved concept for survival purposes, indicating before, now and after. With modern physics and mathematics we have determined some of the peculiarities of time. Einstein's theory of relativity showed that as we travel faster, time slows

---

7. Suzman, *Affluence without Abundance*

down for us, relative to a stationary observer. For example, if you went in a spaceship to our nearest star Alpha Centauri, and then returned, flying at half the speed of light, time would pass 15 percent slower than for people left on Earth. Alpha Centurai is 4.4 light years away, so going there and back at half the speed of light would take 17.6 years for the observers here on Earth. For the traveller, time moves 15 percent slower, so it would only be 15 years for the traveller. If we were travelling at 95 percent the speed of light, time travels at around one third that of a stationary observer, so it would take us only 5.8 years as the space traveller. With longer distances this can cause the amusing effect of being younger than your children when you return home.

Gravitational fields also affect the passage of time. This was shown in 1971 with the Hafele-Keating experiment. Three extremely accurate atomic clocks were synchronized. One remained on the Earth's surface, another was flown in a plane at high altitude i.e. in a lower gravitational field heading east around the world, and the other on a plane heading west around the world. On landing the clocks disagreed due to time dilation: the plane moving westward against the spin of the Earth was moving slowest, so recorded the later time, next was the clock on the Earth, which was travelling at the speed of Earth's rotation, and the clock with the earliest recorded time, was that on the plane that was going fastest, travelling around the Earth eastward. This was all explainable by special relativity i.e. that time slows down as you travel faster. However, in addition to this effect, general relativity explains that for the airplanes further away from the Earth, time moved faster because there was less gravity. The effect was smaller than that due to velocity, but the difference relative to the clock on Earth could still determine that this effect occurred. Thus, time is not consistent throughout the universe, and varies depending on both the speed at which you are travelling and the strength of gravitational field in which you are in. Indeed, Einstein stated that this is because time was not separate from the three dimensions of space, and considered that the four were inextricably linked and should be called *space-time*.

Our perception of time moving in one direction (forward) is also considered to be due to how we perceive nature as biological organisms. We perceive time to move in the direction of increasing disorder, or more accurately *entropy*. Our physical laws appear to work perfectly well whether time is going forward or backward. I have wondered whether the basis of prophetic vision is because somehow certain people are able to see beyond our biological predisposition to see time only moving forward. A girlfriend of mine many years ago had a specific prophetic dream that she related to me at the time, and that I later saw come true. Close to where we lived in Devon, there is a broad dual carriage-way called the A30. She dreamed we were living by the A30, but the road was a much smaller single carriage-way, and had a level crossing for a train. I remember her telling me this dream because at the time she told me it was quite distinct from a normal dream and seemed so realistic. One and a half years later our work there had ended and we had found new jobs in Ascot (outside London). After moving into a new home, we took a brief walk outside, and she told me she recognized the single carriage-way road from her dreams, with the level crossing. I thought nothing of it, until around a month later I realized that this was the A30, the same road that stretched all the way from Devon to Ascot. A second prophetic event also occurred, while we were living in Ascot. She dreamed that a mutual friend at work had appeared to her and hugged her, then said goodbye. Again she identified it as different and more realistic than a normal dream. Two days later, at work, we heard that this friend had gone on holiday, and had died from a heart-attack while swimming.

God lives outside of time. If heaven is an eternity, what is it there for? Do you really want to live with your family for an eternity, even those that may have abused you? And this isn't just your parents and children, it's their parents and children, stretching back to the whole of history and forward to the whole of the future. How is that possible? If we're all related, it will be everyone, or will some members of your family be absent? Though I love my father, three days staying with him is enough for us to start arguing. Are we all there in heaven as one unified spirit? For me death is death, and is simply the end of our human consciousness. I could accept that in some profound way we return to God as one collective whole, and possibly we are part of God and will all be reunified after death, but it's an esoteric concept that logically I'm unable to describe even if something like this were true.

More important than the inability to make logical sense of heaven, is that it doesn't seem to be necessary nor have a real purpose. Since the direction of time is illusory, each moment of time you have spent alive in the universe will always have existed. If you do a kind act, such as offering a hungry person food, this event will always be a part of the reality of the universe and will always have existed, and will have shaped the universe.

Certainly there appears to be a clear separation between the concept of an afterlife and the 'Kingdom of Heaven' in the Bible. The

Kingdom of Heaven is clearly either an idealized society here on Earth, a revelationary understanding, or a form of earthly enlightenment that gives us peace and contentment beyond that we can get from our normal mundane material lives.

> "Again, the Kingdom of Heaven is like treasure hidden in a field. When a man found it, he hid it again, and then in his joy went and sold all he had and bought that field. Again, the Kingdom of Heaven is like a merchant looking for fine pearls. When he found one of great value, he went away and sold everything he had and bought it."[8]

Compare this with a Buddhist parable from the Lotus Sutra (adapted):

> "Suppose there were a man who came to the house of a close friend and went to sleep after becoming intoxicated with wine. The intimate friend, having to go out on official business, sews a priceless jewel into the inside of his friend's garment and, giving it to him, leaves. But the man who was drunk and asleep is totally unaware of this. After getting up he leaves and roams around until he arrives in another country. Although he diligently seeks for food and clothing they are very difficult to obtain. He is satisfied if he just obtains a very meager amount. Later on the intimate friend happens to meet this man. Seeing him, he says: O poor fellow! How have you come to this state through lack of food and clothing? Once, on such-and-such a day in such-and-such a month and year, I sewed a priceless jewel into the inside of your garment, wanting to make things easier for you and to let you enjoy the desires of the five senses as much as you wished. It is still there, although you aren't aware of it, and you seek your livelihood with great effort and hardship! You have been very foolish. Sell this jewel and use it to buy what you need. From now on you will know neither poverty nor want and can live as you wish."[9]

Heaven being a form of reward, or heaven and hell being a form of justice or retribution don't make sense. There is a paradox of doing a good act in the hope that your reward will be living in heaven. Are you doing the good act out of kindness and love, or out of selfishness, knowing that the current life is temporary and instead focusing on the real

---

8. Matt 13:44
9. Kubo, *Lotus Sutra,* 146–47

prize? The later takes the humanity out of the act, and indeed it becomes an entirely selfish enterprise. You're effectively storing up good deeds so you can go to heaven. The Bible is explicit that good acts don't save our souls, and that our sins are forgiven only by the grace of God. Even from a personal viewpoint, the concept of heaven as a reward clearly removes the intrinsic value of doing a good act. The kind or self-sacrificing act that will help another is completely devalued by it being tied to a reward. Instead, we can see that there is no ultimate reward apart from knowing our actions exist forever in time, and echo far into the future. These kind acts, even if not seen, carve a permanent mark, however small, into the fabric of the universe.

A person once asked me, "what is the most valuable thing you have ever done?" My answer would surprise you. Given we don't know the complete consequence of our actions in this huge web of cause and effect, it's very difficult to step outside of ourselves and see the final consequences of our actions beyond what we are doing here and now. Of course acts of kindness are likely to spark positive acts in others, and have positive consequences. When I was young I wanted to change the world, but then as you get older you realize that big ambitions don't always add-up to having big impacts, or even positive impacts. Often the tiny acts of kindness influence people around you in profound ways. When I was asked about the most valuable thing I have done, it wasn't actually something particularly beneficial. The answer for me was surfing! This is an activity which provides no direct benefit to others, does not contribute to society, and for most surfers it isn't even a sport where you get status. Few surfers surf to win prizes. Even though there are professional surfers entering competitions, that's simply to get money to sustain the surfing lifestyle, and not principally driven by winning. Indeed, when professional surfers go on holiday, what they do to get away from the daily grind of competition, is go on surfing holidays. They relax with nature, surf with the waves such that they can really feel them; not to show tricks that will score points. Surfing can become such an obsession with some people, that they drop out of society. Their whole world revolves around the simple joy of surfing. How can such an activity be considered valuable? For me it is because it has intrinsic value. It is not done for anything else than for what it is. When you surf you are *in the moment*, reacting instantaneously to a shifting, swelling, shrinking, breaking wave. Of course there are physical fitness benefits, but there are easier ways to keep fit. Indeed some days you can spend most of your time simply sitting afloat on your board, staring at the horizon and waiting for a decent wave. The value of catching a wave is completely intrinsic; the natural beauty of the environment, the movement, the fun, and the comradery. It isn't utilitarian. You're not surfing for a purpose beyond that of surfing. Similarly, a kind act has its own intrinsic value. We're not doing it to go to heaven, we're not doing it to get social status, we're not doing it so the other person reciprocates, we're not doing it to build a better world. A person in a concentration camp destined for execution is not sharing their morsel of food with a starving neighbour to change society, to build a better world or for a reciprocal act that they'll never live to receive. They do it out of compassion and for its intrinsic value. Sure, surfing and doing something kind for a stranger will both give you a rush of dopamine such that you feel happy. But there is more than just a chemical response; there is memory and expression, and more importantly a beauty beyond the act itself. Indeed everything truly glorious in this world, is glorious intrinsically. It is because the value is intrinsic and not utilitarian, and that's why we rejoice in it. Thus while big acts can be admirable, it is often the small acts that are most touching. Fritz Haber developed the *Haber Process*, in which nitrogen from the air could be extracted to make fertilizer. This is probably the biggest advance in history for reducing famine, and indeed allowed human population to expand by an estimated 4 billion. However, dividing your food with a stranger who is hungry, in some way feels far more beautiful.

In Zen Buddhism, the idea of doing a good act to improve the world is backwards. Their perspective is that we don't do good acts to achieve a goal, but instead the good acts are done because we have achieved a peaceful and loving heart. Developing yourself as a compassionate person comes first, then the kind acts are a product of that. We don't need to measure kindness, compare our kind acts to others, seek for ways to be kind, or constantly evaluate whether we are kind enough. We need to develop a kind heart, and when the situation arises the appropriate action will naturally be a part of who we are. Sometimes we're not in the correct position financially, psychologically or just because of circumstances, to express the compassion we wish to. There are many people in the world and many problems; we have our individual role to play, and so do others, so don't expect yourself to help or heal everyone; we simply help as we can and play our part.

Wait, wasn't this Chapter about the Crucifixion of Jesus? Yes—but the theme I have been addressing is that many actions aren't a means to an end, but they have intrinsic value. Our problem solving minds are often obsessed with the chain of cause and effect: we do this to achieve that, this happened because of this. This isn't a good representation of reality, it is simply a logical overlay, or logical blanket if you will, covering something much more solidly integrated and profound underneath.

I do believe the crucifixion and rebirth has huge symbolic power. For many of us that have suffered, we can get to the point where life seems to be just pain without meaning. Our own sense of self, hope, and life as we know it, is completely destroyed, leaving us spiritually and emotionally dead. The recovery from that can only be rebirth. Certainly I feel that being 'born again' as a Christian is a real event. We leave our old selves behind, because that self could not exist in the world. We literally renounce our life to follow the teachings of Jesus. This is immensely powerful, because we are saying that our ideals have more value than our life. That conviction can only occur when you have died inside, and maybe our trials in life are leading us to a point where we say "I can't take any more! I don't want to live this life. I must have something beyond this material existence." This can be a point for many people where they allow a profound change in their life and a rejection of their material existence, to enter a spiritual life.

The Crucifixion also has Christian symbolism as a method of Jesus absorbing our sins, and thus cleansing us. This comes from it being a replacement for animal sacrifice which was prevalent in the Jewish tradition. That symbolism can help us forgive ourselves, enabling a transformation into a better person. Clearly the act of dying for the whole of the human race represents God's immense immeasurable love for the human race. That love is something I experienced, as I'll discuss in the final chapter. Whether or not that absolution of sins through crucifixion is real, for me it is simply nice and touching symbolism. Since I believe Jesus was a person who gave us in much clearer terms God's message, but was not God himself, and while I see forgiveness of *sins* as important (as previously described), I do not see that as the major point of the crucifixion. Indeed, I see that the crucifixion isn't a necessary part of Christian belief, and didn't necessarily have to have happened, but did occur because Jesus lived by his convictions, and by being crucified, gave us a powerful illustration of what it can mean to be a Christian, and the immense personal power we have as Christians.

As humans, we are under many different social pressures, some we may not even agree with. For example, I have no problem with nudity, but I know that where I live I would be arrested for being naked: there is a dress code I have to abide by in my society. I don't worry too much about that because wearing clothes is not a big imposition for me, and often it can be cold or windy. How much do we abide by society's rules and subvert our own personal values? An interesting human behaviour is that in public, people are less likely try to stop a crime such as theft, rape or assault if others are also not intervening. However, when someone tries to do something to help, others then feel confident to join in. People are often afraid of going against group-think or authority, even when they have the capacity to stop serious damage to another human.[10, 11]

Much of the Bible is stories of people who do not follow the crowd, but instead follow God and use their own strong values to follow a path different from that of the masses. Christianity is quite clear about us having a personal relationship with God.

> "If you belonged to the world, it would love you as its own. As it is, you do not belong to the world, but I have chosen you out of the world. That is why the world hates you."[12]

It is vital that we maintain our values in the face of the masses or within a coercive society, no matter how difficult it can be; to speak up and intervene when we see injustice. In such situations most people will try to keep you in-line and force you to conform. They may say you have no right to make judgments, maybe even devising a reason why you cannot make such a judgement, such as your age, your social status, your different nationality, your race, or your gender. However, as a fellow human you do have the right to object to things you believe are wrong. Henry David Theroux went to prison for not wanting to pay taxes that were supporting slavery. That may seem a simple act of protest now, but at the time he was directly contravening the law of the United States. Your society wants you, indeed needs you, to comply. Of course, others have different views, and we need to compassionately listen to and try to understand the views of others. It's not simply about forcing our view on others, but about maintaining values and supporting the oppressed. I understand why people would be upset seeing me naked, because the body has become sexualized. For myself a naked body is less sexual than a clothed body, with men and women looking more similar when naked than when dressed (due to gender oriented clothing). However, I don't feel

10. Haney, "Study of Prisoners", 1–17.
11. Darley, Bystander Intervention, 377–83.
12. John 15:19

it is problematic or detrimental to society that we have to wear clothes, and it does create benefits, such as cultural uniqueness, comfort, utility and sexual attraction. Thus, we need to be tolerant of differences in viewpoints, and only when we need to, to object to injustices. Often people are persuaded more by kindness, cooperation and understanding than by confrontation. Even if we do need to act, we must act with compassion.

Similarly humans often defer responsibility to others, pretending that we have no power to make a change. The soldier who tortured Abu Ghraib prisoners had a commanding officer who had told him to do it, and that chain of command permitting torture had led all the way up to the US Secretary of Defense. However, no matter the authority of the person ordering your actions, if they are your actions, you are responsible for them. Nobody has power over you unless you give it to them.

You don't want to be an old person, laying in hospital at the end of your life, and blame others for your decisions. We make mistakes, we make misjudgments—that is the process of life. We learn and often change our personal values, but no matter what, we should never blame others for decisions that were ours. Personal responsibility is empowering. It allows, you to realize that so much of what you do in your day to day life is not really decided by others, but decided by yourself. This can be difficult to accept, because sometimes we want an easy life with no conflicts, to make others happy, to do our job well. We also live with balances; you may not approve of your bosses behaviour in having multiple affairs with women at work, but you want to keep your job, so you keep quiet. That decision on what to do is on your shoulders, and you simply have to accept that you have to use judgement and make practical decisions; but ultimately you have responsibility for all you do and don't do.

"Money is power". Do you agree? This is identical to the belief that you have to do something because someone in authority told you. Yes, it's coercive, because in modern society most of us feel we need money to live. However, the Bible specifically tells us that money is not power. It tells us that only God has power, and we have free will. As with an unjust order from someone else, we can choose whether to follow God or money. Notice that the bible does not say money is evil, it says: "For the love of money is a root of all kinds of evil. Some people, eager for money, have wandered from the faith and pierced themselves with many griefs."[13] The love of money is a root (not the root) of all kinds of evil (not all evil).

13. 1 Tim 6:10

Money is useful. Social and national development can be aided by the appropriate use of money and well structured market mechanisms that assist in effectively rewarding work and productive output. Jesus states "it's easier for a camel to pass through the eye of a needle than for a rich man to enter the Kingdom of God."[14]

Jesus does not state that a rich man cannot enter the Kingdom of God (which at this point we are presuming is a Kingdom here on Earth). He just infers that it is incredibly unlikely he will enter the Kingdom of God. Why? "No one can serve two masters. Either you will hate the one and love the other, or you will be devoted to the one and despise the other. You cannot serve both God and money."[15] In the Old Testament, there is advice on investing well and looking after money, there is advice on giving to the poor and tithing. It is the love of money that can cause immoral acts, and the lack of desire to help those in need around us, that can be a problem with money. There are three factors which may indicate that a rich person is coming into conflict with his spiritual needs: (i) if the money was gained through immoral means; (ii) if they are ignoring the needs of those that are worse off; and (iii) if they sought money for purposes other than service to God.

Crime and abuse of others does pay: selling illegal or damaging products, or creating wealth for some through causing a detriment to others. This could be as simple as unnecessarily paying exploitative salaries, or selling a second-hand car that you know is damaged for an inflated price, without being honest about its condition. As we increase in wealth, our responsibility to others increases as we have the power to improve other's lives. This doesn't necessarily mean giving away money. It could be investing in useful or beneficial businesses, setting up a trust fund when you die, mentoring others to get out of poverty. Many famous singers, footballers, and actors have contributed greatly to philanthropic projects.

Money represents an exchange of goods and services, and it doesn't matter so much if you are high or low earning but that your work is contributing to society, and not taking away from society. Selling addictive drugs may make you a muti-millionaire, and maybe you could donate all that cash to a worthwhile charity, but you are attempting to solve one problem while creating another problem. Better to be poor and kind to

---

14. Matt 19:24
15. Matt 6:24–26

those around you, than to be rich but destroying people's lives. The money you have does not represent your value to society, simply what people are willing to pay for those goods or services in the structure of your current society. A doctor in Sudan may be saving as many lives as a doctor in the USA, but their income is likely to be very different. Money is not something to be looked up to, but neither should we despise people because they have money. By generating wealth through fair and beneficial means, we can provide jobs, improve the economy, be of service to others, and help those in need. Money is only power to the people that will commit immoral acts for money; the love of money above God. Such people give power to money, and to those with money.

Thus, power isn't held by people nor material objects such as money. We as individuals give them power. It is actually ourselves that hold the power. A president is voted in, and they are expected to represent the population. They can maintain power partly through their security, police and the military, who are paid. But if there is insufficient will from the people for the president to stay in power, protests and dissent can force an election or a coup. Of course the security personnel may control this action, but they themselves have a choice if they feel that the government should not continue. Power is never taken, only given. Henry David Thoreau's decision to go to jail rather than paying taxes which supported the slave trade was a small act by one individual. Indeed it had little direct impact: to his annoyance his aunt paid his tax debt, completely counteracting his protest. However, it did have a huge subsequent influence. Mohandas Ghandi (better known by his title Mahatma (*Great-soul*) Ghandi) was influenced by this action and used it as a model for his successful campaign to free India from British rule. Each of us has more power than we realize, but understandably most of the time we want an easy life, usually prioritizing our immediate needs above those of others. For money especially, we can give away our power to others. It's difficult quitting a job that you need to support your family even if you know that job is causing harm. This is why corrupt regimes continue to be supported, and innocent people are persecuted. However, if we are to treat our neighbour as ourself, we must accept that those suffering also have families.

As Jesus become more popular with the public, others felt their authority was being challenged and tried to trap Jesus, such that he would insinuate himself:

"Then the Pharisees went out and laid plans to trap him in his words. They sent their disciples to him along with the Herodians. 'Teacher,' they said, 'we know that you are a man of integrity and that you teach the way of God in accordance with the truth. You aren't swayed by others, because you pay no attention to who they are. Tell us then, what is your opinion? Is it right to pay the imperial tax to Caesar or not?'"[16]

There is a back-story to this event. The taxes has to be paid with a Roman coin (denarius), however this coin had the image of Caesar on the back. Emperor Caesar considered himself a God, so some Jews considered using such coins to be idolatry. Thus if Jesus said yes, they should pay taxes, he would be supporting idolatry, whereas if he said no, he would be in trouble for supporting rebellion against Rome.

"But Jesus, knowing their evil intent, said, 'You hypocrites, why are you trying to trap me? Show me the coin used for paying the tax.' They brought him a denarius, and he asked them, 'Whose image is this? And whose inscription?' 'Caesar's,' they replied. Then he said to them, 'So give back to Caesar what is Caesar's, and to God what is God's.'"[17]

Thus, Jesus turned what was a deceptive trap into a strong statement about government authority, money and God. He was not suggesting rebellion against the government, nor the non-payment of taxes, but highlighting the world of money and the world of God are two entirely different things. So what are we to give to God?

"Therefore, I urge you, brothers and sisters, in view of God's mercy, to offer your bodies as a living sacrifice, holy and pleasing to God—this is your true and proper worship."[18]

Thus we are to give our lives to God. This is through service to God, but also through giving up our mundane material life and being transformed (born again), as illustrated in the next passage "Do not conform to the pattern of this world, but be transformed by the renewing of your mind."[19] Our lives are literally what we give to God.

One month after the bus-boycotts had brought Martin Luther King to prominence in the US civil rights movement, his house was bombed.

16. Matt 22:15–17
17. Matt 22:18–21
18. Rom 12:1
19. Rom 12:2

That same night, on 30 January 1956, he had a terrible choice to make. Would he continue his civil rights activity and risk the lives of his wife and two young daughters, or would he put his family first. He tells how he prayed the whole night in his kitchen, asking for guidance from God and torn between these conflicting responsibilities. In the end he believed the path God had chosen for him was to continue his fight for equal rights for black people in America. Though he was finally assassinated only 12 years later, on 4 April 1968 in Memphis, by that time he had achieved so much, and became an inspiration to the world. The truth is, even when we feel weak, we actually have huge personal power. We are free to love others, to tell the truth, and to speak out against injustice. People may persecute us because of jealousy, because they cannot control us or force us, they may even kill us, but we have already given our lives to God. Neither do we have to defer our power and protect our lives by pretending that what is real is false and what is false is real. The Bible is replete in telling us the importance of truth:

> "Dear children, let us not love with words or speech, but with actions and truth."[20]
>
> "God is spirit, and his worshipers must worship in the spirit and in truth."[21]
>
> "Do your best to present yourself to God as one approved, a worker who has no need to be ashamed, rightly handling the word of truth."[22]
>
> "Having put away falsehood, let each of you speak the truth with his neighbour, for we are members one of another."[23]
>
> "Love does not delight in evil, but rejoices with the truth."[24]
>
> "And they sent their disciples to him, along with the Herodians, saying 'Teacher, we know that you are true and teach the way of God truthfully, and you do not care about anyone's opinion, for you are not swayed by appearances'"[25]

---

20. 1 John 3:18
21. 1 John 4:24
22. 2 Tim 2:15
23. Eph 4:25.
24. 1 Cor 13:6
25. Matt 22:16

"The Lord is near to all who call on him, to all who call on him in truth"[26]

"To the Jews who had believed him, Jesus said 'If you hold to my teaching, you are really my disciples. Then you will know the truth, and the truth will set you free'"[27]

Thus, for me the main message of the crucifixion is not that Jesus bore our sins. It was a strong message in being faithful to God with our lives and our bodies, and being faithful to truth.

""You are a king, then!" said Pilate. Jesus answered, "You say that I am a king. In fact, the reason I was born and came into the world is to testify to the truth. Everyone on the side of truth listens to me. "What is truth?" retorted Pilate. With this he went out again to the Jews gathered there and said, "I find no basis for a charge against him.""

Thus I do believe Jesus was a messenger for the truth, the Messiah. Through his crucifixion he showed us that no-one and no-thing has power over us. Only God has power, and if we have dedicated our lives to God, we too are part of that power. Martin Luther King stated ". . . when I took up the cross I recognized its meaning. It is not something that you merely put your hands on. It is not something that you wear. The cross is something that you bear and ultimately that you die on."[28] While being in God's service, being God's eyes and hands in this world, while giving ourselves to God, we may suffer and we may pay the ultimate price, but also we empower God, and in turn ourselves are empowered by God.

The crucifixion then is a demonstration of our own personal power. We have the power to live truthful and unashamed lives. We will not change the world by resentment and anger, but Jesus shows us we can change the world through truthfulness and love. Though it may cost our life, we will retain our integrity and our power. Paul in the Bible presents beautiful imagery, the importance of truth in resistance against injustice and in service to God; through not being led into negative words and actions and not utilizing anger and violence to achieve our ends, but achieving them with peace:

---

26. Ps 145:18
27. 1 John 8:31–32
28. Clayborne, *Autobiography Martin Luther King*, 327.

"Stand firm then, with the belt of truth buckled around your waist, and with your feet fitted with the readiness that comes from the gospel of peace.[29]"

Thus, there is much powerful symbolism that can be taken from Jesus' crucifixion. It is undeniably a touching event in the Bible and a powerful moment in Jesus' life. While for some the forgiveness of sins will be prominent in this symbolism, I would like you, whether Christian or not, to take another message: that Jesus demonstrated we have complete personal responsibility for our lives; that no one and no thing has power over us (unless we give it to them); that through walking in truth, love and peace we can serve God on Earth, and we can retain this power until death. As a consequence of taking responsibility, having faith in God, and not being under the power of anyone or anything, we also gain freedom.

"It is for freedom that Christ has set us free. Stand firm, then, and do not let yourselves be burdened again by a yoke of slavery."[30]

"Now the Lord is the Spirit, and where the Spirit of the Lord is, there is freedom."[31]

---

29. Eph 6:14–15
30. Gal 5:1
31. 2 Cor 3:17

5. Happiness and Suffering

WHAT DO I DO to get money? What do I do to get a husband or wife? What do I need to get on in my career. What do we do to make our nation successful? Life can seem like a constant game of power and grasping. This is the material world we live in. Society, every day, whether through the television, social media, our church, national authorities, our work or our friends, is telling us what we should or should not do; to be a good person, to be successful. But how do we measure that success and does this striving ever end? Think of those people you consider to be successful? Maybe a famous singer like Michael Jackson or Whitney Houston. For the more spiritually minded it may be people like Nelson Mandela, Mahatma Ghandi or Martin Luther King Jr. Do we define success by happiness? Were any of these people happy? Michael Jackson appears to have had so much pressure to perform as a child that he never truly had a childhood, and he spent much of his adult life lonely and surrounded by people whose main interest was his money. After a promising career Whitney Houston became a drug addict and died at the age of 48, drowning in a bathtub with cocaine use as a contributing factor. Her daughter died only three years later, also drowning in a bathtub after drug use. Both Ghandi and King struggled immensely in their lives, both finally assassinated, at 68 and 39 years old respectively. Nelson Mandela spent 27 years in prison. None of these can be considered to have had what is typically considered 'happy' lives. I hope most of you would agree that happiness is not really what we admire when we assess the greatness or success of a person.

Great people do not pursue happiness. Indeed happiness is elusive, temporary and difficult to substantially define. Usually we are happy when our child is born, when we win money, when we see a long lost friend, when we pass an exam. But all these are transient events. You are not happy all the time after your child is born; when you win money you spend it or get used to more wealth and the happiness wanes; seeing a long lost friend is great, but then after a long time with them they become simply a friend; although happy when you pass an exam, the same joy isn't there throughout your career. The way our animal brain works is to seek out dopamine and serotonin, the *happy chemicals* that are released into our body when we achieve something. It's like we're drug addicts for dopamine and serotonin. Indeed cocaine stimulates dopamine production. Even alcohol can temporarily help us feel happy. Sugary foods and meat can trigger dopamine release. Hopefully the more mature of us will restrict these short-term dopamine highs and instead get our dopamine high from activities that are less damaging long term, and more beneficial to health, such as exercise, competing to win a prize, or studying to pass an exam.

Very few animals exercise. Though they may actively play or stretch, it's not an efficient use of calories. You also don't see tigers studying for exams. However, humans have a great capacity for projecting their thoughts into the future and understanding that an action now can result in positive (or negative) outcomes in the future. Thus, we play a trick with our own brain, and do things we don't necessarily want to do now, in the understanding that there will be some future dopamine reward or benefit. This may mean not eating the whole packet of cookies, getting up at 5am to run, or spending the evening studying for the next day's exam rather than going to a party. The benefit is also that your body and brain can learn from these productive activities. I am sure you've experienced the feeling after stopping exercising: it's difficult to get yourself to start again but still you miss it. The short term pursuit of happiness, at least in a hedonistic way, is rarely worthwhile because of its temporary nature, and it often leaves us feeling worse in the long term, or even caught in a roller-coaster of highs and lows. While we may usually assume our subconscious brain simply regulates the body and knows what's best to make us happy, in fact we need to manage and train the brain and our short term desires if we want longer term and more consistent happiness.

A Taoist story I've heard, goes something like this: A group of young men decide to play a practical joke on their good friend. Coming back from the friend's home village they tell him "We're sorry to bring this bad news to you, but your father has died and you have to go to a funeral in your home village." The friend wails at the news of his father's death, tears flow down his face, and he contorts in despair.

Feeling sympathy they tell him "We're sorry, this was just a joke. We met your father and he is alive and well; as healthy as an ox in fact. He simply told us to send his love and best wishes to you." At this news, the friend was relieved and indeed overjoyed that his father had not died. This joy soon turned to anger and he rebuked his friends for this cruel joke. They laughed back at him and commented "People are strange. Indeed, nothing had changed in reality. When you thought your father was dead you were so sad, then when you learned he was not, you were even happier than before we met you. Now you are angry. The reality hadn't changed at all; your emotional response was simply due to the thoughts inside your head."

Grief is a natural preparation for what is a necessary psychological adaptation for a huge change in our personal world and reality. Such grief isn't something that we necessarily really overcome, but instead gradually work our way round until we get to a new normality. The purpose of the story isn't to illustrate the foolishness of grief, but how our perceptions of reality can be so much more devastating than reality itself. That there is an external world that we interpret through our thoughts and feelings, and while we may have little control of much of what happens in the external world, we do have some degree of control over our thoughts and feelings. Pursuing happiness indeed has less to do with the external world, but much more to do with our internal thoughts and reflections about that world. What we deserve, what we need, how people have treated us: all of these things have more to do with our personal opinions and views than they do with the external world. We know that the world isn't just, and that bad things happen to good people, but it is very easy to fall into a psychological trap that the world is somehow specifically victimizing us, that things are worse than they really are, or that the unknown future will be a disaster. Also this applies to how we compare ourselves with others. We may feel that everyone around us is better off, or that we haven't received what we should have for our efforts in life. Usually when thinking such thoughts we ignore those that are indeed much worse off. It's like we can develop a relentlessly craving mind, always looking at how it could be better for us. It's natural; it's our animal brain. But that is also a curse and it is what we have to control.

The dogged pursuit of happiness rarely has a satisfactory ending. When we chase external experiences and objects, we either don't achieve them and feel disappointed, or we will attain them, and then look around to see what more we want. But I'm not proposing aestheticism, where we deny ourselves material goods or goals, or trying to get rid of emotion. A normal human life has ups and downs. A more worthy pursuit than happiness is contentment. This contentment can be found by having meaning in our life, as well as accepting that in the pursuit of our goals we will have dissatisfaction, loss, and indeed may even have to reassess what gives us meaning in our life. By stepping back slightly from life and not chasing short term gratification not only do we calm the immediate ups and downs of emotion, we can also see and plan on a larger scale. Just working toward fulfilling that meaning can provide satisfaction and contentment. People with meaning in their life will suffer, will have periods of unhappiness or discontentment, but that external meaning will provide a structure that allows them to surpass it, re-orientate and continue trying.

Viktor Frankl, the Jewish psychologist and concentration camp survivor, wrote

> "If there is meaning in life at all, then there must be meaning in suffering. Suffering is an eradicable part of life . . . Without suffering and death, life cannot be complete."[1]

In the same book he also quotes philosopher Friedrich Nietzsche: "He who has a Why to live can bear almost any How."[2]

In Christianity we accept that we will necessarily suffer, and even that it is noble or redemptive to suffer. The question of suffering is fundamental to Christianity, with the central role of the crucifixion of Jesus which is considered a model of severe suffering: a man dying for the salvation of humans, while at the time being ridiculed, and tortured, by those he loves and aims to help. Such a model behaviour can indeed give us strength when we are feeling persecuted or treated unjustly. I draw attention to Christian acceptance of suffering in part to draw a distinction with Buddhism. Within Buddhism the central tenet is the Four Noble Truths:

1. The truth of suffering i.e. that suffering exists.
2. The truth of the cause of suffering i.e. it has a cause; usually assigned to the three poisons of hate, greed and ignorance.
3. The truth of the end of suffering i.e. that it is possible for us to end our own suffering.

---

1. Frankl, *Man's Search for Meaning*, 76.
2. Frankl, *Man's Search for Meaning*, 84.

4. The truth of the path that leads to the end of suffering i.e. that there is a method to end suffering, which in Buddhism would be the Noble Eight-fold Path (right understanding; right thought; right speech; right action; right livelihood; right effort; right mindfulness and right concentration/Nirvana (enlightenment).

Buddhism accepts that we suffer, and suggests we can alleviate suffering by a proper approach to the world. Underlying this is that suffering is caused by undue attachment to things in the world. This is entirely logical, and indeed it is the logic and clear parallels with discoveries in psychology that often attract westerners to Buddhism. However, I feel that this prime focus and pursuit on ending suffering, particularly if this entails greater detachment from the world, does not help us to live as fully involved humans. Instead of accepting that suffering is a part of how we move forward, develop and achieve fulfillment, it is an attempt to shield ourself from that suffering. So I wouldn't discredit the immense benefit of such techniques in living a more peaceful life, but instead question whether we necessarily should be living such a life without suffering in the first place.

Taoism takes a slightly more naturalistic approach than Buddhism, and accepts that we may suffer, but simply recommends not making suffering out to be more than it should be; not over-indulging in suffering. For example in this (edited) story from The Book of Chuang Tzu:

> "Chuang Tzu's wife died. When Master Hui went to offer his condolences, he found Chuang Tzu lolling on the floor with his legs sprawled out, beating a basin and singing.
> 'She lived together with you,' said Master Hui, 'raised your children, grew old, and died. It's enough that you do not wail for her, but isn't it a bit much for you to be beating on a basin and singing?'
> 'Not so,' said Master Chuang. 'When she first died, how could I of all people not be melancholy? But I reflected on her beginning and realized that originally she was unborn. Not only was she unborn, originally she had no form. Not only did she have no form, originally she had no vital breath. Intermingling with nebulousness and blurriness, a transformation occurred and there was vital breath; the vital breath was transformed and there was form; the form was transformed and there was birth; now there has been another transformation and she is dead. This is like the progression of the four seasons: from spring to autumn, from winter to summer. If I were to have followed her

weeping and wailing, I think it would have been out of keeping with destiny, so I stopped."[3]

In Christianity, although we accept that suffering is part of life, the main focus is that through having a *Why* (to serve God) we can overcome suffering. That isn't to say that we should indulge in suffering. However, with faith we can not only overcome it, but suffering even has some value.

> "Not only so, but we also glory in our sufferings, because we know that suffering produces perseverance; perseverance, character; and character, hope"[4]

That suffering brings redemption is a controversial claim in the Christian, and particularly Catholic church. In 1259 following crop failure and Europe wide famine, a group of Catholics in Perugia, Italy, felt that they should cleanse themselves through self-flagellation. This practice spread to much of the population, with parades through the city, and condemnation of those who were not self-flagellating. In 1349, when the Black Death plague had swept through Europe, many countries (including England) saw a resurgence of Catholics self-flagellating. Following on from this period the Catholic church tried to suppress self-flagellation and declared it heretical. However, even today in areas of Spain and in Campania in Italy you'll see self-flagellation performed by Catholic devotees around the period of Lent, and in South America and the Philippines some Catholics will even be seen to practice self-crucifixion.

I would strongly distinguish actively inflicting a damaging forms of pain on your own body, such as self-flagellation, from pain which occurs in attempts to improve health e.g. from exercising. Also I see it very differently from acts where we are demonstrating control over bodily desires such as celibacy or fasting. The biblical quotation christian flagellants often use to justify self-flagellation is:

> "Everyone who competes in the games goes into strict training. They do it to get a crown that will not last, but we do it to get a crown that will last forever. Therefore I do not run like someone running aimlessly; I do not fight like a boxer beating the air. No, I strike a blow to my body and make it my slave so that after I have preached to others, I myself will not be disqualified for the prize"[5]

3. Mair, *Wandering on the Way*, 169.
4. Rom 5:3–4
5. 1 Cor 9:27

However, in this case, rather than the New International Version above, which is generally an accessible translation, I would instead refer to the translation from the New American Standard Bible, which most scholars consider more accurate.

> "Everyone who competes in the games exercises self-control in all things. So they do it to obtain a perishable wreath, but we an imperishable. Therefore I run in such a way as not to run aimlessly; I box in such a way, as to avoid hitting air; but I strictly discipline my body and make it my slave, so that, after I have preached to others, I myself will not be disqualified."[6]

Certainly this does not suggest self-flagellation, nor does it anywhere in the Bible. Instead it suggests control over our bodily desires such that they are subjugated to our spiritual needs. Saint Paul is simply alluding to the practice of bodily self-discipline, which I will discuss later in the chapter on fasting. Thus, while as Christians we accept that suffering is a necessary part of life and that it can bring redemption, this should not be equated either with self inflicted suffering, nor bodily self-discipline. Martin Luther King stated that "redemption comes through unjustified suffering". Let me illustrate this from my own personal experience:

I was in Portugal during the European Economic Crisis around 2009. Similar to many at the time, though we were working, we simply were not receiving salaries. Myself, my partner and my step-daughter were in severe financial difficulties. We lived in a large shared house with others similarly suffering. An engineer living in the house decided there was no point continuing work in Lisbon without a salary, and returned to the countryside where he could help his grandmother farm. The landlord, knowing that none of us had an income, had stopped asking for rent, although he asked for a contribution to the money necessary to bribe the man who came to cut off the electricity for non-payment. Food banks had been established in the country, and seeing each other's desperation, we had all begun sharing food when we managed to obtain it. At Christmas, I remember eating nothing but spaghetti and onions. I did not want to leave Portugal, but with having a step-daughter and my wife being pregnant with my child, I decided that we needed to return to the UK so I could support my family. Unfortunately I hadn't foreseen the effect of UK politics: the UK independence party were anti-immigration and campaigning to leave Europe, and the Conservative party who were

---

6. 1 Cor 9:25–27 (NASB)

in power felt they were stealing their votes with such campaign policies. Thus, though my family (Angolan partner and Portuguese step-daughter) had the legal right to enter the country under European law, they were denied entry. Appeals to the European Union fell on deaf ears because they were concerned about the UK leaving Europe and though they had legal authority, did not want to be combative with the UK. At that time legal applications of British people to get their families into the UK were being consistently turned down by the Home Office . The Prime Minister Theresa May even illegally threw out 50,000 foreign students simply because they had done English exams at a college where two students had been found cheating. For myself it ended up being a four year battle against the UK government, with an intransigent and illegally operating Home Office. Indeed the Home Office ombudsman eventually resigned in protest at the disgraceful conduct of the government. During this four year battle I had to support my struggling family in Portugal, hold down a job in the UK, and had to pursue visa after visa for my family while keeping up with the rapidly changing UK immigration law. Eventually, despite the UK trying to block opportunities to appeal rejections, I managed to get the case to court, and the judge immediately determined that my family had the right of entry.

The suffering during all this time was immense. I had to move house regularly since some visas required me to have a home suitable for housing my family, yet I wouldn't even know if these visas would be approved. My family could not visit me in the UK because ironically the Home Office see visitor visas for a partner being a risk because there is a motive to overstay. However, this suffering changed me in major ways. I met two supportive church goers, one from Nigeria and one from Kenya, who helped and supported me psychologically and often sent me verses from the Bible when they saw I was deeply suffering. I read Martin Luther King and could deeply feel and understand what he meant and what he felt when he wrote his famous *Letter from a Birmingham Jail*. I read Henry Thoreau's book *Civil Disobedience*. Not knowing from month to month when I would ever be with my family again, through constant applications, I felt deep compassion for Nelson Mandela having been in prison and not knowing when he would be released. Thankfully for me it only ended up being 4 years of not knowing, rather than the 27 years of not knowing that Nelson Mandela suffered. I wept over the plight of Iranian Zaghari-Ratcliffe and her husband Richard Ratcliffe when she was detained by Iran on false charges of plotting to overthrow the government because they wanted leverage on an unrelated financial dispute between Iran and the UK. At the time she was still imprisoned but thankfully was released in 2020, four years later.

None of these injustices did I see through the lens of logic, or through a political science degree. I saw these people's suffering through the lens of my own day to day suffering, through my personal experience. I would love to say I am not bitter. I left the UK eventually and vowed to myself never to return. I saw that governments around the world crush individuals for their own political objectives. I didn't just have sympathy for Martin Luther King, Nelson Mandela and Zaghari-Ratcliffe, I had empathy. I would never want anyone to suffer like that, but I can fully believe that like me, there was great redemption in their suffering.

"Praise be to the God and Father of our Lord Jesus Christ, the Father of compassion and the God of all comfort, who comforts us in all our troubles, so that we can comfort those in any trouble with the comfort we ourselves receive from God."[7]

Indeed, I had more suffering to come. Soon after getting into the country my partner became extremely violent, triggered by the long period of separation exacerbating her depression, which due to a distinctly discriminatory anti-male view of domestic violence, resulted in me losing my family again. But certainly now I am a stronger person, and I have empathy with those in real pain. I don't even expect to stop suffering in my life, but I have tools to help me, one of which is my faith. Instead of destroying my faith, eventually the suffering strengthened it. I realized that our whole life can collapse and we come to the brink of being completely desperate, a point where really we cannot know anything for certain and absolutely the only thing we are left with is our trust in God. A trust that somehow, despite terrible pain, everything will be alright.

God did give me a second chance. Out of the bitterness of being a political basketball between right and left wing ideologies, I left the UK and settled in Africa where I married a beautiful and compassionate wife. I do know I will suffer in the future, but God has given me opportunities I could not have dreamed of. I trust and pray to God that my daughters are happy and healthy, and I trust that whatever their struggles, God will care for them. This whole process humbled me in the presence of God, such that I understand this passage from Deuteronomy:

---

7. 2 Cor 1:3–4

"He humbled you, causing you to hunger and then feeding you with manna, which neither you nor your ancestors had known, to teach you that man does not live on bread alone but on every word that comes from the mouth of the Lord"[8]

Though I did not know it at the time, it deepened my faith and even opened my eyes to injustice and suffering I had not seen before in the world. It allowed me to peak behind the dirty curtain of politics and how it mindlessly steamrollers over people, but more importantly, it brought me much closer to God. I saw parallels in my feelings of injustice and hopelessness, that required a deep necessity for faith, with the imprisonment of Joseph in the Bible. In a similar way, the redemption found through suffering made me realize that exactly because we are frail and weak humans, we should do what is right, regardless of the consequences, because otherwise we are at the whim of selfish people; and that I'd rather be in the service of God. Ironically that service of God is what gives us immense power. It is that very renouncement of everything in life except for God, that allows us to be free, to choose, and to have that immense power.

> "While he was still speaking, yet another messenger came and said, 'Your sons and daughters were feasting and drinking wine at the oldest brother's house, when suddenly a mighty wind swept in from the desert and struck the four corners of the house. It collapsed on them and they are dead, and I am the only one who has escaped to tell you!' At this, Job got up and tore his robe and shaved his head. Then he fell to the ground in worship and said 'Naked I came from my mother's womb, and naked I will depart. The Lord gave and the Lord has taken away; may the name of the Lord be praised.'"[9]

If you have suffered greatly, it is very likely, like me, you have cursed God for what was happening in your life. Forgive yourself for that; it's a stage. Through your suffering you can find redemption. When you come out the other end you'll see such suffering from a larger perspective. If you are able to renounce everything except God, you may be able to reach the point Job reached; to die that internal death, but then find yourselves completely dependent on that trust in God. Even our Taoist friend Chuang Tzu echoes this sentiment of humility in the face of suffering:

---

8. Deu 8:3
9. Job 1:18–22

"Four men got in a discussion. Each one said 'Who knows how to have the void for his head, to have life as his backbone and death for his tail? He shall be my friend!'. At this they all looked at one another, saw they agreed, burst out laughing and became friends.

Then one of them fell ill and another went to see him. 'Great is the Maker,' said the sick one, 'Who has made me as I am! I am so doubled up, my guts are over my head. Upon my navel I rest my cheek, my shoulders stand out beyond my neck. My crown is an ulcer surveying the sky. My body is chaos, but my mind is in order.'

He dragged himself to the well, saw his reflection and declared, 'What a mess he has made of me!' His friend asked, 'Are you discouraged?' The ill man replied, 'Not at all! Why should I be? If He takes me apart and makes a rooster of my left shoulder I shall announce the dawn. If He makes a crossbow of my right shoulder I shall procure roast duck. If my buttocks turn into wheels and if my spirit is a horse I will hitch myself up and ride around in my own wagon!'"[10]

---

10. Merton, *Way of Chuang Tzu*, 62

6. Gratitude and Humility

PREVIOUSLY I ASSERTED THAT happiness is short lived, and that we're all going to suffer at some point in life. This doesn't mean we should close down our emotions. If you have meaning in life, and are striving, you will endure. But how do we find that meaning? Usually specific goals are illusory. When we have attained them we then just set another goal. If you want to be a millionaire by the age of 30, if you achieve that what is the next stage? Become a billionaire by the age of 50? The meaning doesn't have to be self-orientated, it could be to bring pleasure to other people in your life; to look after your ill parent. We can create these meanings artificially by setting goals. Maybe you want to be a champion marathon runner. While such goals are laudable and can bring satisfaction during the journey to the goal, they're rarely sustained throughout one's life. Usually we don't choose arbitrary goals, but develop these goals from early interests as a child, or due to an event or struggle we've passed in life. Maybe we have been deeply affected by something we've seen in society that we wish to change. Maybe a chain of events simply put us in the position to make a fulfilling impact. Martin Luther King did not plan to lead the civil rights movement. He was simply a popular pastor at the church, who others looked to during the civil rights movement; they had to persuade him to take up that mantle.

For many Christians the belief in a purpose in life comes from their faith, and they will either pray to God for guidance on what work they should do, or they may feel obliged to spread the faith, or to help those that are suffering. Most Christians will also trust that they are where they are supposed to be at that moment, because God has a plan for them.

Stoicism would consider that the goal in life is to do the best we can with what we have available. There is this model *eudaimonia* or *good spirit* which is the ideal we could be, and that we should strive to be that ideal, even if in reality it is difficult to achieve. Having a mentor, model person or idealized hero to live up to can certainly help align ourselves to our goals of being who we want to be. Modern Christianity even adopted the "What Would Jesus Do" phrase to create such model behaviour, though personally I feel too detached from that era and Jesus' life to really translate it to my own life. Slightly differently to Stoicism, Christianity puts faith in God that we are where we are supposed to be at this time, and that we have a path we need to walk, and God will guide us there. This in many ways can be more calming than the frantic desire and sense of dissatisfaction that could come from having an ideal that you consistently do not achieve. We can all look back in life and see a period which we thought at the time was superficial or useless, but on reflection actually provided us with useful insight, shaping us to be the person we are today. Whether real or not, this belief we're on a path also gives a sense of cohesion within our life. We can be satisfied packing dog biscuits in a factory while we're saving money to further our education, knowing God is guiding us.

> "Commit to the Lord whatever you do, and he will establish your plans. The Lord works out everything to its proper end."[1]

Conversely, if we use Stoic logical analysis to determine what is the best we can be, there is a danger of frustration or feeling that logically that we cannot achieve our dreams. Christianity gives you more space to dream big even if it seems logically impossible at the moment. The basis in Christian faith can thus have both a calming effect in knowing that we may not have everything we want or need to achieve our goals in the current situation, but that we can and are continually moving forward in a positive direction.

Our character is continuously shaped by both our good and bad experiences, and we can use positivity and faith to take positive lessons from both such experiences. I've often reflected that old people seem to typically fall into two categories: bitter and resentful, or gentle and caring. Inevitably almost all old people have gone through some profound pain, disappointment or suffering in their life. The difference has only been in the way they responded to that trauma: as something that grew like a cancer within them, or something that, while shaping them, they learned from and moved beyond. I certainly believe that this type of happiness and contentment is eventually a choice.

1. Prov 16:2-4

For all of us, we have this path in life which is different from what we expected. When I was a child I would never have reflected that I would be living on a different continent, learning a Bantu language, and indeed working in an area outside my main area of higher education. The world is unpredictable and events conspire to push us in a different direction to that we initially planned. Instead it forces us to take advantage of what is in front of us rather than wishfully thinking for things we hoped were in front of us.

We all have our ups and downs, and we know we will be happy at times and suffer at times. What we want in life also changes as we get older. In Zen Buddhism there is a saying 'not a roof overhead, not a tile underfoot' i.e. everything is transient and temporary, so what is it that we can rely on? For Christians, this is simply God, and the knowledge that God loves us. That faith in God provides us with confidence that despite all the changes in life, there is purpose and where we are now is where we are supposed to be, even if we don't understand it yet. God loves us, and knowing that helps us understand that our suffering is not meaningless, even though at the time it may appear to be. With such understanding some individuals can show extreme courage in the face of difficulties. What we need to trust in, is not even the end point itself, but the process. With a purpose and faith we are able to endure enormous suffering. We will of course cry and feel disappointed, but these are simply rocks in the road.

> "Nevertheless, each person should live as a believer in whatever situation the Lord has assigned to them, just as God has called them."[2]

> "And we know that in all things God works for the good of those who love him, who have been called according to his purpose."[3]

Thus, while goal setting is useful for progress, we still need flexibility and adaptability, because life changes. Judging when to continue and when to change is part of the skill of life. While Stoicism may expect you to strive to be the best you can be, usually taking the societal context into account i.e. contributing to your society, Christianity doesn't expect you to be of this world. There are Christian values that may not relate to your society, and indeed you should not be swayed by society. As Christians

---

2. 1 Cor 7:17
3. Rom 8:28

our purpose very much derives from the concept that we are God's tools on Earth.

> "Do not be conformed to this world, but be transformed by the renewal of your mind, that by testing you may discern what is the will of God, what is good and acceptable and perfect"[4]

Thus, while as Christians we will set some specific personal goals, these are aligned with what we perceive to be God's will. This can sound flaky and mystical, and indeed Christians themselves question their direction and lives in their prayers. We do know that as Christians we are called to serve others, though this is not necessarily through conforming to society. We may even feel later in our lives that we have a specific path we must walk. We should also accept that not all Christians have the same task. We are not all on Earth to be great leaders, famous artists, or inspirational speakers. There is something unique that we are contributing to a larger picture, even if it seems small to us at the time.

> "So neither the one who plants nor the one who waters is anything, but only God, who makes things grow. The one who plants and the one who waters have one purpose, and they each will be rewarded according to their labour."[5]

> "Each of you should use whatever gift you have received to serve others, as faithful stewards of God's grace in its various forms."[6]

The concept that God is everything, yet we are the ones who fulfills God's plans; effectively God's eyes and hands, the tools of God, is evident in many places in the bible:

> "You are the light of the world. A town built on a hill cannot be hidden. Neither do people light a lamp and put it under a bowl. Instead they put it on its stand, and it gives light to everyone in the house. In the same way, let your light shine before others, that they may see your good deeds and glorify your Father in heaven."[7]

> "For it is God who works in you to will and to act in order to fulfill his good purpose."[8]

4. Rom 12:2
5. 1 Cor 3:7–9
6. 1 Pet 4:10
7. Mat 5:14–16
8. Phil 2:13

"No one has ever seen God; but if we love one another, God lives in us and his love is made complete in us."[9]

I heard a similar sentiment in a modern Buddhist story: A lay Christian and lay Buddhist monk were walking down the street of a bustling city together. They passed a young man in rags, picking through discarded rubbish looking for a morsel to eat. As they continued on, the lay Christian, looking pensive, finally asks his friend "If there is a God, how does he allow such suffering to happen?" The Buddhist stops, thinks, and then questions "Did God create all these conditions?" "Yes, I guess", the Christian replies sheepishly. "And did God create us and our conditions?" the Buddhist asks. The Christian remained silent. "And so, were we not given the capacity to do God's work?" At this they both rushed back to assist the young man in rags.

As we get older in life, we can develop the feeling that we have not achieved the things we are really capable of. We know we capable of so much more. This feeling can keep us moving forward and attempting to do what we believe is valuable, but sometimes the relentless pressure to do and be more can be psychologically exhausting and entirely unsatisfying. While we may curse our situation in life and think everyone else is doing better than us, for Christians it isn't about what we achieve. We must not forget that we are simply in God's service. We are the tools of God, or maybe more prosaically, we are God's employees. While the progress toward certain larger objectives can be long, most of us are repeatedly placed in small situations where we can act to improve the lives of others. This doesn't entail rushing around trying to do as much good as possible. We also trust in the path given to us, and that there are certain things we can act on. Some of these will be tiny gestures that are required of us, some of them large or challenging actions. We can also recognize that not everything is for us to do, and sometimes that task is better for another to complete. God guides us on the path to fulfill his service. The overall meaning in our life is thus much larger than our smaller goals, and encompasses a selfless duty to God.

> "Do nothing out of selfish ambition or vain conceit. Rather in humility value others above yourselves, not looking to your own interests but each of you to the interests of others"[10]

---

9. 1 John 4:12
10. Phil 2:1-4

As children, we may find it difficult to see clear choices of how we serve God because we are dependents and working with little autonomy and power in our world. There are some opportunities where a child can demonstrate kindness instead of cruelty, and honesty rather than deception. Then, as we develop we're indoctrinated by society's views of what it is to be heroic; through film, television and books. This model of heroism can often include being physically strong and dominating the enemy by force to get the young woman, by deceitfully outwitting the enemy, or through violent revenge. This is contrary to the model provided by Jesus, of personal sacrifice, truth, and love for others. We could believe that the adult choices of what is right or wrong becomes more blurred. However, in my experience the opposite is true. With years of reflection on what is appropriate to do, as an adult we should have developed our values. Through our own suffering it is likely we have become more empathetic to the plight of others. The problem in making choices as an adult is not that we do not know what is right, but that we can have much more to lose through making the right choice. For many of us, that extra bit of money we can get through corruption or theft can improve our family's quality of life, or even pay for your grandfather's life-saving operation. Often it's not just personal greed that causes us to make knowingly unethical choices, but the pressures to support dependents such as wife, children and family members. Martin Luther King had exactly this dilemma when he prayed for guidance in continuing the civil rights movement, at the risk of his family. Following the straighter path becomes easier when we trust in God, and this often means we have to make an immediate sacrifice, for a much later (even beyond our lifetime) benefit.

How do we really help people? Just providing or being generous can create dependency and is open to exploitation. Should we all give up our jobs and property and become dependents ourselves? In Jesus' times most communities were much closer together and people understood each other's true need much more. In large cities, we do not know whether a beggar is desperate to support his hungry family, is a drug addict fueling an expensive cocaine habit, or is a professional beggar owning a car and house. Large cities and extensive movement of people have made it difficult to know the person asking for money.

As a child I was torn about Jesus requesting that we give to the poor and destitute:

"Sell your possessions and give to the poor. Provide purses for yourselves that will not wear out, a treasure in heaven that will never fail, where no thief comes to near and no moth destroys. For where your treasure is, there your heart will also be."[11]

Already at that young age I wondered, who were we selling our possessions to, if we were all to follow this advice? Would the receiver also have to sell them? Also, I realized that many beggars are there through a consequence of their own actions; whether alcoholism, desire to withdraw from society, drug abuse, or simply as a way of making money. In some locations begging can bring in significant tax free revenue, such that for some it is a profession. In the USA it is estimated that beggars can make $8 to $15 an hour (more than the federal $7.25 minimum wage), and in tourist locations in Spain it's possible to make up to 200 euros a day through begging. Once in London I gave to a disheveled young man begging on the subway and another person reprimanded me, explaining that he was a known drug addict. Another time a man desperate to get home was asking for train fare; but I later saw him chatting with friends on the street, and drinking from a large bottle of whiskey. Another beggar late at night in Wales explained how he needed the money to sleep somewhere safe, and I dropped him off in the car, at a hotel that most of us would not be able to afford.

Should we help such people? As Christians, we are called to love people. However, supporting drug habits, creating dependency and facilitating a life which is not conducive to their mental and physical health is not help. Our obligation to those with drug habits is to help them lose this habit. Our obligation to those deceiving others to obtain cash is to bring them back into society where they can make a positive contribution. If a thief enters your house, is it better to advise them on the problems of their lifestyle, or to give them what you have and wish them good luck in the next household? We also have obligations to others that may be victims of their fraud or theft. We do know that simply giving in to lies and deception does not help anyone, but it is essential that our approach still has to be with a loving heart.

In Jesus' time most communities would have been much more familiar with each other's situation. When we are asked to give hospitality to strangers, or help the poor, Jesus does not also talk about supporting those who use deception to beg or obtain wealth; he is simply telling us

11. Luke 12:33–34

to help the needy. We are obliged to care, but not to facilitate bad behaviour. Thus we have to attempt to distinguish from those that are honestly in need of help, and those that are exploitative. I can't suggest firm guidance, because people adapt in their strategies, but often talking more fully and getting to know a person can help with your assessment, and may help you avoid supporting criminal activity and drug abuse. Where I live many Malawians routinely beg for money from white people as there is a perception that all white people are very wealthy. It is a habitual act with requests around four to ten times a day such that it is impossible to financially support. It took me time to realize that most of the begging wasn't from desperation, but from a perception of white people. I could only determine this through a long time talking and getting to know people. You can help people in more constructive ways than simply giving money. Maybe someone needs food, maybe someone needs directions or a lift. You should get to know those within your community; maybe you can help people get a job, or maybe its a friend that has become homeless and they need somewhere to stay temporarily. Of course personal safety is important, but we should also not to be overly fearful. Saint Paul gives a balanced statement about giving what is "decided in your heart", neither reluctantly nor under compulsion.

> "Remember this: Whoever sows sparingly will also reap sparingly, and whoever sows generously will also reap generously. Each of you should give what you have decided in your heart to give, not reluctantly or under compulsion, for God loves a cheerful giver. And God is able to bless you abundantly, so that in all things at all times, having all that you need, you will abound in every good work."[12]

Within each person's life there are things we believe we need. Abraham Maslow was an American psychologist who developed a well known *hierarchy of needs* which is a theoretical pyramid of requirements, with the most essential to survival at the bottom, and those needs that are more emotional and social at the top. At the bottom are physiological needs such as food, water and sleep. When these are lacking we tend not to think of much else except attaining them. At each level we believe that fulfilling these needs will solve our life's problems, but then when those needs are fulfilled, we develop higher level needs that we believe will make us more fulfilled. The next level, is personal security and health.

12. 2 Cor 9:6–8

Following this level is love and belonging, such as having friends, family and a sense of connection. Above this is esteem, status, respect from others, recognition. Finally there is a level called *self-actualization* which is a desire to fulfill your own perceived potential. What's often omitted in this theory, but which I myself experienced when homeless and hungry, is that you usually resent those that have fulfilled the needs that you don't have. When you don't have food, you not only feel that your life would be solved if only you had food, but also you resent those who have food and are focusing on their own needs at higher levels of the pyramid. Naturally you ask yourself why they have it and you don't. Watching someone spend money on an expensive fashionable hat can be difficult when you know that money could feed you for a month.

What rarely happens is the converse. When you have what you need at that level, you rarely look at those who have less; they are usually forgotten about. It's in our animal nature to compete and to want more, and to look at those with more and work out how to get that. When I was living in Portugal during the European economic crisis, there were educated working people who had lost everything, and some were on the street picking through waste to find food or sell anything they could salvage, such as discarded electronics. At the time I was staying in a second story flat where I could see the activities in the street and remember seeing one such man in a suit, in an organized fashion, picking such material out of waste container, and laying it into small piles depending on utility. Only a few yards away a middle aged woman was shouting at a young girl for painting her plant pots the wrong colour. She was completely devastated about the events going on in her life. All of us tend to walk around with the problems of our own life in our head, and forget of the problems of those around us.

Apart from our obsession with wanting more, blinding us to other's needs, another problem we have is the belief that everything good we have in life is due to our own hard work and personal ability, yet everything bad in our life is due to other people's actions. As humans we live in complex human societies, and while having focus and purpose combined with dedication and hard work can bring rewards, other people have built the social structure we rely on. Much of us earn salaries from money paid in taxes, or through an organization that has developed through other's hard work. Some societies reward doctors handsomely, some don't; some reward engineers well, some don't; some reward ministers well, some don't; some permit you to make money from unethical activity, some don't; some have low inheritance tax, some don't. Your assets and income doesn't necessarily represent your contribution to society, but also how society is structured.

While we need to take personal responsibility for our lives, and do what we can, we are still buffeted by good and bad fortune which is outside of our direct control. Possibly you performed excellently in a humanitarian organization, but politics has changed and your area of speciality is now redundant. Maybe you invested in something worthwhile, but it didn't work. Maybe you had to give up your career to care for someone. What helps us both cope with these ups and downs in life, as well as allows us to see the suffering from others, is humility. While we try to be as effective as we can in our lives, elements outside of our control, and often self-sacrifice for an ethical greater benefit, can limit our success. A trite example is when I once helped a blind man take his luggage off a train, only to miss my connection and have to spend a cold night sleeping on a railway platform in Spain. Through humility we can do the best we can, but recognize that some will gain and some will lose and often because of external events. This will help us understand that not everyone suffering is because they didn't try, and not every success is down to just personal effort. Humility is an important method of recognizing that each of us can go through very difficult times, and helps us maintain empathy for others.

Gratitude for what we have naturally arises from this since we understand that it is completely possible, like in the Biblical story of Job, to lose everything. Remembering gratitude for the things we have is one tool to lesson the animalistic craving for more, and the temptation to be jealous of what others have. Because, as part of our natural human problem solving mental mechanism, we are psychologically built to put more focus on our problems than on our blessings, we easily forget all the amazing things we have achieved and attained.

As a short exercise, think about the amazing things you can still contribute to the world because of your ability to move your body, smile, think, speak. What if you lost your legs? You could still carve wooden objects with your hands, type at a keyboard, write a novel. What if you lose your arms too? You can still speak. Several people with *locked in syndrome* where they are completely paralyzed from the neck down have written books with the help of electronic equipment and using their eyes or a small tube to push air down. If you are still able to think and can move at least some part of your body, you are lucky: you have the ability to impact the world, no matter how dire it appears. This is much better than being dead. Many years ago the director of the research institute I worked in, whenever there was a panic, would stop everyone and ask "Is anyone dead? No? Then everything is fine." Of course, even if others are dead, things are fine because you can still act. If you're dead of course, the worrying is over. The reggae singer Bob Marley also had quite a stoic take on the difficulties of life when he sang "If you're not wrong, then everything is alright" i.e. if you're following a good path, nothing else matters.

Gratitude has been shown by science to have positive psychological and health benefits, build stronger relationships, create more positive emotions, and help you enjoy good experiences. A simple practice that can achieve this is each day is to think of the things for which you are grateful. Not just on great days, but more especially on those terrible days where everything is a disaster. Realizing that you still have some amazing things in your life, maybe a healthy body, people that love you, food, a beautiful sky or fresh grass to look at, a nice aroma in the air; all these things will help you counteract that animal-brain that wants to just focus on what you are missing. Particularly this negativity can come when you think about past things, that you no longer have control over, or future things that haven't happened. That gratitude for your current benefits, the things you can do now, is really empowering. For those that pray, gratitude can be the start of your prayers. Instead of praying for things you don't have, pray with gratitude for things you do have. While prayers can be useful for helping us to focus on what we really need in life such that we work toward it, I've often found that through first expressing gratitude, what would normally be a request in my prayers actually then turns to others, knowing that they don't have the things that I am extremely grateful for.

Being grateful also creates a positive mindset by reducing wishful thinking: it makes you evaluate all the resources you have to achieve your desired objectives. Sometimes desperation and loss makes us cynical and locks us in the belief that our life is a tragedy. By stopping and re-examining what the real situation is, and the tools for action we still have, we can "pull ourselves up by our boot-straps" and find another path to our objective. Gratitude is thus an extremely important tool in our day to day lives and in our coping strategies. Rather than give examples, my suggestion is simply to try it. Every day for a week, tell God (or even speak to yourself if you are not a theist) at least five things you are grateful for in your life. I can guarantee that this simple exercise will bring you joy and a new perspective on life.

I believe gratitude also results in us being more likely to help those truly in need, since instead of jealously and looking up the pyramid to those we perceive to have more or better lives than us, we look down the pyramid and see how others are suffering. We can see a part of life and society many often ignore, including the poor, homeless, and those suffering loss. We also realize that we are indeed blessed to have what we have, even if that previously appeared to be very little when we were trying to climb the hypothetical *ladder of success*.

Gratitude walks hand in hand with humility. To be grateful usually requires humility: we realize that others who are just as worthy as us, often have less through no fault of their own. Similarly gratitude creates humility. Through gratitude we connect not only with those that help us, we understand that we have some level of dependence on those that cook our food, look after our children, those that drive on the correct side of the road, and we also start to understand that we have an intimate dependence on the oxygen we breath, the earth on which we stand, the sunlight, nature, and the wider universe. Knowing that we must have gratitude for so many many things puts our life in context and creates humility.

Humility places us correctly in our place, as God's servant. As a child we probably prayed for God to do things for us, and maybe even became frustrated because of the apparent lack of action. What was a big turning point in my life was finally understanding that God doesn't serve us, we serve God. At this point I stopped feeling like a child who had been left out, feeling like I had fewer toys to play with than those around me—no big car, no big house, no off-shore bank account filled with money. As an adult I had an important task to do external to my own day to day life, and I need to work with others and even illicit their help in achieving that task. Humility allows me to see life isn't just about me, but that I was a functioning part of a greater whole.

> "As a prisoner for the Lord, then, I urge you to live a life worthy of the calling you have received. Be completely humble and gentle; be patient, bearing with one another in love. Make every effort to keep the unity of the Spirit through the bond of peace"[13]

---

13. Eph 4:1–3

6. GRATITUDE AND HUMILITY

"Do nothing out of selfish ambition or vain conceit. Rather, in humility value others above yourselves, not looking to your own interests but each of you to the interests of the others."[14]

Though I have previously mentioned the benefits of Christianity for our personal selves, with praying, gratitude and humility having distinct psychological and life benefits, please do not take from this that I see personal benefit as the purpose of Christianity. I want non-Christians to understand that there can be such non-theistic benefits, but I think without being sincere in service to God, such benefits are superficial. One such trend I have seen in some Christian groups which I refer to as *Life-style Christians* is the advice to only associate with people who are materially successful if we want ourselves to be materially successful. I have no doubt that this advice is correct: if you associate with investors, you will learn how to invest. If you associate with high level people within your organization you will undoubtedly be near the top of the list when they are looking to someone to promote. You will learn much from those who are the wealthiest and most successful in society. But certainly that is not what God calls us to do. We are called to be humble, and welcome everyone equally, from president to pauper.

> "Live in harmony with one another. Do not be proud, but be willing to associate with people of low position. Do not be conceited."[15]

This humility is also important in taking us away from our (often theoretical) religious, scientific or philosophical preaching to others based on the our self-perception of superior wisdom. Instead we should speak with simplicity and indeed, the best teaching is often through our own personal demonstration:

> "Who is wise and understanding among you? Let them show it by their good life, by deeds done in the humility that comes from wisdom"[16]

I am sure all of us as children have held strong opinions, that now have changed. Even as an adult we can change strongly held views. The whole of science is based on our ability to change strongly held views through new evidence. We can thus gain humility through understanding

---

14. Phil 2:3–4
15. Rom 12:16
16. Jam 3:13

that our own opinions may change, and indeed because other people's opinion may change but they may need time to understand; we're all on a journey of understanding. Although we may disagree with others, it's useful to understand where they are coming from. When we are humble we can understand that in fact no-one has reached the destination, and we are all travelling on our own unique path. When looking at life from a larger perspective I sometimes use the analogy of a burning building. We're all inside, and we know we won't get out alive. The question then becomes, what do we do when we realize that? Do we run around crazily pushing others out the way, do we claw at the windows desperately, or do we comfort and help each other.

The practice of humility is a sign of maturity. At some point in our life we realize that understanding can be superficial. We go to school and learn some basic knowledge, go home and tell our parents about the "truth" we have discovered. We may go to do a degree in university, where we then discover that what we learned in school was a huge over-simplification. When we then progress to a PhD we realize that this knowledge that we "discovered", is actually a work in progress and that even specialists may be disputing important aspects of this "truth".

Knowledge and understanding is always a work in progress; something we define and develop. Up to around 1,400 AD educated people in the Middle East and Europe had seen that all the stars, the sun and the moon revolved around the Earth and thus concluded that the centre of what they considered the universe must be the Earth. During that era, the concept of the universe was very different, with the Earth simply being considered the centre of a series of concentric celestial spheres, with each planet, the moon and the sun in their own celestial spheres. The outermost sphere contained the stars, but at the time people didn't even consider that these stars were like our sun. Some even considered the stars to be holes in the outer sphere through which the light of God shined.

In 1543 AD Copernicus, based on careful observations of the movements of celestial bodies, published the ground breaking work "Revolutions" in Latin. He detailed that the Earth and planets actually rotated around the sun. He died shortly after publication, avoiding persecution by the Catholic Church. At the time declaring that the Earth was not the centre of the universe was considered heresy. Galileo, having read Copernicus' book then later published his work "Dialogues" in the Italian language in 1632, making it accessible to the whole Italian readership. He also added additional material on tides which helped further justify this theory of *heliocentrism* i.e. the sun being the centre of the solar system. Pope Urban VIII then famously requested the inquisition to try Galileo for heresy. It wasn't so much that heliocentrism contradicted the Church, but that much of learning still lay heavily on ancient Greek and Roman writing, and it contradicted Aristotle's and Ptolemy's theories, which the Church supported. After an eight month trial Galileo admitted he had violated the injunction against heliocentrism and was allowed to return home, but the book was banned. A censored version was eventually released in 1744. It took until 1820 for the Catholic Church to finally admit that the Earth went around the sun; 277 years after Copernicus first published. Some people also associate the church of the Middle Ages with the belief that the Earth was flat, but no historical records show that Europeans ever believed the Earth was flat.

Now we have much better instruments and a more rigorous scientific structure, with investment in science and around nine million scientists doing research, so we know even more about our universe. However, our comprehension still seems tiny compared to the vastness of the universe. The greatest distance from Earth humans have travelled so far is only 384,400 km: the distance to the moon. That's less than 10 times the distance around the world. Proxima Centauri, our nearest star (apart from Sol, our sun) is 4.24 light years away. That's 40,208,000,000,000 km! The size of the universe is 94 billion light years across; and that's just the observable universe: Because light takes time to travel everything we see is in the past. Even the light from the sun takes 8 minutes and 20 seconds to reach us, so we are actually seeing the sun 8 minutes and 20 seconds in the past. Thus when we keep looking further and further to the edge of the universe we are looking further into the past until we get to the point where the universe started. We cannot see beyond that. At the edge of the observable universe there is just background microwave radiation, at a time before all the stars formed. Thus, what we can observe of the universe is only as far as the distance the light from the very start of the universe has taken to reach us. We cannot see any more of the universe than that.

In our discussion on knowledge, I hope you don't miss the irony that we believed the Earth was at the centre of the universe, then we realized that the Earth rotates around the sun, but now we once again understand the Earth is at the centre of the universe, albeit what previously was considered the universe was really the local sun and planets, whereas the centre of the universe for us now is the centre of the observable universe i.e. light is travelling at the same speed in every direction from the edge of the universe, so we're inside this sphere 47 billion light years radius.

Interestingly, the age of the universe isn't 47 billion years, which would be the time it took light to reach us from the start of the universe. This is because also the fabric of the universe has expanded. This means, as a small particle, or *photon* of light left the edge of the universe, the universe was expanding; even behind it, so the distance it has actually travelled is further i.e. the observable universe is larger than the age of the universe due to expansion. Indeed, while the edge of the universe is 47 billion light years away, the age of the universe is just 13.7 billion years.

You may ask, "why, if the universe started from a single point, is the edge of the universe all around us?" This is because, contrary to popular conception, the universe didn't start from a single point and then expand from that point. It wasn't an explosion like a hand grenade. Everywhere was expanding. The Big Bang is really a misnomer for what is a rapid expansion of the whole of space. A common analogy: imagine baking a loaf of bread with sultanas in it. As it bakes it expands, and the sultanas, which are analogous to the stars, are all moving away from us. This is what we see in the universe, with the stars rushing away from each other. However, this isn't a small bun expanding, it is an infinitely large loaf of bread, but all we can see is as far as the time it took light from the start of creation to reach us. We may never know if the universe is infinite, since we cannot see beyond the start of time, but it does seem likely.

It's not just the vastness of the universe that makes our knowledge seem insignificant, it is the understanding that on the whole, as humans we have a subjective way of viewing things. This is usually based on their utility. Take, for example, a chair. Everyone knows a chair. But do they? When I say "chair" it is an object in your mind defined by the function, for sitting. In Papua New Guinea there are forest tribes that don't use chairs. What is it to them? Probably it is firewood, or maybe even a work of art. But is it that? To trees, that chair is a dead brother that has been stripped and shaped. In a bar fight it is a weapon. Which of these is it really? It's all of these, and none of these, and indeed much much more. The way we split up the universe into defined objects really says more about how we think as a biological animal rather than how reality is. You see yourself as an individual, but you cannot exist as a human without consuming matter in the form of food, which is recombined to form your body and internal organs, and the oxygen around you which you breath, the water that you drink. Then parts of your body are broken down and excreted in faeces. We are in-fact an integral part of the environment, and depend completely on that environment. This inter-relationship is described regularly in Taoism, with a concept of all existence being one complete and indivisible whole.

We can see that much of our knowledge is based on a predefined structure of logic, and in that respect has an element of subjectivity, which to some extent may come from the way we see things as a human organism that evolved. Usually that logic is based on apparent distinctiveness in structure or function, despite strong inter-relationships between all things in the universe. We have, however, developed powerful abstract logical structures that can be considered objective. A prime example is mathematics. Within the field of science, mathematics is the only thing that we can actually "prove" since a mathematical calculation is simply reiterating the logical structure we have created. 1 + 1 = 2 simply because of the definitions of the symbols 1, 2, + and =. Unlike pure mathematics, with science we are creating a theory which we compare to a reality we do not fully understand. Thus we need to do testing to see if our theory matches reality. You do not, and indeed cannot, test if 1+1=2 since it is abstract. You can prove it, through the cohesive logical structure of mathematics, but it's only when we are making comparisons with reality that we must test our concepts. If we drop an apple it will fall due to gravity, and we know the rate at which it will fall. We can test this. Our theories on gravity are very robust, and thanks to Isaac Newton's (or possibly to Robert Hooke, who said Newton had stolen the idea from him) publishing the universal law of gravitation in 1687, we could predict the movement of objects under gravity. Notably Einstein developed the laws of general relativity, publishing in 1915. It was derived mathematically, but made slightly different predictions to the universal law of gravitation. All planets orbit the sun in an ellipse, having a point at which they are closest to the sun, called the *perihelion*. Due to the gravitational influence of other planets in the solar system, this perihelion point moves to different locations around the sun. It was observed that the planet Mercury doesn't obey Newton's universal law of gravitation, however it does move in accordance with Einstein's theory of general relatively. Many more tests showed that general relativity was a much more precise model of gravity, especially when looking at large scales in the universe. However, this is not the end of the story: the edges of distant galaxies spin faster than expected under general relativity, and we don't really know why. Some cosmologists propose that general relativity is correct but that there is undetectable dark matter, whereas other evidence suggests a new modified theory of gravity.

From these examples we can see that science is not "truth" in the conventional sense. They are models that predict what will happen, but often there are gaps in our understanding. No well informed scientist would say any science is "true" outside of abstract logic such as maths. Usually experiments are done that the probability of your hypothesis being correct is tested. The most we can do is improve the likelihood that something is true. New evidence can always overturn our current understanding of science.

The philosopher Karl Popper developed what was and still is a cornerstone of modern science—the "null hypothesis". He stated that while we can gather evidence to support a theory, we only need one piece of evidence to disprove it. Einstein's quote "a thousand experiments can prove me right, but it only takes one to prove me wrong", is simply a restatement of the development Karl Popper made as a cornerstone of modern science: science is that which is falsifiable i.e. we don't test to prove something: we develop a theory, and then test to try and disprove it. Let me give you an example...

Maybe you laughed at the previously mentioned Middle-Ages belief that the Earth was at the centre of the universe. However, this belief is not as illogical as it sounds. I'm sure you've looked up at the constellations in the sky. Now, while the stars move around the sky because the Earth is spinning on its axis, the constellations don't change shape. Ursa Major in January looks exactly the same shape as Ursa Major in June. If the Earth was not the centre of the universe, but instead was moving in an eliptical orbit, these constellations would distort. To make this more obvious let me give you an analogy: You are running around in big circle on a football pitch. When you are at one side of the field, close to where you would kick a corner, the two poles of the goal posts look close together—holding your finger up to your face you could probably cover both posts with it. As we run toward the goal posts, and then in front of them, they seem very far apart—one finger or even a whole hand cannot cover both goal posts. Similarly the relative distances between the stars in Ursa Major should change as the Earth moves in a rotation, but that is not what we see. Thus we must be at the centre of the universe with everything rotating around us. That is logical.

While logical, there was information they were missing. They didn't know the vast distance between Earth and the stars. Alioth, the star in the constellation Ursa Major which is closest to us, is 766,300,000,000,000 km from Earth. Going at 10,000 km/hr it would take six time longer than the age of the universe to reach it. It takes 83 years for light to reach us from this star. Stars are very far away. Imagine the football posts are 20 km away, but you running around in a circle 4 m diameter, you wouldn't notice the apparent distance between the posts changing because the effect is so tiny. Similarly, it took modern telescopes to be able to detect the very tiny changes in the shapes of the constellations as the Earth does its orbit around the sun. Thus, while something can seem very logical at the time, based on weight of evidence, it only takes one experiment to prove it wrong. Science doesn't "prove" anything, it simply develops more effective and precise models of reality.

Maybe you're not convinced that some things can't be proven in science. Let's go back to 1+1=2. We know that is an abstraction, but also we know if we add one apple to another apple, we get two apples. This is the power of maths. But it is also not reality. We call them two apples because that is how we classify them. But in reality they are not identical objects. Each apple is fundamentally a different entity. One may be larger, a different colour, a different shape, have a stalk, be older and definitely it is in a different location. Thus, mathematics abstracts the real world into classifications such that we can apply it. For most people in the market they don't care if it has a stalk or not, so one apple plus one apple equals two apples for the use to which those apples will be put; eating. If one of the apples was rotten, then you'd have to question your classification.

Thus maths works very effectively with our categorization of things, but to say two very similar objects are identical, an assumption common in mathematics and applied to science, is often incorrect. A problem in ecological modelling is that members of the same species are not identical. We can classify an animal as a rabbit, and it will probably eat grass, run away from foxes, and hop around. But their behaviors, sizes, appetite, speed, are not identical. Indeed a fundamental aspect of evolution is that members of the same species vary, such that the species can adapt to different selective pressures. Life is diverse, it seeks to be different, to find its own niche, to experiment. But making ecological models are notoriously difficult to the points that precision is less important than general rules.

All we understand about reality is a model. Usually a model in our heads, but we can also use books, and now computers, to make predictive models that are far more complex than anything we can imagine in our heads. Reality is out there, but everything we think about it is an approximate model of how reality really is. Understanding this basic principle of science should help you to be humble in the little knowledge we have, and that there is such a vast amount of understanding that we are completely unaware of: not just because we are limited in how we are able to conceive of things, not just because the observable universe is immense and the actual universe may be infinite, but also because anything we do "know" is just an approximation, a fluffy interpretation, of reality.

In our short lives we often expect those with more experience in life to guide us. The concept of wise elders and the benefit of our grandparents stories, is that they can tell us things that we have no direct experience of. Of course life is different for us than for even our parents era, but there are occurrences that all humans have to deal with in their lives, such as falling in love, death, disease, coping with the ups and downs. One of human's most important inventions, writing, helps us to learn from people far into the past and from people that that have experienced things we have not and even could not experience. Through books we can learn how it was for people to reach the antarctic, to live in the times of the Great Plague, to go fishing in Maine, to build the Eiffel tower, to dive to the bottom of the ocean. In many ways the Bible contains such wisdom, carried down the generations by scribes putting what were originally oral wisdom, on to parchment.

One such story in the bible, while I don't believe it to be a completely factual account, is a very powerful message about how major events can be outside our living memory. The Great Flood is a story in the Old Testament, thought to be based on an original story from the oldest surviving literary work, called the Epic of Gilgamesh. The Epic of Gilgamesh was written in Mesopotamia (current day Iraq and Eastern Syria) around 2000 BC, but itself likely came from even earlier traditional oral stories. Flood stories are common in various cultures to symbolize unexpected destruction or cleansing, it is thought the myth in the Old Testament could relate to real events at the end of the last Ice Age and even a specific flood event in the Mediterranean basin. It is thought that historically the whole Mediterranean sea basin had dried up, evidenced by a thick five mile layer of salt underneath the sea base. At that time a small spit of land at the Strait of Gibraltar was all that separated that drying basin from the Atlantic Ocean. Then, approximately 5.3 million years ago, that spit of land began to collapse and the whole ocean began to fill the Mediterranean basin again. The Mediterranean Sea today is up to 5 km deep, averaging 1.5 km, and contains 3.8 million km^3 of water.

6. GRATITUDE AND HUMILITY

It still wasn't the whole world that was flooded during that event. However, there was a time in history when the whole world was covered in water: around 3 billion years ago. The Earth is thought to have been a water-world, with only a few tiny islands formed at the tip of oceanic volcanoes. This is so long ago, that at this time there was no complex life, just archeabacteria (primitive bacteria), with the earliest evidence of life just 0.7 billion years earlier. The Earth itself only formed 1.5 billion years before this. The water-world period was also long before there was even oxygen in the atmosphere. It would take 2.998 billion years (2.3 million years ago) for photosynthesizing cyanobacteria to evolve and release oxygen into the atmosphere in the "great oxidation event". Even after that it would take a long time for the dinosaurs to evolve, who in their various forms would roam the Earth for 165 million years. That era would end with the impact of a large meteorite, affecting the climate and changing oxygen concentrations in the atmosphere from around 33 percent to something similar to today's 21 percent; resulting in the large reptilian dinosaurs dying off and being functionally replaced with more oxygen efficient mammals. Thus there is no convincing evidence that there was global flood in the last 350,000 years that humans have existed, and certainly the biology behind putting animals on an ark to survive makes absolutely no sense. But this doesn't take away from the important message in this and many other culture's flood stories: there are dramatic and unexpected events that can occur completely outside of our living memory, knowledge, and understanding.

Chuang Tzu also speaks on the limits of our knowledge and lived experiences, in a picturesque passage from the Book of Chuang Tzu:

> "Prince Mou leaned against his table and heaved a great sigh and said, 'Haven't you heard about the frog in the broken-down well?'
>
> 'I really enjoy myself here!' it said to a turtle of the Eastern Sea. 'if I want to go out, I jump along the railing around the well, then I come back and rest where the brick lining is missing from the wall. I enter the water till it comes up to my armpits and supports my chin. When I slop through the mud, it covers my feet and buries my toes. Turning around, I see crayfish and tadpoles, but none of them is a match for me. Furthermore, I have sole possession of all the water in this hole and straddle all the joy in this broken down well. This is the ultimate! Why don't you drop in some time, sir, and see for yourself?'

But before the turtle of the Eastern Sea could get his left foot in, his right knee had already gotten stuck. After extricating himself, he withdrew a little and told the frog about the sea, saying,

'A distance of a thousand tricents is insufficient to span its breadth; a height of a thousand fathoms is insufficient to plumb its depth. During Yu's time, there were floods nine years out of ten, but the water in it did not appreciably increase; during T'ang's time, there were droughts seven years out of eight, but the extent of its shores did not appreciably decrease. Hence, not to shift or change with time, not to advance or recede regardless of amount—this is the great joy of the Eastern Sea.'

Upon hearing this, the frog in the broken-down well was so utterly startled that it lost itself in bewilderment."[17]

Outside science, people regularly argue based on weight of evidence and rhetoric—clever but not necessarily true arguments. Culture and politics is heavily swayed by these subjective, unproven arguments, that are often built up to support advantage in one social group or another. This leads to endless wrangling between opposing opinions: republican and democrat, left and right wing, socialist and capitalist. Many of these arguments are simply to pick holes in the opposing tribes view and offer little to help with understanding. Because of a lack of understanding of how science works, people are swayed by anecdotal evidence. Single events are quoted to give weight to an argument rather than people objectively weighing all the facts. Emotive photographs are used to sway public opinion. Governments, because of a desire to rule rather than a desire to serve the public, try to follow the public opinion rather than lead it, so there is an ebb and flow of policy and opinion based purely around the influence of lobbyists, politically motivated media and pressure groups. Unfortunately this is the world in which most people live, and which affects most people's view of reality. How can we work against this?

The first step to clearer understanding, it to realize that much of what people say and do is to influence your behaviour, such that you will think and act in a way beneficial to their interests. If you hate someone, or want something someone else has, why waste time in direct confrontation? Easier to convince others that this person is bad and they should give you their resources. Almost always when you hear someone is bad or evil, especially groups of people, it is simply a battle for resources.

17. Mair, *Wandering on The Way*, (edited) 153

The second step is critical thinking about all the information you receive. Is there a political motivation behind it, is the provider of the information independent? Within science we have *peer review*, which means that peer reviewed articles have had a group of direct competitors critique the article and judge whether the statements are acceptable. This works most of the time. Also, any statements in a scientific paper, which aren't directly evidenced from the experiment within that paper, have to be referenced so that you can can find and read the original research and judge for yourself. Unqualified opinions are not allowed. This thoroughness does not happen in most media outlets, statements and data are presented without sources, and opinions are gathered and circulated as if they have value. To be a critical thinker you need to thoroughly engage with different and conflicting evidence and determine yourself what seems most likely, and that takes objectivity and experience.

The third step that is useful to have is a rock of personal values, which you may have to develop from some time living in the world. Why do we need personal values? Because we are inevitably influenced by the society we live in, or the groups of people we associate with (including churches). When we are younger we can consistently question and refine our values by thoughtful reflection. This will gradually solidify with an understanding why we think a certain way and enable us to compare the consistent shower of other values with those values we hold. When I was younger I attempted to rid myself of all conditioning, thinking I could be an objective and logical human. However, humans are social and we are constantly influenced by others. Those that don't hold that they have a certain philosophy toward life, inevitably absorb the philosophy of the group or society around them. We also know that many people are selfish and manipulative, trying to convince you to support one opinion or another; this is the basis of politics, and it is problematic if you want to live as an independent thinker since before you know it you're hating people you have never met because of what you have been told about them or because of sweeping generalizations. We must treat people, as they come, as individuals. Many people act subconsciously in a tribal behaviour, wanting your support to take resources from one group and reallocate it to another, or to themselves. Fundamental to Christianity, is to treat people equally, as individuals, to forgive people, and to love people. Having that basic attitude prevents you being manipulated to hurt others because of political, social and ideological pressure.

"There is neither Jew nor Gentile, neither slave nor free, nor is there male and female, for you are all one in Christ Jesus."[18]

In such a way we can retreat from public and political opinion, and instead focus on our values. We can determine what we think of the world, but continue to have an attitude of gratitude and humility; always able to return to personal values of love, forgiveness and fairness regardless of the pressures and manipulation to adopt hatred, resentment and discrimination.

---

18. Gal 3:28

7. Knowledge, Love and Jealousy

This attitude of gratitude and humility is not just about being grateful for the things we have, and being humble in the face of other people's understanding. It is a much broader attitude where we understand that the universe can take things from worthy people and give things to cruel people, and that people will pretend to know things, but fundamentally we all come from a limited perception. Just as a parent would not get into an intellectual argument with children about which toy is the best, we must place ourselves in the perspective that, while holding values (because necessarily we have to act on our values) we understand that neither ourselves nor others understand everything. A passage from Taoist Lieh Tzu, amusingly reflects this attitude:

> "Once, when Confucius was walking through a marketplace, he saw two children who looked like they were arguing heatedly over something. Confucius got curious and went over to ask them what their contention was. One child said, 'I say the sun is nearer us when it is rising and gets farther away at midday.'
>
> The other child immediately said, 'I say the sun is farther away when it is rising and nearer us at midday.'
>
> The one who spoke first then said, 'The sun looks bigger when it is at the horizon and gets smaller as it reaches noon. Don't things look smaller when they are far away and bigger when they are near?'
>
> The second child was not daunted. He said, 'The sun is hotter at noon than when it rises in the morning. Isn't something hotter when it is near and cooler when it is farther away?'
>
> Both children then pestered Confucius to answer their questions. Confucius was stumped. He told them he couldn't tell which of them was correct. The children laughed and said,

'Hey, you're supposed to be a learned man, and you can't even answer our questions!'[1]

For us we can laugh and think that, despite using logic, both children were wrong. But that isn't the point. The point is that using clever arguments and logic won't necessarily get us the answer. Christianity also condemns haughty or clever words, when the reality of what we are trying to achieve is beyond showing-off our intelligence:

> " If I speak in the tongues of men or of angels, but do not have love, I am only a resounding gong or a clanging cymbal. If I have the gift of prophecy and can fathom all mysteries and all knowledge, and if I have a faith that can move mountains, but do not have love, I am nothing. If I give all I possess to the poor and give over my body to hardship that I may boast, but do not have love, I gain nothing"[2]

Most of have seen the Christian proselytizer on the street corner shouting at people about the sin they are living in, and demanding that they repent. Maybe they're correct, but it doesn't work, because they're a resounding gong, and they are showing neither humility nor love. A simple and humble kind act is what would convert people. When I was nineteen I was traveling across Europe on an adventure with a close friend of mine. We had boarded a train and entered Germany but had no German currency; this was before the single European currency and people paid in Germany in Marks. A German woman and her grand-daughter had overhead our moaning about being hungry but not having any currency, and she sent her grand-daughter to give us each their sandwiches that they had thoughtfully prepared for themselves for the trip. Despite being thirty-three years ago, this tiny act of complete selflessness stuck with me, and continues to inspire me.

It is only through humility that we can really love others. Saint Paul asks that we love each other in humility. This passage is commonly used at weddings, and comes from instructions to the church at Corinth:

> "Love is patient, love is kind. It does not envy, it does not boast, it is not proud. It does not dishonor others, it is not self-seeking, it is not easily angered, it keeps no record of wrongs. Love does

---

1. Wong, *Lieh Tzu*, 139.
2. 1 Cor 13:1–3

7. KNOWLEDGE, LOVE AND JEALOUSY

not delight in evil but rejoices with the truth. It always protects, always trusts, always hopes, always perseveres."[3]

Following this St Paul reiterates a very powerful message: that love is more important than any abilities, or any knowledge:

"Love never fails. But where there are prophecies, they will cease; where there are tongues, they will be stilled; where there is knowledge, it will pass away."[4]

I purposely separated these here, because sometimes the Bible is so terse and dense that it can be difficult to take in everything is says line by line. Indeed, even biblical scholars may argue with each other over different meanings, which is not without its merit. However, there is no confusion in the Bible that the overall single instruction is to love one another, and this is more important than abilities or knowledge. Everything else in the Bible is background compared to this message of love.

Saint Paul was highly educated for his time. Initially called Saul of Tarsus, because he was born a Roman citizen in Tarsus, a Mediterranean coastal trading centre now in modern day Turkey. While young he was sent to Jerusalem and received an education in Jewish law and history from a leading Rabbi, Gamaliel the Elder. He could speak both his first language, Greek, as well as Aramaic, and could fluently read and write in Greek, which for that time was the sign of being an educated man. Saul was a devout Jew, living at the time of Jesus, and persecuted Christians relentlessly, seeing them as heretics. At around age thirty, heading from Jerusalem to Damascus, he saw a flash of light from the heavens and a voice from God that said "Saul, Saul, why do you persecute me?" Paul writes that it was Jesus, who was talking to him. This was around five years after the crucifixion of Jesus.

While I don't believe that Jesus is God nor the son of God, I can completely relate to this religious experience, not only because of my own religious experience which I'll describe later, but because following that religious experience Paul's words in the Bible (which is at least seven of the New Testament books) started to make sense to me. I had read much of the bible before, and had logically understood what was written. These words had not changed, but now I saw the words were reaching to get to some pure truth beyond the words on the page; like it was laying

---

3. 1 Cor 13:4–7
4. 1 Cor 13:8

just behind a gauze like layer of the logical interpretation of these words. Unfortunately, as I think may be the case with many religions, words are often an unsatisfactory method of trying to communicate a deeper meaning. As such, words can be confused and either intentionally or unintentionally misrepresented.

Christianity isn't a system of human logic or human knowledge, and as with Saint Paul on the road to Damascus, it is meant to be transformative and take you beyond your previous understanding and the mundane thoughts of the world. That's not to say that thinking illogically is thinking correctly. We have science and our logic is a vitally important tool for understanding the material reality around us. However, our understanding of reality has its limits; as humans we have our limited minds. There is something behind this that we cannot interpret with logic and science. Discovering what is behind that calls for humility but also personal introspection. We must come to the understanding that there is more than just what we know. Then how possibly can we reach this understanding? I know many Christians reading this will call out "through faith", but this seems a shallow and unfulfilling answer. While I believe faith is important, I think our deeper understanding is in fact, given to us by God. It is God who shows us, and then when we have seen, we are able to follow with faith:

> "Above all, you must understand that no prophecy of Scripture came about by the prophet's own interpretation of things. For prophecy never had its origin in the human will, but prophets, though human, spoke from God as they were carried along by the Holy Spirit."[5]

When Paul says "Love does not delight in evil but rejoices with the truth"[6] he was clearly not talking about scientific proofs or conventional knowledge, but something beyond that which we can see for ourselves with our logical brain.

> "But the natural man does not receive the things of the Spirit of God, for they are foolishness to him; nor can he know them, because they are spiritually discerned."[7]

> "And I will ask the Father, and he will give you another advocate to help you and be with you forever—the Spirit of truth.

---

5. 2 Pet 1:20–21
6. 1 Cor 13:1
7. 1 Cor 2:14

The world cannot accept him, because it neither sees him nor knows him. But you know him, for he lives with you and will be in you"[8]

"God is spirit, and his worshipers must worship in the Spirit and in truth"[9]

Christianity expects us to take a step back from the binary arguments of who is right and who is wrong, and simply to love those around us despite our differences, our different opinions, the bad or misguided things we each have done—to create a bridge of hope and love that is beyond subjective arguments. With humility we can get away from our desire to be "right" and see to the depth of where this originates. Maybe the person is afraid, maybe they are simply defending their reputation, or maybe you are! At a basic level, as with children, we want to love, and to be loved; regardless of any superficial arguments. Taoism also warns against binary right or wrong approaches, and suggests a way to get beyond them:

> "Tao is obscured when men understand only one of a pair of opposites, or concentrate only on a partial aspect of being. Clear expression becomes muddled by wordplay, affirming one aspect and denying others. What use is this struggle to set up *No* against *Yes*, and *Yes* against *No*? Better to abandon this hopeless effort and seek true light!
>
> Life is followed by death, death followed by life. The possible becomes impossible, the impossible becomes possible. Right turns into wrong and wrong into right—the flow of life alters circumstances and thus things themselves are altered in their turn. But disputants continue to affirm and to deny the same things they have always affirmed and denied, ignoring the new aspects of reality presented by the change in conditions.
>
> The wise man therefore, instead of trying to prove this or that point by logical disputation, sees all things in the light of direct intuition. He is not imprisoned by the limitations of the *I*, for the viewpoint of direct intuition is that of both *I* and *Not-I*. Hence he sees that on both sides of every argument there is both right and wrong. He also sees that in the end they are reducible to the same thing, once they are related to the pivot of Tao.
>
> When the wise man grasps this pivot, he is in the center of the circle, and there he stands while *Yes* and *No* pursue each other around the circumference. The pivot of Tao passes

---

8. John 14:16–17
9. John 4:24

through the center where all affirmations and denials converge. He who grasps the pivot is at the still-point from which all movements and oppositions can be seen in their right relationship. Hence he sees the limitless possibilities of both *Yes* and *No*. Abandoning all thought of imposing a limit or taking sides, he rests in direct intuition. Therefore I said: 'Better to abandon disputation and seek the true light!'"[10]

Discussion is important: to improve our understanding, to gain knowledge, and to see other's views and resolve problems. However, confrontational or overly picky arguments devolve into petty battles over power or standing. The Bible specifically warns against such arguments:

"Don't have anything to do with foolish and stupid arguments, because you know they produce quarrels. And the Lord's servant must not be quarrelsome but must be kind to everyone, able to teach, not resentful. Opponents must be gently instructed, in the hope that God will grant them repentance leading them to a knowledge of the truth."[11]

"Avoid foolish controversies and genealogies and arguments and quarrels about the law, because these are unprofitable and useless."[12]

"Keep reminding God's people of these things. Warn them before God against quarreling about words; it is of no value, and only ruins those who listen."[13]

This desire to beat others rather than reach a truth, sometimes motivated by greed or jealousy, can be overcome by maintaining humility and gratitude. Anyone who has spent extended times in isolation, either on a round the world yacht race, isolated imprisonment, or long distance solitary walks, feels grateful of the company of all the humans they finally meet. Though we have personal disagreements, it's good not to be pulled into a power battle. With humility we are grateful for all we have, and can be sympathetic to others. We can understand the ebb and flow of life that may provide good fortune to the undeserving, and bad fortune to those with merit. If we received good fortune for being good and bad fortune for being bad, the spiritual path would be easy, but we don't. What most

10. Merton, *Way of Chuang Tzu*, 42–43.
11. 2 Tim 2:23–25
12. Titus 3:9
13. 2 Tim 2:14

people respect day-to-day is not wealth, fame or skill, but a good character that can weather the ups and down of life with fortitude and love. Some churches will tell you that you'll get material rewards for giving, and for being a good christian, and some pastors justify their own wealth because of blessings, but this is simply not the truth. Many will help you when you have yourself been kind, but others may exploit your kindness. Corrupt and deceptive people can gain wealth and status. Jesus did not gain wealth from being good. Instead for teaching, for healing and for loving people, he was repaid with hatred and jealousy. Martin Luther King Jr. said "The cross is something that you bear and ultimately that you die on."[14]. We don't maintain our values just because we benefit, but because we know it is what we should do. It provides value in our life, beyond wealth and status. This is the immense power that comes from a Christian approach: the decisions are made because we know it is truthful and right, not because we materially benefit.

When we are caught in seeking material gains, we can easily become jealous. Indeed, jealousy is a by-product of greed. If we always want more we will search around us and work out how. Jealousy can even be a natural response. It may be an evolved mechanism to enforce other members of the community to share. Anthropologist James Suzman, relates how the tribal Khoisan people in Africa have social controls, expecting those who have been lucky in hunting to share their food, or else be exposed to ridicule[15]. This behaviour seems to be especially the case in hunter-gather tribes where hunted food can be sporadic. In a more commercial environment, especially under capitalism, sharing wealth conflicts with a notion of productivity and meritocracy, where the more skilled and harder working are duly rewarded, as well as the accumulation of capital for investment. Where I live in Malawi, there seems to be a friction between rural communal sharing and city entrepreneurs. Those in the city have an urgency to invest, buy land, and build, and those in the countryside, while sharing resources, have an expectation of help from their rich city family members, the government, and foreign aid. Probably similar to many other sub-Saharan countries, it can create a culture of greed and jealousy which makes everyone feel that they are poorer than those around them and probably is a significant driver of corruption, theft and other crime.

14. Clayborne, Autobiography *Martin Luther King*, 327
15. Suzman, *Affluence Without Abundance*

Why is resisting jealousy important? For a Christian, it is primarily because jealousy tends to relate to material wealth, and what a Christian is trying to achieve in life is spiritual. There is a clear understanding we will lose all our material goods when we die. Even though all Christians are not specifically directed to be poor or to hate money, it is clear that Christians have a binary choice, of serving God or serving money[16] i.e. wealth isn't a problem, but not being considerate of the poor and seeking to accumulate wealth to the detriment of others is not Christian. Also, by being embroiled in jealousy a Christian is evidently not working for God, but instead is craving for material things (or status) that their neighbour has.

> "Who is wise and understanding among you? Let them show it by their good life, by deeds done in the humility that comes from wisdom. But if you harbor bitter envy and selfish ambition in your hearts, do not boast about it or deny the truth. Such "wisdom" does not come down from heaven but is earthly, unspiritual, demonic. For where you have envy and selfish ambition, there you find disorder and every evil practice. But the wisdom that comes from heaven is first of all pure; then peace-loving, considerate, submissive, full of mercy and good fruit, impartial and sincere. Peacemakers who sow in peace reap a harvest of righteousness."[17]

> "Do not fret because of those who are evil or be envious of those who do wrong."[18]

Again, Saint Paul reiterates that we should not be of the mundane material world, or acting like an animalistic human, but spiritual people:

> "You are still worldly. For since there is jealousy and quarreling among you, are you not worldly? Are you not acting like mere humans?"[19]

But how can we get what we want? Well, that's the point really. We're not here to get what we want. We're here to serve God. As such we are supposed to align our desires with what is good in the world.

---

16. Mat 6:24
17. Jas 3:13–18
18. Ps 37:1
19. 1 Cor 3:3

"Do nothing out of selfish ambition or vain conceit. Rather, in humility value others above yourselves."[20]

"When you desire but do not have, so you kill. You covet but you cannot get what you want, so you quarrel and fight. You do not have because you do not ask God. When you ask God you do not receive, because you ask with the wrong motives, that you may spend what you get on your pleasures."[21]

We each have a greater destiny than buying a 4x4 Humvee that will eventually look outdated and rust. We have a role to play in God's world. Such humble actions may seem tiny in our small small lives, but as mentioned previously, small kind acts can have profound consequences. Jealousy doesn't even help us achieve what we want. Maybe we're jealous that someone else has been promoted, or that someone has received a huge sum of money which they used to build a successful business. Being jealous does not help us attain those things ourself. We look at other people's lives through a very narrow lens, thinking "I wish I had John's car", or "I wish I had Angela's house", or "I wish I had Peter's family life", not realizing that each of them probably made sacrifices to get those things. Maybe John has a tiny house because he spent his money on his car, Angela is going through a divorce, Peter is struggling to educate his children. Ironically they may even be jealous of you for something you have. Again, the animal brain is active, wanting to get more. Rather than focusing on individual parts of other people's lives and think that you would be happy if you could cherry-pick all the best things from other people's lives, it is much more effective to understand in what way you can serve God, and how to find the things you need to do to achieve that. In this way you are not "chasing two rabbits" i.e. running after two different goals, neither of which you'll catch because your focus is too broad. By determining what you want to do, and simply planning and working towards that goal with committed time, persistence, and faith you will eventually fulfill that goal or at least move further toward it. You should be blinkered to the successes of others in their own goals, because that is what they are doing, you are doing something specific to yourself. Your path is unique. You will have different challenges, different failures, different successes. Jealousy has no part of working towards that goal and is simply a distraction. Jealousy is considered so negatively in the

20. Phil 2:3
21. Jas 4:2–3

Bible that it comes in as number ten in the ten commandments, and it is considered even worse than anger and hatred:

> "Anger is cruel and fury overwhelming, but who can stand before jealousy?"[22]

Wasting time and energy on jealousy is wholly pointless. The world is not fair, it is not just; it is us as humans that bring justice and fairness into the world. However, by consistent and diligent effort we can achieve things and we can do the best we can with the resources available. Maybe we will have to work harder than others to achieve this, but what matters is that we're working toward it. With this approach we will be recognized for our struggle and commitment, and often supported by others because of the hardships we suffer. Indeed, through injustice and hardships we can develop a more resilient and deeper character and when the good times shine on us, we can value what we have and the successes we gain all the more. Without struggle, would we really find fulfillment? Without struggle would we really feel we have attained something?

---

22. Prov 27:4

8. Do what is Possible

THE TITLE OF THIS chapter is a motto. It probably sounds to you like an uninspiring and dismal motto. You would laugh to hear a eulogy that went "he did what was possible", or a motivational speaker telling you "do what is possible". People want to hear "do the impossible", "never give up", "break all barriers". However, this motto doesn't come from an aspirational speaker, it comes from a rule I made for myself during difficult times, when I was at my lowest: when I was homeless, and when I lost my daughter, and it felt that the world was collapsing around me. So how can this be inspirational? It's because much of our life we live in a mental fantasy: it's easier dreaming than doing. We think to ourselves "one day I will be rich" or "one day I'll be the best doctor in the world" and we smile to ourselves. Yet we don't plan, we don't look at what we need to do to make the first steps, we don't make it happen. It just remains a dream.

Let's break down "Do what is possible", which has two equally important aspects. The first is to determine what is possible: not to dream, not to think "if only such and such", but to think objectively of all the options, even the less likely ones. When we're in difficulty a common initial reaction is to deny or ignore that something bad has happened. We pretend everything is normal and how it used to be; nothing has changed. We just weren't mentally prepared for it. Another coping mechanism is to day-dream that something unimaginable will happen, and suddenly everything will be better. You've lost your house, but tomorrow you will win the lottery! But that doesn't happen. If you're going to cope, you need to take action based on what you already know. If you want to buy a loaf of bread, you have to get out of bed. You may fantasize that you'll go to the kitchen and it's in the cupboard, but if you know it isn't, you have to go to the shops.

The "what is possible" is to separate the fantasy from the reality, but also to really think about new possibilities. This situation has changed, there are lots of day-dreams, but you need to really think, what are all the options? You want to learn to fly, but you have no money for lessons. Do you just dream that one day you'll find a job that pays enough so you can get flying lessons, or that a wealthy relative will die and you'll inherit the money? Better to think: what is possible. You calculate how much money it will cost; so how will you get that money? Look for a new job? Ask a loan? Maybe you could join a club where you can get discounts for flying. Maybe you could apply to join the Army Air Corps or the Royal Air Force. Maybe you can befriend people that fly and ask them how they afforded it, or even through these friendships try and get a discount. When you stop dreaming, a host of real options can appear and you can determine the best options to try first and to strategize how to get there. The motto isn't about limiting your options, it's about seriously considering all the alternatives, even the more outlandish alternatives, even if they might be very unlikely. When you stop dreaming of a magical solution, suddenly you can get the tools to create many real alternative solutions. Can you teach yourself the theory, and then pay just for some practical lessons?

Working out various possible solutions is a key to discovering previously unconsidered actions. For me, it was when I was homeless and with very little money for food, and thinking how I could get a job to support my family who were themselves being supported by a friend in Portugal. At that stage I was ashamed to ask for money. I realized I would have to ensure the little money I had would only be for the purposes of food or travel for a job interview. That travel had to be the cheapest possible travel. While I felt very down and quite cynical, thinking to myself "do what is possible" kept me moving forward one more step, kept me acting in a positive direction. I couldn't afford accommodation, so I slept in a forest. I bought some very cheap cheese and the cheapest bread I could find, which I could stretch over four or five days. I found a tap in a public gardens from which I could drink. To prepare for interviews I had to go to the organization's bathrooms early, and wash and change into a suit surreptitiously. There were solutions. I didn't day dream. I understood at that point that, when necessary, I could find food in bins, and I knew I would eat it. Such a thought had disgusted me before, but now I needed to, it was an option. I had to change who I was, I had to do things I would not have expected.

The next part of the motto is "Do". While the "what is possible" stops us day-dreaming about how things should or could be, the "Do" is a call for action. Stop thinking, start doing. There are options. Be practical and do it now. Maybe your whole family died in a fire and you are the only survivor; maybe it was your fault because you left the electric heater on, and it fell over. You're devastated with guilt, your reality has been destroyed, you feel that you'll never recover, maybe you even feel suicidal. First, stand back. Breath. Stop thinking that you wish they were still alive. Stop thinking about what you could have done, what you should have done. Do what is possible, here and now. In such a situation your psychological state is no doubt at its lowest and you may feel physically and mentally incapacitated. What's possible may be as simple as making yourself a cup of tea, or walking outside for a while. Even phoning a counsellor and asking for help. As someone that has suffered from depression I can attest that it is absolutely debilitating. Getting yourself back to a normal life when you've fallen into the black hole of depression can be difficult, but by looking objectively at the situation, and making a first step—by doing what is possible, you can gradually get back into social contact with people, doing exercise, doing other activities, working, productive activities that help pull yourself together.

It can seem difficult to reconcile a pro-active approach with a Christian concept of dependence on God for everything. Fundamentally, while following God's will, we are still expected to be pro-active and work hard, effectively, and with wisdom.

> Go to the ant, you sluggard; consider its ways and be wise! It has no commander, no overseer or ruler, yet it stores its provisions in summer and gathers its food at harvest.."[1]

> "The plans of the diligent lead to profit as surely as haste leads to poverty"[2]

And in the New Testament:

> "Anyone who does not provide for their relatives, and especially for their own household, has denied the faith and is worse than an unbeliever."[3]

---

1. Prov 6:6–8
2. Prov 21:5
3. 1 Tim 5:8

This approach seems to conflict with some passages in the New Testament:

> "Look at the birds of the air; they do not sow or reap or store away in barns, and yet your heavenly Father feeds them. Are you not much more valuable than they? Can any one of you by worrying add a single hour to your life? And why do you worry about clothes? See how the flowers of the field grow. They do not labor or spin. Yet I tell you that not even Solomon in all his splendor was dressed like one of these. If that is how God clothes the grass of the field, which is here today and tomorrow is thrown into the fire, will he not much more clothe you—you of little faith? So do not worry, saying, 'What shall we eat?' or 'What shall we drink?' or 'What shall we wear?' For the pagans run after all these things, and your heavenly Father knows that you need them. But seek first his kingdom and his righteousness, and all these things will be given to you as well. Therefore do not worry about tomorrow, for tomorrow will worry about itself."[4]

However, we should not take these passages out of context. Directly proceeding this is the passage previously highlighted "No one can serve two masters. Either you will hate the one and love the other, or you will be devoted to the one and despise the other. You cannot serve both God and money."[5] which itself is the conclusion of passages calling for you to follow God rather than Earthly material goods. Also, just as these passages in Mathew are not a call to walk around naked, neither are they a call to avoid planning and preparation. Reading closely you can see that the admonition relates to anxiety over the future: we should plan and prepare, but we should not be anxious. Instead we should trust that we will do what is necessary when the time comes. If we are following God, these things will take care of themselves.

For non-theists you may want to view problematic anxiety over the future in a different way: First: we truly don't know what is in the future, so we should not be anxious about what hasn't happened. Second: that we will almost certainly be wiser in the future than now, and we will also have more information about such a catastrophe and possibilities to deal with it, than we can know now. Third: to recognize that we have passed through difficult events in our past, and we have coped with them, so we can expect

---

4. Matt 6:26–34
5. Matt 6:25

to cope with such events in the future. Just because the future is unknown, it doesn't mean we will drop into some black-hole. The anxiety over the future is almost always worse then the future itself.

Some Christians also ask whether we should be poor, again citing the Gospel of Matthew:

> "Jesus told him, 'If you want to be perfect, go and sell all your possessions and give the money to the poor, and you will have treasure in heaven. Then come, follow me.' But when the young man heard this, he went away sad, for he had many possessions. Jesus looked around and said to his disciples, 'How hard it is for the rich to enter the kingdom of God!' The disciples were amazed at his words. But Jesus said again, 'Children, how hard it is to enter the kingdom of God! It is easier for a camel to go through the eye of a needle than for someone who is rich to enter the kingdom of God.'"[6]

Should everyone do this? It would make no sense as who can we give our possessions to, if everyone is renouncing their possessions. Jesus and the apostles themselves were dependent on the generosity of wealthy patrons. What Jesus is really talking about here is not about giving up wealth, but about putting God first and not being attached to wealth. Proceeding this verse is:

> "Jesus called a little child to him and put the child among them. Then he said, 'I tell you the truth, unless you turn from your sins and become like little children, you will never get into the Kingdom of Heaven. So anyone who becomes as humble as this little child is the greatest in the Kingdom of Heaven.'"[7]

What Jesus is requesting is that we should be humble, and give up who we think we are; to understand that to follow God material things can tie us down. While we may need material things to achieve certain goals, we can easily become obsessed with the material things themselves. Jesus didn't ask everyone to give up their wealth, he was directing his teaching to a specific man who was following all the commandments. Jesus knew that what was stopping him following God was his attachment to wealth, not that he was wealthy.

---

6. Matt 19:21–23
7. Matt 18:2–3

Underlying all this is simply that money or material goods is not the primary concern. When we are following a plan aligned with God, we can plan and prepare (but not be anxious about the future).

> "Commit to the Lord whatever you do, and he will establish your plans."[8]

Following that plan we can take the first step, and work out how to continually push forward. With faith we can keep looking for solutions for the next step—not always having a hypothetical plan, but being flexible such that we can take advantage of new opportunities as the future gets revealed to us.

> "In their hearts humans plan their course, but the Lord establishes their steps."[9]

Also, what we often fail to take account of in our grand future plans, is that if we have a worthy goal people often see our diligence, see the value of our goal, and see our hard work and faith. They then often begin to believe themselves in this mission and that it can be achieved and may even feel willing to assist us in such a worthy goal. While we obsess over money to achieve these goals, believing that's what we need, often goods and services can come for free when people themselves see the value in what we are doing.

Many people think "if only I had money I could do . . .". The truth is we don't have time to commit to all the dreams of the future we have, and also this view is completely inverted. If we decide what we want, we can then find the resources to achieve that. If it is money we need, we will work to find the money to achieve that.

If you just seek money, when you get it, what will you spend it on? Probably a large beautiful car that will eventually seem outdated and decay into rust; an expensive holiday, where you have everything catered for but realize it doesn't capture the culture of the country you are visiting; a private jet, which means that you're increasingly isolating yourself from people; an over-priced watch, that functions like a normal watch but attracts the attention of thieves and those who want to use you just for money. There are advantages to not having wealth: travel with less hassle, no need to second guess people's intentions, not having to manage your assets, being able to change your direction in life rapidly without material

8. Prov 16:3
9. Prov 16:9

attachments, not having to worry about maintaining or losing your assets. Money is only a tool (but not the only tool) for achieving things.

This is why you must not start with "if only I had the money" but start with "I must do . . ." By starting with your objective, you don't waste money, you don't waste time. Think what you need to do, make a realistic plan, and take steps to achieve that. You won't know all the details, in part because things, yourself and those around you, will all change as you progress. You just make that first step in faith, then the next step will appear. Christians may say "God will provide" the next step, or as an atheist you may want to alternatively reflect that, when you have made that step, you will be able to focus more clearly on the new problems that arise. Each moment is different: planning each stage too precisely means you don't appreciate that things will be different by the time you reach that stage, and you can only see that stage clearly in all its context, up close.

But surely Christianity is about miracles, and God providing when we have nothing; God doing extraordinary and unexpected things for us when we need them? Through our own lives we see that the unexpected happens, both positive and negative. Faith is important, such that we can prepare for success. If we are expecting failure, when an opportunity arises we don't see it, and are unable to take advantage of it. Just trying, despite the odds, gives us a better chance than not trying, and usually we learn an immense amount through the starting and the trying. You want to write a book but you're not a writer? —through the act of starting and trying to write a book, you will become a writer. You'll see where you're bad and you'll try to correct it, the necessity to understand how to write well becomes more urgent. Your choices and thoughts are geared to what you're doing to be a good writer, not to a fantasy of some future that you haven't even started engaging with. Of course, we all have limited time and energy, so we need to choose where we put our focus. Trying to do everything gives us experience but tends to result in not being an expert in anything. However, where we choose to invest our energies isn't based on what we think is easiest. In a humorous play on a popular quote I once read "We don't do this because it's easy, but because we thought it would be easy." The original quote come from John F Kennedy, talking about the moon landing in 1969: "We do these things, not because they are easy, but because they are hard." If we have meaning in our lives we can see that life is a challenge that we are rising to, and that reason inevitably ties in to our personal values. We need those challenges; quoting a popular YouTube Stoic, Ryan Holiday: "all growth is on the other side of resistance".

The purpose of having faith that things will work out for the best, is partly a positivity and faith in the ultimate functioning of the universe. This helps us push forward and continue, even when we feel pain and resistance. It prevents negativity and helps us raise the spirit of ourselves and others to find alternatives, to seek another path where we can achieve our objective. How is this different from just hard work and optimism? In part it's about getting that balance point between being over-stressed and under-stressed. It's not healthy lying back and thinking we don't have to do anything, and nothing matters anyway. Similarly, if we put too much pressure on ourselves we end up blindly sprinting toward a goal that requires a marathon. We want to achieve that relaxed sensitivity to a situation where we are responding most effectively. Through trusting that God will give us opportunities, rather than that God will do it for us, we may achieve that balance point. Certainly the world is much bigger and more complex than what can be contained in your own mind. By both actively seeking what you need to achieve your goal, and having faith, these two can work together to produce beneficial outcomes.

Educated people usually shy away from the concept of miracles in Christianity. It's difficult to evaluate the veracity of the miracles that Jesus performed since they are only recorded in the bible, and thus critics can consider these biased accounts. I see them as having important Christian symbolism, as well as being literary tools used, particularly by Mark, to gain followers to Christianity and increase the status of Jesus. We now live in a modern era that has more critical logical systems and scientific approaches to knowledge, so this strategy has backfired: whereas Jesus being reported to have performed a miracle may have attracted followers 2,000 years ago, now it is likely to drive people away from Christianity. This isn't helped by modern pastors, particularly in some African and evangelistic churches, using deception and tricks to recreate "miracles" of healing, knowledge and prophecy. These fake performances can be a well intentioned attempt to attract people to the church, erroneously thinking that deceiving people to being church members is a sin worth the cost. But everything built on foundations of falsehood is likely to eventually crumble. Maybe this is being generous to some pastors, as some are undoubtedly using deception to build a congregation which will financially feed their business.

Whether we believe miracles or not, we do love religious miracle stories. It touches on part of us that wants to believe in magical power and that against all odds something positive can happen. However, as adults we know that if magic was real, then it wouldn't be magic: something is either part of reality or it isn't. Are these miracles part of a reality that we don't fully understand, whether this is God's power or something beyond our current knowledge? As humans, we need to have humility about our understanding, because one thing we do know, is that we know and understand very little of the entirety of reality. Part of this humility is accepting that we cannot accurately predict the future for most things, but if we work with faith we can adapt to the bad times when they come, as well as fully utilizing the unlikely opportunities provided by the small "miracles" in our life. Through faith in the good work which we are doing, we can also enjoy our life and feel value in what we are achieving, even if these achievements are small.

Some people believe that on a military mission, where you're under extreme psychological and physical stress, that it's awful. This isn't true; most revel in the excitement, the clear purpose and the struggle. There is a mission, there is meaning, and we know and even expect struggle. In the 1997 Italian film *Life is Beautiful* (La Vita è Bella) a father is placed in a Nazi concentration camp with his young son, whom he is trying to protect. He lies to his son and tells him that it is just a game, and his son asks, "what will we win?" and his father responds, "a tank". His father is simply trying to ensure that his son can have purpose and survive the awful ordeal. With purpose we can not only endure so much, we can also get satisfaction out of that perseverance and passing through trials. A fundamental question you need to ask yourself is, "in life, does truth and love prevail?" Your answer to this I believe says much about your faith, even if you're not religious, and says much about your outlook on life. Christians would undoubtedly say yes to this question. In a life filled with suffering and persecution, it can be difficult to accept this positive attitude. Some people spend their lives being abused and exploited. The transatlantic slave trade lasted 450 years and slavery in Africa existed even long before that. Under those conditions and for that duration can you accept that truth and love prevail? Looking back, we can say yes—slavery became illegal, in a major part due to the faith in truth and love by the people that worked in the movement to abolish slavery. Slavery is still prominent throughout the world, but people see it as an injustice, actively fight against it and certainly slavery is not institutionalized in the way it was during the transatlantic slave trade. How can truth and love prevail? It is because we can see people who are abused and exploited, and through being aware of it, we can act. Certainly, there were generations of slaves that prayed and hoped for a better future for themselves and their family, only to see their children and grandchildren in turn become slaves. What we want and need may not come in our generation, but if we are working toward it, and if we have faith that truth and love prevail, it can be achieved. Martin Luther King stated "The arc of the moral universe is long but it bends toward justice."

The Taoist Lie Yukou, better known as Lieh Tzu, lived between 500–400 BC. From Lieh Tzu we also see this concept of faith that stretches beyond our own short life:

> "In a valley surrounded by two high mountains lived an old man. He was nicknamed the Old Fool by his neighbors because he was always thinking up impossible projects. One day, the Old Fool got tired of having to take a long and roundabout hike to get out of his valley. He called his family together and presented them with the proposal that they remove the mountains that blocked their way. His son and grandson were very excited about the idea and wanted to start the project right away. The old man's wife, however, was not enthusiastic. She shook her head and said to her husband,
> 'You are ninety years old. You don't even have the strength to remove a small mound of dirt. How can you level two high mountains? Aren't you a bit too ambitious? Anyhow, where would you place the dirt after you've taken down the mountains?'
> The old man was not discouraged. 'We can dump the rocks into the sea,' he said. His son and grandson agreed.
> The next day, the Old Fool, with his son and grandson, took shovels and picks and headed for the mountains. On their way, they were joined by a seven-year-old boy from a neighboring family. The four of them worked from sunrise to sunset and did not return home to rest until the winter came.
> A wise man in the village who had heard about the Old Fool's attempt at leveling the mountains came to talk the old man out of his foolish project.
> He said, 'At your age you should be wise enough to know that your project is impractical. You are old and weak. You can't even pull up the weeds in your garden. What makes you think you can move a mountain?' The Old Fool sighed and said, 'Your mind is as set as a rock. Even a seven-year-old child is smarter than you are. Can't you see that if I don't finish the project, my son and grandson will continue with it? And if they can't finish moving the mountain, their sons and grandsons

will continue, and so on. The mountain, on the other hand, does not grow. So if each generation keeps chipping away, then one day the mountain will be leveled.'"[10]

The Old Fool's ridiculous project illustrates several important points: (i) he chose to do it, not because it seemed easy, or even possible, but because it was important (ii) he started immediately, even though he knew it would take longer than several generations to complete it; he had to make that first step (iii) when others saw him doing it, they realized it was important and joined him (iv) some ridiculed him, but he realized that with perseverance it could be achieved. Now of course, I have been talking about "do what is possible" throughout this chapter. What the Old Fool realized was that this project, while improbable, was possible. The full story explains that the Gods, seeing his determination and that what the Old Fool said was indeed true, performed a miracle and moved the mountains for him. Again, this illustrates that recognition by others of a task that we may have started on our own, can attract the assistance of others as they get engaged in the value of that task and the dedication and interest we show. This concept has been shown at a much more personal level in psychology, with the previously mentioned *bystander effect*[11]: if someone is assaulted in public, people tend not to intervene unless they see someone else intervening first. In our life, we can be that first person that starts something, with faith, and eventually people will recognize its value and help. So in the chapter, don't be discouraged with the title "do what is possible" or feel that it is in someway limiting, because it isn't only you doing it. If something is good and useful, with time and patience, others will help, but this often requires faith.

One of the most common popular quotes from the Bible used to illustrate faith is: "'For I know the plans I have for you' declares the Lord, 'plans to prosper you and not to harm you, plans to give you hope and a future.'"[12] This Bible quote is regularly taken out of context, with Christians applying it to themselves in their individual lives. In the original Hebrew the "you" is not an individual you, but a plural you; it is written to the Israelites as a nation in Exile. In the preceding passages we read: "'Do not let the prophets and diviners among you deceive you. Do not listen to the dreams you encourage them to have. They are prophesying lies to you

10. Wong, *Lieh Tzu*, 132–33.
11. Darley, *Bystander Intervention*, 377–83.
12. Jer 29:11

in my name. I have not sent them.' declares the Lord. This is what the Lord says: 'When seventy years are completed for Babylon, I will come to you and fulfill my good promise to bring you back to this place. For I know the plans I have for you' declares the Lord, 'plans to prosper you and not to harm you, plans to give you a hope and a future. Then you will call on me and come and pray to me, and I will listen to you.'"[13]

This is harsh. God is saying, don't believe the false predictions that you encourage the profits to make, you will be wandering for 70 years! For most they'll be dead before they finally return. In no way is God promising them as individuals a happy or easy life, he is talking about the people in general. What he tell us is what will eventually prevail is good for us, as a people. You're here to do God's work. We will be able to achieve what we are on Earth to achieve, but God isn't giving us a life of enjoyment and hedonism. Our satisfaction will not be gained in that way. We probably will experience periods of joy, even in dire circumstances. We're not just working for ourselves, we are part of a destiny far bigger than our own lifespan. We need to make a choice of whether we believe "does truth and love prevail", not necessarily in your life-time, but through your and other's works, and you can be contributing to this truth and love and the arc bending toward justice.

> "And we know that for those who love God all things work together for good, for those who are called according to his purpose"[14]

False prophets during trying times, mentioned in the previous passage of Jeremiah, still occur today. Indeed it saddens me that so many in the church reject science because of a misplaced conviction that science and religion conflict with each other. Similarly there are those in *scientism* who may go so far as to believe that if we have not proven something in science it is not real. Gravity was no less real before Newton formulated a theory of gravity in 1665, than it was afterward. Reality didn't change, our understanding of reality changed. Conversely some modern Christians find ever more convoluted ways of explaining why the Bible should be literally interpreted, though misrepresentation of scientific understanding or through contriving a profoundly false alternative theory. Whether it's a pastor tricking the congregation with "magic-tricks" or making up false narratives to bolster a religious belief, no one should

13. Jer 29:8–12.
14. Rom 8:28.

come to God through lies. If you've been interested in Christianity but you don't believe many things in the Bible or the unusual things your pastor or congregation tells you, then great; we have our own path to walk. We are each individuals called in a different way. St. Paul directed the church through the seed of faith sown in him on the road to Damascus, not through a logical analysis or critique of Christianity. Don't let someone else's truth dissuade you from discovering for yourself what you know deep down in your own heart. The Christian philosopher Søren Kierkegaard said Christianity wasn't a point we reached, but that it was an ongoing relationship with God, and we will always be questioning. This isn't to say we should drive ourselves crazy with religious questions: Do angels exist? Do they have wings? How many can fit on the head of a pin? It's important to separate the important and practical questions from the flippant. Personally my faith doesn't depend on the existence of angels, the existence of Satan, the resurrection of Jesus or even the crucifixion of Jesus. There is only one over-riding theme in the bible. It isn't 95 percent of the Bible, it is the whole Bible and every other single aspect of the bible comes from it: love. How we walk our path in life is something we will and should consistently question. The Bible is a guide, and we can use it as a wisdom document, but we don't have to accept the unbelievable to have faith in God. Such a path easily leads to blind acceptance of false prophets—to giving humans power over us. There is no-one interceding between us and God, we just need humility to listen, understand but still walk our individual path in life. Walk with faith. Now, I want to ask once again: does truth and love prevail? Put this book down, and ask yourself that question seriously. Look around you, reflect on your life, make a choice, yes or no? If no, don't worry about reading the rest of this book as you'll be wasting your time. If you don't think truth and love prevail it's difficult to have meaning in life. It's difficult to pursue all the things that this book is suggesting: humility, doing what is possible, loving others. Best to return to the "practicalities" of life and put this book on the shelf, give it to someone else, or maybe recycle it. Maybe you'll come back to this book when you find life isn't working for you how you expected it. Yep, at times we'll be downcast and sad, but answering this simple question "Does truth and love prevail" once and for all in your life, can make a huge difference. Even if you are suffering or will suffer immensely, answering this question can help.

For those that have answered 'yes', let's continue. Firstly, I'm not giving you a prize. You've given yourself a prize, just don't lose it. Before moving on, I just wanted to meander a bit on miracles. I've tried to pull you away from the need to believe in things you don't know, or to believe in the illogical. Now I'll discuss a little on some of the symbolic meanings around the miracles in the bible. People love miracles; I'm not saying miracles are useless. They serve an important function, but if we just believe all the stories literally, we may in fact miss the importance of the miracle: it is trying to tell us something far deeper than the simple surface facts of a story.

The miracles Jesus is purported to have performed in the Bible were not new, and indeed for the people of Jesus' time they would have resonated with them because other religions that were around them had similar miracles. Larry Holzworth (The History Collection)[15] amusingly asks, in a strangers wedding in Cana, when Jesus turned water into wine, why Jesus felt he had responsibility for the guests' refreshments? He goes on to explain this miracle has a basis in the Roman God Bacchus (or Dionysius for Greeks) who was well known for turning water into wine. Miracles at that time symbolized that the performer of the miracle was divine. With other religions Gods were providing miracles, so it was understandable that Jesus also had to provide miracles to illustrate his divinity. Indeed at the end of this miracle story it is written "What Jesus did here in Cana of Galilee was the first of the signs through which he revealed his glory, and his disciples believed in him."[16]

This miracle also had strong symbolism within earlier passages of the Bible, linking the symbolism of transformation between water, wine, and blood. Through Moses the Nile was turned into a river of blood, and in the last supper wine is turned into blood, creating the Christian communion ritual. In the communion Catholic Priests will attest that it is truly a transformation into the blood of Jesus, though it is clear and scientific tests will show, that it isn't blood. Does it take away from the importance of the ritual? No—but it shows we're not supposed to take this literally. As with all the miracles in the Bible, something important and relevant is being said. Jesus was not a magical bartender at a wedding, the whole scene represents transformation; spiritual transformation. Similarly, the communion symbolizes that we are all one in Christ. It is a ritualistic gesture intended to bond the church together as

---

15. Holzworth, *Biblical Miracles*
16. John 2:11

a Christian community in open love for our neighbour both within and outside the church, to be like Christ and to serve God.

A miracle that I believe is straightforward in both a symbolic and a practical way, while still being very profound, is the miracle of feeding the 5,000.

> "'We have here only five loaves of bread and two fish' they answered. 'Bring them to me' he [Jesus] said. And he directed the people to sit down on the grass. Taking the five loaves and two fish and looking up to heaven, he gave thanks and broke the loaves. Then he gave them to the disciples and the disciples gave them to the people. They all ate and were satisfied, and the disciples picked up twelve basketfuls of broken pieces that were left over. The number of those who ate was about five thousand men, beside women and children."[17]

We can imagine, a huge group of people and many are saying they have little or no food. Someone contributes five loaves and two fishes. The others see this generosity and feel mean for keeping what they have to themselves. As the baskets go around, they put in their food and in turn understand that there isn't much to go around, so they just take a little so others can share. When the baskets come back around the disciple Philip, who was present, may have said something like "Hang-on, everyone said they had nothing!" Fundamentally it's illustrating normal human behaviour, that people will keep things to themselves unless they see that others are being generous, and that when we demonstrate sharing behaviour and modesty in what we take, many others will follow suit. And the point of the miracle? For me, it's a parable: if you are generous with people, it helps them become more generous. It takes away this fear that you'll lose out and enables us to share more openly. This type of ritual happens in bars around the world every day, where someone buys all those at the table a round of drinks at their own expense, and then others feel compelled to reciprocate. Although sometimes an act of generosity doesn't result in reciprocation, in general an act of generosity is a prompt for reciprocation sooner or later. In biology we would call this *reciprocal altruism* i.e. we're good to others in the expectation that others will be good to us. We're being asked to be generous, such that others will be generous, and in this way we will all receive plenty. Within the Bible Jesus wants us to go a step beyond reciprocal altruism. It's not

---

17. Mat 14:17–21

just about serving our own lives; Jesus asks us to give without expecting to receive "When you give a luncheon or dinner, do not invite your friends, your brothers or sisters, your relatives, or your rich neighbors; if you do, they may invite you back and so you will be repaid. But when you give a banquet, invite the poor, the crippled, the lame, the blind, and you will be blessed. Although they cannot repay you, you will be repaid at the resurrection of the righteous."[18]

Some of the miracles in the Bible aren't about catering, or Jesus demonstrating his power as a deity, but about self belief and faith. For example, in the Old Testament David defeating the much larger and better trained Goliath, or in the New Testament, the lame man who isn't just told he's healed, but told to pick up his mat and walk. Even the blind man healed by Jesus was not passive in his own healing, he had to do something; to wash in the pool of Siloam. This last miracle also makes a statement about the cause of disease and disabilities, as well as the purpose of the miracles: "As he [Jesus] went along, he saw a man blind from birth. His disciples asked him, 'Rabbi, who sinned, this man or his parents, that he was born blind?' 'Neither this man nor his parents sinned,' Jesus said, 'but this happened so that the works of God might be displayed in him.'"[19]

A prevalent thought at the time (and sometimes even today!) was that bad things happen to you because of your sins, or the sins of your ancestors, but Jesus refutes this. Jesus then goes on to say that the reason he is doing miracles is to illustrate the works of God i.e. he was blind because through that affliction people would see God working, in this case Jesus' healing, though maybe God's work could be expressed through generosity or kindness shown by others. Jesus' miracles in the Bible can be found in many other earlier stories predating the time of Jesus, but which early Christians would have known about, and some of which are in the Old Testament: Elijah raised a widow's son from the dead (1 Kings 17:17-24); Elisha fed 100 people (2 Kings 4: 42-44); Zoroaster (about 1,200 years before Jesus) was said to be born of a virgin mother (Dughdova); Orion, the Greek God and son of Poseidon and Euryale, was able to walk on the surface of the sea even during great storms (recounted in the Iliad, by Homer). The philosopher Greek Apollonius of Tyana, born around 3 BC, has also been compared with Jesus and

---

18. Luke 14:12-13
19. John 9:1-3

indeed the anti-Christian philosopher Porphyry (born 234 AD) mentions Apollonius as having performed similar miracles.

The books of the New Testament were not written during Jesus' lifetime, but some were written just a short time later. The oldest Gospel, The Gospel of Mark, was written around 70 A.D. by Saint Mark the Evangelist, in either Rome or Syria. It is the most miracle dense gospel, hoping to show the divinity of Jesus. Interestingly, not counting the resurrection of Jesus, there is only one miracle that occurs in all four Gospels, which is the feeding of the 5,000. However, the Gospel of Mark is not the earliest book in the New Testament. Predating this Gospel by at least 10 years are the thirteen Epistles (writing directed towards a particular person or group of people) of St. Paul. Only seven of these Epistles are considered to be actually written by Paul: Galatians (48 A.D), 1 Thessalonians (49–51 AD), 1 Corinthians (53–54 AD), 2 Corinthians (55–56 AD), Romans (55–57 AD), and Philippians and Philemon (57–59 AD). There is debate whether 2 Thessalonians, Ephesians and Colossians was written by Paul, but the remaining three (First Timothy, Second Timothy, and Titus) are considered to be falsely ascribed to Paul. The age of the Epistles is from internal evidence relating to events described and the existence of the churches to which Paul was writing. Scholars believe either Galatians or 1 Thessalonians is the oldest book in the New Testament, but we can see that all the Epistles are within living memory of Jesus' crucifixion, believed to have been 30 or 33 AD. St. Paul himself is believed by scholars to have been born around the time of Jesus (which was between 6–4 BC). Paul converted to Christianity around 33 AD, which must have been shortly after the crucifixion of Jesus, and died in Rome between 62 and 64 BC. There is no direct evidence that Paul met Jesus while Jesus was still alive. However, Paul was a resident of Jerusalem as a child (Acts 22:3) and was there (as Saul) when approving the stoning of Saint Stephen (Acts 8:1). That Paul's nephew was in Jerusalem suggests that his family had resided there for some time (Acts 23:16), and since Jesus visited Jerusalem (Mark 11:11, John 2:13, John 5:1) it is possible, though not shown, that Paul could have even have seen or heard Jesus speak there. So St. Paul, who definitely wrote at least seven of the twenty seven books in the New Testament (26 percent), though around half (thirteen books) are attributed to him, was Jesus' contemporary; yet apart from the resurrection, Paul does not mention any miracles of Jesus.

So, in all the writings of the most prolific author of the New Testament, the author who lived at the time of Jesus, clearly knew of him during the time he was alive (Paul previously persecuted Christians, so he must have heard of their leader), and a person who may have even heard Jesus speak, did not mention even one miracle. Mark the Evangelist was born in 12 AD, so Jesus would have been crucified when Mark was around 18-21 years old. However, there is even doubt over whether Mark the Evangelist, despite being credited with starting Christianity in North Africa, wrote the Gospel of Mark. The miracles in Mark reflect prophecies of Isaiah in the Old Testament i.e. the blind shall see; the deaf will hear; the lame will walk; and those who could not speak would be able to do so. In the Old Testament this is probably figurative, a metaphor for how repressed people would become empowered, but in the New Testament of Mark, they have become actual physical miracles. These miracles would also have assured early Christians that Jesus was not only the son of God, but more powerful than all the other Gods that the Romans held dear. Unfortunately in modern times and for educated people looking toward Christianity for guidance in life, these miracles cast doubt on the veracity of Jesus and the Bible, making it look like a falsified magic show. From my personal perspective, while not believing Jesus was God nor the son of God, the Bible still contains good guidance for life. and certainly through Jesus' words and Paul's writing, that both were divinely inspired.

In Chapter 5 we discussed the Old Testament flood myth, where humanity is destroyed and all the animals, except for Noah and his family and those animals he was told to bring on the ark. It is well established that the biblical origin of this myth predates Judaism and comes from the ancient Sumerian writings, the *Epic of Gilgamesh*, dating from around 2100 BC. However, great flood myths are extremely common in many human civilizations including Mesopotamia, North American Ojibwa tribes, Hinduism, Chinese mythology, ancient Australian aborigine tribes and in South American tribes. It is entirely possible that huge flood events actually occurred; such as that sudden flooding of the Mediterranean Basin which is now the Mediterranean Sea. However, these flood stories probably relate to extreme local floods that caused devastation, particularly since most civilizations develop next to the sea or along river flood plains. Since huge flood events may only occur 1 in every 200 years or more, the lesson of the flood story relates to the understanding that things can change over time-scale much longer than our life-span, and so we should not believe that the future will just be like the past just because of our relatively short experience, even written experience. Though we discussed this in relation to humility, here I want to relate it to the theme of "doing what is possible", in that it is important to plan and to do things, but the level of planning relates to how much information we have. If we plan too precisely about events far in the future, many other factors will intervene and we may get caught up on strenuously achieving a precise goal, rather than recognizing opportunities along the way. Also, it may make us less adaptive to the current situation. We know what we know now, but tomorrow will we know more. This gives us thought to both planning and realizing that we should still be adaptable, and indeed review what we're doing.

Unexpected information and unexpected events can seem like a disaster or event that limits us or even blocks our goal completely; something we have to work around, to reflect on and then "do what is possible" to achieve our goal. However, it can also be unexpectedly beneficial, such as a person we meet who can help solve our problems, or learning that makes us re-evaluate what our goal should actually be, and thus increases our understanding of "what is possible". Fundamentally we have to have faith because we simply don't have all the information. We make a best guess, which should be a well reviewed and optimistic one, but there are so many opportunities and road-blocks along the way, we have to use sensible judgement. In one way, "do what is possible" therefore means (i) to collect information and collate it (ii) to make a sensible but optimistic judgement (iii) to be open and prepared to grasp new opportunities when they arise, and (iv) having faith and calm when we are blocked from our objectives, and able to see novel ways of moving around these blockages. Another aspect is also not to be too goal obsessed. Though they're a useful organizational structure, and help us evaluate what important steps we should take, fundamentally the meaning and how we develop good habits to achieve our goals which is more important. Having the goal of being a good writer will not make us a good writer, but having a habit of writing (that we enjoy, otherwise why else would we do it!) will help us on the way; though of course to get recognition as a good writer there are other activities that may seem more boring, such as approaching publishers and editing your work, that must be done and can be part of the thought out plan.

So, we can accept we don't know everything, and if we were to wait to know everything we would never make a decision. Indeed, the timing of what we do is often vital to success. Thinking too much and not doing makes us miss many opportunities and also makes us miss the learning that we would gain simply by starting. By starting to do something we instantly begin to amass directly useful information. We make a judgement and go for it. This is why the concept of faith is also useful; it gets over the self-doubt, the hesitation, the chopping and changing decision making. We need that confidence to achieve, to persevere and to keep going when we get set backs and the times are tough. Indeed, through faith we have a chance, not to do the impossible, but to really see that what is possible is often beyond our vision and understanding; that only by walking the path and trying can we actually determine what is possible. Again, there is a difference between having faith that "God will take care of everything" and faith that "God will provide me all I need to take care of everything"; it is an active, not a passive faith.

So many different events and opportunities can occur, and if you make a start and are prepared to grab those opportunities, that will make success much more likely. Within the Bible we have the phrases "seek and you will find", "knock and the door will be answered"—these aren't passive; they're active. The answers are there, the possibility is there, but you have to actively pursue it. This is well illustrated in the Old Testament story of Elisha and the Widow's Olive Oil

> "'The wife of a man from the company of the prophets cried out to Elisha, 'Your servant my husband is dead, and you know that he revered the Lord. But now his creditor is coming to take my two boys as his slaves.'
> Elisha replied to her, 'How can I help you? Tell me, what do you have in your house?'
> 'Your servant has nothing there at all,' she said, 'except a small jar of olive oil.'
> Elisha said, 'Go around and ask all your neighbors for empty jars. Don't ask for just a few. Then go inside and shut the door behind you and your sons. Pour oil into all the jars, and as each is filled, put it to one side.'
> She left him and shut the door behind her and her sons. They brought the jars to her and she kept pouring. When all the jars were full, she said to her son, 'Bring me another one.'
> But he replied, 'There is not a jar left.' Then the oil stopped flowing.
> She went and told the man of God, and he said, 'Go, sell the oil and pay your debts. You and your sons can live on what is left.'"[20]

---

20. 2 Kgs 4:1–7

This passage contains some significant points. The widow when asked, says she has nothing at all. When we are suffering, feel destitute, or have suffered a loss, we often automatically feel or even tell people we have lost everything. Her husband had died, she was terribly poor, and she was worried her sons would be taken into slavery. Then she realizes she has a small jar of olive oil. It seems negligible, but she has something. We always have something we can work with. If you can think and act, you have something, even if all you can move is your tongue or even an eyeball. Elisha then asks of the widow that she requests help for empty jars from her neighbors. So not only does she have a small jar of oil, she also has a neighbourhood who are willing to help. By the widow asking for only a little assistance she can get out of her problem. Next Elisha asked the widow to use the little she has; the small jar of oil, and pour it out. That tiny last thing that you have left, that tiny remaining resource you have—use it to get more. This is a clear example of both having faith, and "doing what is possible" (with all the resources you have).

Some Christians reading this Chapter will consider my commentary on Christianity to contrast greatly to what they have been taught and what they know. They may have even thrown this book across the room in anger. I would just say, don't just follow humans or the church leadership. If you wish, read widely, find authoritative texts on history, question and probe. So many Christians feel they cannot question what they are told by people within the church. Don't fear that knowledge of what is true or false will stop you believing in a faith that has guided you in your life, there is a beautiful a universal message in Christianity, and that will remain regardless of minor changes in your thoughts over the history of Christianity. There are excellent religious historians and writers on Christianity, with inspiring messages or even critical analysis. You don't have to do that, there is after all one over-riding message in Christianity which is equally suitable for both intellectual academics and the poorly educated. But what about those that want to manipulate religion for their own purposes and deceive us? Well, first we have to stop believing in magic or those acting as prophets for their own status. We have clear advice in the Bible, both not to believe false prophets, and on how to identify false profits: "Beware of false prophets, who come to you in sheep's clothing but inwardly are ravenous wolves. You will know them by their fruits. Are grapes gathered from thorns, or figs from thistles?"[21]

21. Mat 7:15-16

We can see by people's actions what is in their heart. Indeed, for ourselves, we can know the truth by seeing if it reflects what is in our heart, and given that God is love, we can understand this relationship with God through love. Thus we can wipe away all the unnecessary and sometimes damaging flotsam and jetsam of confused and over-discussed thoughts that tends to accumulate around any growing religion. Even Taoism left its highly philosophical origins to become a folk magic religion searching for an alchemic solution to eternal life—in direct conflict with its original concept of accepting death as part of the natural progression of life.

9. Going to Church

As well as having been a Buddhist, an Atheist, a Taoist and an Agnostic, I have also been to many different denominational churches: Catholic, Methodist, Born Again, Pentecostal, Mormon, and Seventh Day Adventist. I don't specifically affiliate with any denomination, but I do feel at home in the Seventh Day Adventist church because it has a clear interpretation of the Bible and there is a strong emphasis on being truthful. This gives me an innate trust in most people I meet from the Seventh Day Adventist church, either inside the church or outside in every day life. I don't believe the end of the world is imminent, but like all the churches I have been in, I never penetrated the church sufficiently to be torn between their beliefs and mine. When I started going to a Seventh Day Adventist church I was pulled there by a close friend, and it seemed a distraction from the seven days a week that I was putting into my PhD, and slowly becoming burned out. Forcing myself to take the Saturday as a complete day of rest completely settled my mind, refreshed me, and allowed me to realize the erroneous belief that if I worked harder, I would do better. We need times to work, times to rest and reflect. That it is a Saturday rather than a Sunday didn't matter to me, though I understand why Seventh Day Adventists prefer to keep the original Sabbath, rather than the Sunday Sabbath created by Constantine and the Catholic Church. Indeed, being in Portugal, where Saturday is called "Sabado" it made sense that the Sabbath in the SDA church was kept to its original day on the Saturday.

Unlike years, months and days, the week day doesn't relate to anything physical and is purely convention. A year is the time it takes the Earth to make a complete revolution of the sun, a day is the time it takes for the Earth to revolve. Hours and seconds are archaic subdivisions of the day. A month was based on a complete cycle of the phases of the moon, although now months have been allotted fixed numbers of days such that 12 months fit more or less neatly into a year, albeit with variable sizes of months. Jewish and Islamic calendars still utilize lunar months, and thus have festivals on dates which change relative to the typical calendar year, using calendar months. Early Rome (around 625 BC) had 10 months in the year and only 304 days. Then by 45 BC Romans had increased this to a 355 day calendar year, but still had to add extra days on some of the months to keep festivals in line with the seasons. It was Julius Caesar who created the 365 day calendar, and Rome would add an extra day as February 29th each four years to make up for the fact that it actually takes 365 and one quarter days for the Earth to circle the sun: creating the Julian calendar. In 1582 Pope Gregory XIII created the Gregorian calendar which further refined the Julian calendar, such that the leap year extra day would be added specifically on the years which could themselves be divided exactly by 4 e.g. 2020. In the modern calendar this was adjusted even more, because being more precise, it takes 365.24949 days for the Earth to circle the sun; slightly less than 365 and one quarter days. Thus, the concept that century years are only leap years if they are divisible by 400. For example, the year 2000 is a leap year, but 2100 isn't, despite it being divisible by 4. The next century year to be a leap year is 2400.

Unlike the rest of Europe, England (and the British Empire) kept the Julian calendar until it adopted the Gregorian calendar in 1752 through an act of Parliament. Its adoption was finally necessary because of the difference in dates between England and other European countries, including Scotland, caused problems in legal agreements. To bring the English calendar into line with the Gregorian calendar which was already in use by countries including France, Italy, Portugal, Poland and Spain, the whole year had to be adjusted. There were two hurdles to overcome. The first was that the New Year in in the Julian Calendar was 25th March, whereas in the Gregorian Calendar New Year started on the 1st January. The second hurdle was that the dates of each calendar mismatched by 11 days. To resolve the first hurdle, the year 1751 in England was cut short: instead of the year ending on the 24th March, it would end on the 31st December. 1751 would thus have only 282 days. The second hurdle required the date to be changed. Therefore it was decided that Wednesday 2nd September 1752 would be followed the next morning by Thursday 14th September, aligning England and the whole of the British Empire's calendar, with Europe. According to legend this caused riots in

England, with people believing they had lost 11 days of their lives, but the riots are now considered to be a myth.

The seven day week comes from the very early civilization (2100 BC) of the Sumerians. They used a lunar cycle to determine the month, which would last 29.53 days. This was broken into four weeks, with each week being 7 or 8 days. The first day of the month would be a new moon (no moon visible), then the 15th day would be a full moon. Thus the 15th and 21st day would have been crescent waxing (growing) and waning (diminishing) moons respectively.

In the Bible, the Sabbath relates to the creation myth of the Earth in Genesis, where God spent 6 days creating the Earth and everything in it, and then rested on the 7th day. Given that numbers in the Bible usually have symbolic meaning, with 7 representing completion, it's difficult to know if this is supposed to literally represent a week. As early as 200 AD some churches had been changing the Sabbath from Saturday to Sunday to help Christianity appeal more to pagans: the Sunday was already considered a day off, since Sunday was the day of the Sun God. We can be certain that originally the Sabbath was a Saturday (following on from Judaism), and that this was officially changed to a Sunday in 321 AD by the Christian Emperor Constantine, supported by the Catholic Church. In this year, Emperor Constantine decreed in law that, on the venerable day of the Sun, let the magistrates and people residing in cities rest, and all workshops be closed[1]. Constantine was himself a convert to Christianity, and as such stopped the persecution of Christians across the Roman Empire, and indeed was instrumental in the spread of Christianity throughout the Empire. As well as Seventh Day Adventists keeping Saturday as the Sabbath, so do Seventh Day Baptists, Sabbatarian Adventists, and Orthodox Tewahedo (a denomination in Ethiopia, Western Asia and India).

Going to church is problematic for many people, including myself. For children and many adults it can be painfully boring. The structure and stage is set up for one individual, a pastor or priest, to dictate from a powerfully positioned raised platform toward a kneeling congregation. This seems a world away from the very earliest Christian communities, where they would usually gather in people's homes and form *housechurches* with the whole Christian community throughout the city being considered a church, in that they were a body of Christians. Church

---

1. Blume, *The Codex of Justinian,* book 3, title 12, law 3.

(ekklesia in Greek) just meaning an assembly of people. These housechurches were sometimes converted into more functional churches, with a teaching area and assembly room and sometimes a separate location for baptisms. Unlike Roman Temples that focused on the offering of sacrifices at an alter for a few individuals at a time, a Christian church with its large congregation, needed more space. With Constantine legalizing Christianity, the Roman Emperor provided government buildings for Christians to worship, which could be adapted with open seating areas and aisles, and also a simple table as an altar. This alter would have less significance than the altar in a Roman Temple, since there was no physical sacrifice. Constantine Christianized Rome in the forth century. With the fall of the Western Roman Empire at the end of the fifth century, traditional Roman religious practice declined and some Roman temples were converted into churches. Early catholic church buildings, while influenced by the Roman architecture of the time, were not necessarily designed like a Roman temple. Some cultural artifacts of Roman culture do still exist in the church, such as the exchange of rings during marriage; though in Ancient Rome this ceremony involved the husband giving a ring to the father-in-law as a bride price, rather than to his wife.

Early Christianity did not just develop in the cities. Between 270 and 400 AD there were groups of Christians who escaped to the desert, becoming desert monks or nuns, often referred to as the *Desert Fathers*. These Christians were informal groups of hermits who formed the model for later Christian monasticism. Most lived in the Desert of Scetis in Egypt, now known as Wadi El Natrun, and others in Nitria and Kellia, also in Egypt. The Desert Fathers were ascetics who gave up their material goods and instead prayed, fasted and had vows of silence. Religious pilgrims would visit them for advice, which increased the Desert Fathers' popularity such that at the end of the forth century a collection of writings called "Sayings of the Desert Fathers"[2], written in Greek, became widely circulated.

Religious festivals and rituals bind a community together. Very much like the Olympics or a football game, there can be special clothing worn, a structured procedure, standing up and singing together, chanting together, and generally creating an emotionally charged environment which is shared by the group. Religious festivals can act to remind people of the common beliefs that bind the group, such as the

2. Ward, *Desert Fathers*

resurrection of Jesus, Mohammed ascending to heaven, of the celebration of the birth of Gautama Buddha. Binding a group together through religion and shared beliefs and values may have been the social origin of religion; reducing internal conflict in the high population density areas of early cities. Though, while binding those of the same belief together, religion can also cause conflict between religions. With many religions based on an irrefutable belief system rather than logical discourse, where two religions meet, those differences cannot be easily reconciled through discourse. Thus warfare and prejudice are easily sparked, which has been common throughout the history of all major religions. Catholics persecuted the Jews and Muslims during the twelfth century with the Spanish Inquisition; Jews and Romans persecuted Christians in the first, second and third centuries. Islam invaded the Jewish and Christian city of Jerusalem in 635 AD. Between 1095 and 1291 the Christian Crusades sent knights to regain Jerusalem from Muslims. Between the fifteenth and nineteenth century Muslims from North Africa (the Ottoman empire) enslaved millions of non-Muslim Europeans (mostly Christians), bringing them back to North Africa, in the Barbary Slave Trade. To hold the social grip religions often had methods to punish those speaking out against the religion, knows as 'blasphemy laws'.

> "Anyone who blasphemes the name of the Lord is to be put to death. The entire assembly must stone them. Whether foreigner or native-born, when they blaspheme the Name they are to be put to death."[3]

The Catholic church utilized capital punishment (death sentences) for blasphemy during the Middle Ages. In thirteenth century France they would instead cut off your lips and tongue. Even in the modern era blasphemy laws exist in many Muslim societies including Afghanistan, Egypt, Pakistan, Iran, parts of Nigeria, Pakistan, Sudan, and the United Arab Emirates. Britain only decriminalized blasphemy against Christianity in 2008; the death penalty in England for blasphemy was abolished in 1676, but before 2008 people could still receive a fine. Pakistan is one of the toughest countries on blasphemy and in 2023 there were 80 people in prison on blasphemy charges, half of which either had a death sentence or life imprisonment.

3. Lev 24:6

Within Christianity there is a powerful passage about forgiveness. The punishment of stoning in that time was not just for blasphemy, but also for adultery:

> "But Jesus went to the Mount of Olives. At dawn he appeared again in the temple courts, where all the people gathered around him, and he sat down to teach them. The teachers of the law and the Pharisees brought in a woman caught in adultery.
> They made her stand before the group and said to Jesus,, 'Teacher, this woman was caught in the act of adultery. In the Law Moses commanded us to stone such women. Now what do you say?'
> They were using this question as a trap, in order to have a basis for accusing him. But Jesus bent down and started to write on the ground with his finger. When they kept on questioning him, he straightened up and said to them,
> 'Let any one of you who is without sin be the first to throw a stone at her.' Again he stooped down and wrote on the ground.
> At this, those who heard began to go away one at a time, the older ones first, until only Jesus was left, with the woman still standing there. Jesus straightened up and asked her,
> 'Woman, where are they? Has no one condemned you?'
> 'No one, sir,' she said.
> 'Then neither do I condemn you,' Jesus declared. 'Go now and leave your life of sin.'"[4]

In a modern globalized society religious tolerance is essential. Any religion that is not tolerant of other major beliefs will find it difficult to stay out of conflict with the rest of the world. Despite the persecution of Jews, Muslims and blasphemers in the Middle Ages by the then powerful Catholic church, Christianity explicitly calls for tolerance of other religions:

> "You have heard that it was said, 'Love your neighbor and hate your enemy.' But I tell you, love your enemies and pray for those who persecute you, that you may be children of your Father in heaven. He causes his sun to rise on the evil and the good, and sends rain on the righteous and the unrighteous. If you love those who love you, what reward will you get? Are not even the tax collectors doing that? And if you greet only your own people,

---

4. John 8:1–11

what are you doing more than others? Do not even pagans do that? Be perfect, therefore, as your heavenly Father is perfect."[5]

"To the rest I say this (I, not the Lord): If any brother has a wife who is not a believer and she is willing to live with him, he must not divorce her. And if a woman has a husband who is not a believer and he is willing to live with her, she must not divorce him. For the unbelieving husband has been sanctified through his wife, and the unbelieving wife has been sanctified through her believing husband. Otherwise your children would be unclean, but as it is, they are holy."[6]

This directly contradicts Deut 7:3-4 in the Old Testament, though I hope we're together in admitting that much of the New Testament revises that which has been previously written in Jewish tradition.

The ancient Romans while conquering nations with diverse religious beliefs, generally allowed them to practice their own religions. With most of the conquered nations being polytheistic, such as the Greeks and Persians, the Romans didn't have a problem incorporating other nation's Gods into their festivals and sacrifices. The Romans not only built temples for other the Gods of other cultures, but sometimes even worshiped these foreign Gods themselves, as they came in to fashion. For example, Mithras, the Persian God of the sun, become popular with Roman soldiers. Roman Gods were affiliated with equivalent earlier Greek Gods e.g. Jupiter (Greek) and Zeus (Roman), and Greek myths were incorporated into Roman culture. Sometimes cults were banned for reasons of social cohesion. For example, Dionysus, the Greek God of wine and drunkenness, was banned because of the debauched behaviour of its followers, though in the interests of religious freedom, the authorities eventually relented. The monotheistic religions of Zoroastrianism (from Persia) Judaism and Christianity were more problematic since these religions would not themselves accept nor incorporate their religion into Roman polytheistic religion and cultural practices. Indeed, the initial persecution of Christians is believed in part to be due to the self-isolation of Christians from Roman culture and their refusal to take part in Roman social religious festivities. While Rome attempted to tolerate Judaism, being a well established religion, there were still frictions, such as when the Roman governor of Judea confiscated money from the Great Temple in

5. Mat 5:43-48
6. 1 Cor 7:12-14

Jerusalem and caused a Jewish riot. This also led to the establishment of Jewish revolutionaries called *Zealots* who attacked Romans and Roman soldiers in Jerusalem and surrounding areas.

When Christianity came on the scene, there was little interest in tolerating it. Roman Emperor Tiberius, asked the senate to legalize Christianity around 30 AD and declare Christ a Roman God, but the senate refused. On 18 July 64 AD, when a fire erupted in the popular arena *Circus Maximus* false rumors led the public to believe Emperor Nero had himself started the fire to create space for a new palace, and Nero directed the blame to Christians, making them a scapegoat. At this time Christianity was illegal and negative gossip circulated such that Christians were cannibals because they ate the body and blood of Christ at communion, and that they practiced incest, because of the call to love their brother and sister. Christians were being martyred in arenas, with lions and wild dogs unleashed on them. Outside the arena Christians were being persecuted through crucifixion or being burned alive. Later, in 110 AD Emperor Trajan ordered Roman officials not to interfere with Christian gatherings, and for over a hundred years persecution subsided. In 250 AD, Emperor Decius was trying to rehabilitate traditional Roman, and recommenced Christian persecution, but Emperor Gallienus, who succeeded Decius, again stopped the persecution and then finally recognized Christianity as a legal religion. In 297, Emperor Diocletian re-initiated persecution, evicting all Christians from the Roman military, destroying churches, prohibiting Christian worship, and torturing or executing Christians with positions in government. Galerius, who succeeded Diocletian, continued this persecution, once again sending Christians into the arena, or making them slaves in government run mines. In 306 AD, Constantine, born of a Christian mother, became Emperor. In 312, at the age of 40, he himself became the first Roman Emperor to be a Christian, promoting tolerance of Christianity. It was written, by the tutor to Constantine's son, that Constantine's conversion was due to a vision. This was after battle, before leaving France to return to Rome, and he and his army saw a large cross in the sky and heard the words "in this sign conquer" and he proceeded to paint the sign of the cross on his army's shields. It is more likely however, that Constantine considered it politically advantageous to be Christian at that time.

The political and social structure of religion is part of why I find it problematic going to church. The Priest or Pastor is usually dictating their own thoughts, though based on the Bible. Sometimes these are insightful and inspirational, sometimes they are prejudicial and discriminatory. Rarely does it match exactly how you as an individual think and feel, so it becomes like a self inflicted brain washing—an attempt to get everyone to think the same for the purposes of social cohesion. Churches, as with all human groups, tend to develop their own power hierarchies. Sometimes this is innocent and for the purposes of organization for spreading the religion, with kind hearted individuals working tirelessly to help others. Sometimes this hierarchy is developed for money, power, or social status.

Lafayette Ron Hubbard developed the Church of Christian Scientists apparently after a religious vision during a tooth operation. He had admitted that as a science fiction author he made very little money and felt that religion was a better route to wealth. Hubbard had previously lived with Jack Parsons, a leader of a *Magick* lodge that were followers of the sexually promiscuous occultist and occult writer, Aleister Crowley. L Ron Hubbard would eventually have an affair with Parson's wife, causing husband and wife to separate, as well as scam Parsons for money.

We can also see Evangelists, particularly from America and Africa, utilizing their huge events and church donations for personal enrichment, including private jets and expensive sports cars. This leads us to seriously question whether a lavish lifestyle is really the model that Jesus was proposing. Jesus, Paul and the other apostles were clearly dependant on donors, including people like Mary Magdalene, for their proselytizing, but they were also extremely humble in their needs and lifestyles. They didn't buy chariots or boats to get to places more quickly, and Jesus famously rode to Jerusalem on a donkey. They lived off the generosity of others on a day to day basis, not through the accumulation of wealth. Similarly, we would expect pastors to act accordingly and be more dependent on assistance such as food, housing, and travel, rather than collecting cash from their congregation to purchase assets.

I live in Africa, and the financial motive of many pastors is very clear. I generally have a rule that if money is mentioned more in a church than God, then it is clearly a church of money, and unfortunately that is common. Even within a congregation the predominant prayers are not for peace, love, and health of others or in the world, but for money and personal success in business. People tend to be very vocal at prayer time, being encouraged by pastors to speak out loud the things that they want in life, and to have extensive tirades of pleading interspersed with speaking in tongues. This does build an atmosphere or fervor in the church, sometimes with people shaking vigorously or even falling to the floor. Speaking in tongues and prophecy is encouraged in the Bible: "I would like every one of you to speak in tongues, but I would rather you have prophecy. He who prophesies is greater than one who speaks in tongues, unless he interprets so the church may be edified."[7] However, these practices are later put into perspective: "Nevertheless, in church I would rather speak five words with my mind in order to instruct others, than ten thousand words in a tongue."[8]

Though 1 Corinthians praises and extols spiritual gifts such as speaking in tongues, prophecy and healing, in my experience these expressions of religion have always been fake. I also don't see any reason myself to parrot these behaviors if they are not truly coming from God. As for prayer, Jesus is quite explicit about the humility and personal approach that should be taken to prayer:

> "And when you pray, do not be like the hypocrites, for they love to pray standing in the synagogues and on the street corners to be seen by others. Truly I tell you, they have received their reward in full. But when you pray, go into your room, close the door and pray to your Father, who is unseen. Then your Father, who sees what is done in secret, will reward you. And when you pray, do not keep on babbling like pagans, for they think they will be heard because of their many words. Do not be like them, for your Father knows what you need before you ask him."[9]

My main concern is also that most of the prayers are either for personal success in business or for money. Prayers for money have become so important to the religious culture that the concept of *Miracle Money* has developed in America and Africa: pastors promise blessings of wealth to their congregation, particularly if they give large donations to the church. Sometimes collection time is even heralded as "Now for the time of blessings". The pastors will say "give and you will receive" and there may be two, three or more rounds of collections, the first being for the church, another for the needy and other subsequent collections for specific needs such as buying a mini-bus or car. Almost inevitably these donations are done whereby the person walks up to the front, making

---

7. 1 Cor 14:5
8. 1 Cor 14:19
9. Matt 6:5–8

those who don't give a donation clearly visible. This is in direct contrast to what Jesus asks when we give to the needy:

> "Be careful not to practice your righteousness in front of others to be seen by them. If you do, you will have no reward from your Father in heaven. So when you give to the needy, do not announce it with trumpets, as the hypocrites do in the synagogues and on the streets, to be honored by others. Truly I tell you, they have received their reward in full. But when you give to the needy, do not let your left hand know what your right hand is doing, so that your giving may be in secret. Then your Father, who sees what is done in secret, will reward you."[10]

Unfortunately most religions get associated with profiteering. Probably one of the most shocking actions of Jesus in the Bible is when he drove out the money-lenders from the temple. What made Jesus so uncharacteristically angry?

> "Jesus entered the temple courts and drove out all who were buying and selling there. He overturned the tables of the money changers and the benches of those selling doves. 'It is written,' he said to them, 'My house will be called a house of prayer, but you are making it a den of robbers.'"[11]

There of course is a back story to this event. The priests in Judaism had become wealthy from the annual temple tax, which was equivalent to one day's wages for each of the around 3 million Jews, each year. They were also making money from other profiteering activities. One was the exchanging of money at the temple, because it was not permitted to use the Roman silver coins in the temple (which had the image of the Roman Emperor, who was considered a God), only the coins from Tyre. Ironically the coins from Tyre had a pagan god on one side (The God Melkart, son of Baal). However, it was likely the priests demanded this coin instead because it was around 95 percent silver compared to the 80 percent silver Roman coins. So as well as demanding a temple tax from fellow Jews, this tax had to be paid with a high value coin, which itself had to be purchased from the priests at huge profit. These coins also had to be used when purchasing sacrifices outside the temple. Although people could bring their own sacrifices, such animals had to be judged to be without a blemish—and it was the priests who checked this, ensuring

10. Matt 6:1–4
11. Matt 21:12–13

that the fellow Jews had to purchase sacrifices at an inflated price. The profit made in Jerusalem from these activities was so huge, that when the Roman General Marcus Crassus looted the temple in Jerusalem in 54 AD he took 80 metric tons of gold: worth today around 4.8 billion dollars.

The extortion conducted by the priests was not the only factor annoying Jesus. Gentiles (non-Jews) were not permitted to worship in the inner temple. A balustrade blocked the entrance to the inner temple with notices in Greek and Latin, warning foreigners and uncircumcised people that crossing to the inner courtyard was punishable by death. The common people and gentiles (non-Jews) would therefore have to pray in the outer courtyard. However, instead of seeing an area of prayer there, it was occupied by money changers and dove sellers. Why doves? Doves were cheaper sacrifices that women and the poor generally purchased. There is a lot to unwrap here, but Jesus' bold action was a strong statement about (i) giving the right of gentiles to worship (ii) the exploitation of women inside the temple and (iii) the profiteering of the priests. Of course these actions only further upset the Jewish priests whose income was being threatened by Jesus. Paul declares that the temple is not the buildings where we go to pray, but the body of Christian people themselves: "Don't you know that you yourselves are God's temple and that God's Spirit dwells in your midst? If anyone destroys God's temple, God will destroy that person; for God's temple is sacred, and you together are that temple."[12]

There is no doubt that many evangelist preachers, and leaders of many religious cults, are profiteering from their congregation and the promotion of Christianity. We have Kenneth Copeland (American Televangelist), worth 300 million dollars; David Oyedepo (Nigerian Preacher), worth 200 million dollars, TD Jakes (American Bishop) worth 147 million dollars, and many many more that have turned religion into a profitable business. This is not to specifically accuse any of these people of crime. However, when we give money to the church or religious leaders, we should be told where that money is going, and within Christianity we should expect that the leadership of the church is humble and not taking from the poor to increase their wealth, but ensuring that the poor and needy are prioritized.

One the largest scams perpetuated almost universally within the church, and certainly in the spirit of the extortion by Jewish priests during

---

12. 1 Cor 3:16–17

Jesus' times, is tithing. What is tithing? *Tithe* means *one tenth* in Hebrew. According to many ministries it is a biblical practice, whereby Jews and Christians give a tenth of their income to the church, for the purposes of supporting the church as well as the poor and needy:

> "'A tithe of everything from the land, whether grain from the soil or fruit from the trees, belongs to the Lord; it is holy to the Lord. Whoever would redeem any of their tithe must add a fifth of the value to it. Every tithe of the herd and flock—every tenth animal that passes under the shepherd's rod—will be holy to the Lord.'"[13]

Evangelists will argue that tithing is not just about helping the poor, but for bringing blessings upon ourselves:

> "'Bring the whole tithe into the storehouse, that there may be food in my house. Test me in this', says the LORD Almighty, 'and see if I will not throw open the floodgates of heaven and pour out so much blessing that there will not be room enough to store it.'"[14]

These are two passages from the Old Testament, but what does the New Testament say about tithing? Nothing. The word tithe or tithing is never mentioned. Tithing simply is not a Christian doctrine, it is neither asked for nor is it obligatory. Paul, in appealing to the believers in Corinth to give generously to help poor Christians in Judea, said this:

> "But since you excel in everything—in faith, in speech, in knowledge, in complete earnestness and in the love we have kindled in you—see that you also excel in this grace of giving.
>
> I am not commanding you, but I want to test the sincerity of your love by comparing it with the earnestness of others. For you know the grace of our Lord Jesus Christ, that though he was rich, yet for your sake he became poor, so that you through his poverty might become rich. And here is my judgment about what is best for you in this matter. Last year you were the first not only to give but also to have the desire to do so.
>
> Now finish the work, so that your eager willingness to do it may be matched by your completion of it, according to your means. For if the willingness is there, the gift is acceptable according to what one has, not according to what one does not have. Our desire is not that others might be relieved while you are hard pressed, but that there might be equality. At the present

13. Lev 27:30–32
14. Mal 3:10

time your plenty will supply what they need, so that in turn their plenty will supply what you need. The goal is equality, as it is written: 'The one who gathered much did not have too much, and the one who gathered little did not have too little.'"[15]

So notice: Paul states that giving is a *grace* i.e. voluntary. Paul is not commanding them to give, there is no obligation, he is simply appealing to them. He is also not asking to give such that they would be without, but to give such that there will be equality. It is not to give to the wealthy, but to give to the needy. And not just this—it is to give to the needy such that they can return the favour when you are in need. He is actually appealing for them to be the first in initiating reciprocal altruism. Note also, this was not a gift to a church, nor another church, it was a gift to the individual believers in Judea who were suffering greatly from poverty.

Note that Paul is speaking about a specific matter to a congregation in Corinth; not necessarily making broad universal conclusions, but what is clear is that there is no obligation to give: "Each of you should give what you have decided in your heart to give, not reluctantly or under compulsion, for God loves a cheerful giver."[16]

Even for the Jews, it is important to remember the tithe was not based on all they owned, and indeed it wasn't even taken from their financial wealth: it was a tithe of food. Only food from the farms and herds of Jewish people who lived in Israel. It was only ever a tithe in food, as illustrated in the above verses in Leviticus. Sometimes Abraham's tithe to Melchizedek is considered part of the biblical basis for tithing:

> "Then Melchizedek king of Salem brought out bread and wine. He was priest of God Most High, and he blessed Abram, saying, 'Blessed be Abram by God Most High, Creator of heaven and earth. And praise be to God Most High, who delivered your enemies into your hand.' Then Abram gave him a tenth of everything. The king of Sodom said to Abram, 'Give me the people and keep the goods for yourself.'"[17]

However, this tithe was from spoils of war, not from Abraham's own property. Neither was it freely given nor directed to the poor, nor to a church, but was a demand by the kings Melchizedek and the King of

---

15. 2 Cor 8:7–15
16. 2 Cor 9:7
17. Gen 14:18–21

Sodom. This is entirely different to the requirement to help the poor and needy that we see in the New Testament.

So, within the Old Testament tithing are of four types: (1) a first harvest tithe to the servants of the priests (Levites), who would give a tenth of what they received themselves to the priests[18]. This was in part because neither could inherit land i.e. could not grow food themselves[19]; (2) A feast tithe to the worshipers in Jerusalem during three holy festivals (Deut. 12:1–19); (3) A tithe for the poor, whereby every three years a tithe would be given to widows, fatherless, foreigners and Levites[20]; and (4) a tithe to the occupying Romans as tax[21].

Thus, in Jewish tradition the only relevant tithes today are to the poor, or those servants of priests who cannot own land. For Christians, the New Testament has replaced tithing with charitable gracious giving to widows, the fatherless, and foreigners; not the church. Also, the act of giving is voluntary, is for the poor and needy, and is there to achieve a form of financial equality. Thus, it is fraudulent for a church to say that there is a biblical obligation to provide a tithe, and if a tithe is asked (voluntarily) the money should be for the poor and needy. This does not preclude the church asking for money for upkeep, and services and for the pastor or priest, but it is not an obligation in Christianity, and it certainly cannot be called a tithe.

The *Prosperity Gospel* movement which originated in America, then spread to Europe and Africa, relies heavily on tithing and convinces its congregations that they should be tithing. The *Word of Faith* movement is one organization that convinces their congregations that they can and should get power and money through prayer, and indeed is linked to many of these extremely wealthy charismatic preachers. The Prosperity Gospel preaching convinces followers that God wants you to be financially prosperous, and that we are each, as individuals, like "little Gods", as in the passage:

> "'We are not stoning you for any good work,' they replied, 'but for blasphemy, because you, a mere man, claim to be God.' Jesus answered them, 'Is it not written in your Law, 'I have said you are "gods"'? If he called them "gods", to whom the word of God came—and Scripture cannot be set aside—what about the

18. Neh 10:37–38
19. Deut 12:12, Deut 14:27
20. Deut 14:27–29
21. 1 Sam 8:14–17

one whom the Father set apart as his very own and sent into the world? Why then do you accuse me of blasphemy because I said, 'I am God's Son?'"[22]

To put this in to context, Jesus was making a point that those who were accusing him of blasphemy were acting like "little Gods" because they were seeing themselves as self-appointed persecutors of the wicked. It is a direct reference to the Psalms in the Old Testament, which was also a rebuke of religious leaders who were acting as if they were God.

> "They do not know, nor do they understand; They walk about in darkness; All the foundations of the earth are unstable. I said, 'You are gods, And all of you are children of the Most High. But you shall die like men, And fall like one of the princes.'"[23]

Charismatic pastors and televangelists will also tell people that tithing and donations are a way of "sowing a seed" whereby we will reap greater rewards. Congregations will then happily pass money to them such that these pastors can purchase huge homes and private jets. Even in Malawi, which has smaller scale abuses than in America or Nigeria, pastors will convince the impoverished congregation that by giving to the church, they will get more in return. The poor giving to the rich is certainly not what Jesus, Paul or any writer in the New Testament asked of us. Thus, to identify if your church is more of a business than a house of God observe if either the service focuses on talking about money; if the church declares how much money individuals have given; if you have to visibly give money in front of others; or if the pastor has a congregation that is far poorer than he is.

Charismatic pastors may perform "miracles" and tricks to convince the congregation of his power or blessings. Costi Hinn, the nephew of Benny Hinn the famous (and rich) evangelical faith healer himself details how he observed the fraudulent activity of his uncle, e.g.: people without illnesses that are paid to feign illness and then be miraculously cured. These churches have *screeners* who will remove those going to the stage that have a real affliction, so only the fake illnesses will be "healed". With the infamous "leg growing trick" someone with uneven length legs will go to the stage and the healer will lengthen one of the legs, healing them, when in fact the person simply changes the position of their hip back to a normal position. No different to snake

22. John 10:34–36
23. Ps 82:5–7 (NKJV)

oil salesmen of the wild west, these healers are con-artists, exploiting people's desperation. Those that need healing will be asked money as "donations of faith". As well as receiving those donations, the fake healings will also act as advertising for the church, to grow the congregation and get a greater income for the leadership.

The atmosphere of such churches is purposely raised, with people crying and chanting together, creating a hysteria. Pastors will shout and then repeat the same phrase maybe five, ten or more times, to put people in an almost hypnotic state, making some in the congregation open to suggestion. The congregation are asked to give generously, "not so the church can be blessed, but so you can be blessed in return". These churches are not about God, and they use the power of affirmation to stir people up, getting the congregation to shout out "I am wealthy, I am blessed, I am strong, I will receive" over and over.

Giving to others often does mean you will receive when you need help; that's reciprocal altruism. And, the power of positive affirmation does have benefits—but then you have to ask yourself, why are you going to church rather than to a motivational speaker? Why do you pay to see fake healings rather than going to a magic show? Listen to the way charismatic leaders speak, the rising and dropping volume of their voice, the repeated words—eliciting social conformity. Is this how Jesus spoke? It does not seem so from the Bible. From the words we see in the Bible, it seems Jesus preached with deep, well thought out parables and stories, with terse sayings that were extremely relevant to the situation, and often with more than one layer of meaning. He was not hosting a concert, he was not hypnotizing a crowd. He was appealing to their minds and their hearts. There are organizations, such as the Trinity Foundation, and pastors, such as the American John Piper, who are actively working to fight exploitation by charismatic pastors and televangelists.

So this has been a critique of the problematic practices found in many churches. My advice is simply to have a healthy scepticism of everything you hear—don't believe there is a God just because you are told to have faith, or because you are in a social group or society that compels you to believe. Remember that the closest contemporary to Jesus (Paul) never ever mentions miracles. You don't need to believe in miracles to be a Christian. In Christianity faith is through God's grace. It's not that we wake up and decide we need to choose to believe in God. Faith coming through God's grace means that it is God that chooses at some time in our life to reveal himself to us. Of course, we can notionally believe there is a God, and we can be a Christian from a very young age, but you don't have to *buy-in* to religion. Be who you are. Accept the truths that are evident in front of you, and adjust your understanding as you learn and travel on your own spiritual journey.

A difficulty with our short human lives, is it can take us a long time to learn fundamental lessons. Particularly if we have irresponsible parents, no parents, a disturbed childhood, or schooling which focuses on making cheap productive workers to power the economy. It can be as late as our 40s or 50s when we start to understand ourselves and solidify an effective set of values and strategies for living a contented life. These values may come from religion, from personal experience, from philosophy, or simply reflective analysis. Indeed, the unconsidered adoption of religious values as a child may result in rebellion and rejection as an adult as we examine the religious assumptions we previously inherited without question. Partly why I am writing this book, is for readers to understand how I have found that philosophically considered personal values do relate well to Christianity. We are able to find our strength, our growth and our contentment in Christianity without having to simply believe a host of doctrines of the local church that we may feel are logically erroneous. As we know, the first and only principle of Christianity is to love, and St. Paul specifically tells us: "Love does not delight in evil but rejoices with the truth."[24] Truth appears as a word 109 times in the New Testament. We cannot be Christians and simply absorb things we don't believe are true. Christianity is a quest for the truth, even if this truth isn't what we first thought it was. We need space and personal reflection to question what we are told.

My intention in this book, while adding some tidbits of information for interest, has been to keep the view of Christianity straightforward and simple, with no need to argue over the details. I had previously been a Christian and rejected it, in part because of the questionable logic that some pastors and churches insisted that I must believe, only finding out later that not all churches hold even the most core beliefs about Christianity, and indeed beliefs that historians of Christianity question existed in the early church, such as the resurrection of Jesus[25, 26]. For myself, the benefit of latching my values onto Christianity has been that it creates a simpler framework from which I can approach life, and some solidity in

---

24. 1 Corinthians 13:6
25. Mach, *Lost Gospel*
26. Ehrman, *How Jesus Became God*

practicing my personal values. Simplicity in Christianity? Well yes and no. When I was younger I would reflect endlessly on the philosophical implications of various teachings, question the legitimacy of the creation myths, see contradictions in the Bible—particularly between the Old and New Testaments. However, I implore you to understand one simple all encompassing message of Christianity that overshadows any other petty discussion: God is love. Not to say, it's just another word for love; this I will explain in the final chapter. However, the overwhelming understanding should be that we are all entirely and completely loved by God, and we don't have to worry if we know this, and can trust that this is true. This is why arguing over the minutia of the Bible, while it may be historically or intellectually interesting, does not at all change the message of the Bible— and indeed, if we are arguing aggressively over such points, or shouting at people to repent or change their ways, we may be speaking words from the Bible, but we are not living as Christians. From knowing God loves us, we derive these values: faith, hope, optimism, inner strength, contentment. From the fundamental principal of loving others, comes another set of values and practices of the Bible: humility, gratitude, forgiveness, charity.

Modelling ourselves as a Christian, although we will question our beliefs and attitudes toward Christianity at times, provides a simple but secure rock on which to live. If I were an atheist I may have personally philosophized that having sex with a person other than my wife is morally wrong because it would cause her pain, and I need to ensure that she is happy in her marriage with me to be able to have an ongoing relationship, and maximize the opportunity of success for my children through both of us providing for them—then I start to philosophize, what happens if we can't have children? Does this still count? What happens if she says she is happy if we have an open relationship? What happens if she doesn't know, is it still fine? All these philosophical questions can constantly be raised. I could take a philosophical view point that is slightly different: adultery is wrong because it is an indulgence in the physical world rather than intellectual or spiritual, then my philosophical musings may go down another path. By taking on board Christianity, but in a considered manner, it enables me to accept the wisdom found in the bible, but without having to accept it unquestioningly. I will not have to go down a logical rabbit hole, and reflect endlessly on this issue, forgetting maybe my justifications for one behaviour or another. Instead I can use the teachings in Christianity to help build my character and create a firmer barrier against performing actions that would make me think less of myself. So, to some extent we do need to put trust in the Bible, but it is a measured trust, that we have evaluated. I feel fortunate that I was outside of Christianity when I then recognized that some of the values I felt were important in my life were intrinsic to Christianity. This is why I also encourage those that are outside Christianity to examine their lives and what they believe is important, and see if it is reflected in the New Testament. For the question of adultery that I raised, indeed for myself the real point for me is that when I got married I made a promise to God that I would be faithful to her.

Given all these terrible reasons for being involved in a church, many would choose to have a more private belief system, such as Zen Buddhism, or a polytheistic Roman cult that requires private sacrifices at a household shrine. Some philosophies can adequately fill in for many of the moral and psychological beneficial aspects of Christianity, Stoicism being a prime example. I don't doubt that these religions and philosophies have great value for people. However, Christian churches can offer more. On the whole, congregations are welcoming, and contain kind people who are trying to follow God regardless of any commercial structure or politics that the organizational structure of the church has. There is a benefit by being surrounded by people that have similar values, and when you have questions or problems about your faith, with whom you can discuss these problems. Although church goers vary in their commitment to different values, you can generally see good modeled behaviour, and often it is easier to emulate behavior that you yourself want to be like, or at least use such model behavior to remind you of how you should be. The church can thus give you strength and stability in following Christian values.

Many churches do use donations to help the poor in structured ways, and can reach those that we would not normally reach through our day to day interactions in public. If a church is functioning effectively in its community, it is aware of many of the people in the community struggling for basic necessities, and can provide for them through the congregation's donations. As an individual, while we may help those in need in our work or through personal donations, the church can help remind us of our commitments to the needy and provide a structured way of providing that assistance, particularly within the local community.

As humans we need connection to others. Churches provides a relatively cheap, welcoming and instant way to reengage with people which can be particularly beneficial to those that are lonely or rejected from their family or community, such as the highly introverted, homeless, ex-criminals or old people. This social activity can provide a diverse range of people of different professions and ages to associate with, and a social life that generally avoids the use of alcohol and drugs associated with many other social arenas. We can expect to be with a community of fellow humans that hold certain values including forgiveness and acceptance of others (including toward non-Christians), to treat all people equally, and to demonstrate a more-or-less ethical lifestyle, as well as spreading compassion and love. Indeed, if your church is not following such principles, you can be assured they are not faithfully following Christianity. The assistance the church gives should not be just to other Christians, but to those most in need. The pastor can earn a living from the church but should not be gathering unnecessary assets or living a wealthy lifestyle from his/her ministry. He/she must be humble and lead by example. A Christian minister is not a lifestyle coach. They are preaching a very specific way to live and treat others, a way to inner peace, and a connection with God. The preaching in a service should not be about how to build your businesses, how to build your church, or how to get rich.

The Christian life in the time of Jesus and early church was clearly a communal life. Reading the Bible from a modern (especially Western) perspective can be misleading because we have developed a society of individual rights, individual destiny and individual values. Maybe some practices and beliefs are more suited to such a modern lifestyle, such as yoga, meditation, philosophy, Buddhism? Christianity was undoubtedly designed, not for just personal worship, but for a congregation to come together—it is communal and indeed gets much of its power from being a communal movement; whether that is helping each other with charity, or influencing politics in positive ways. Certainly in Malawi many people find benefits in the church because of the wider communal assistance; with often large crowds at marriages or funerals, frequent hospital visits if you are ill, financial assistance when you are destitute. Globally, the largest correlate with a country having many religious practitioners, is wealth division. Both rich and poor in those societies, tend to be more religious than in countries with lower wealth division. Possibly this occurs because governments help those in countries that are more equitable in their wealth, but countries with high wealth inequality need social networks: the wealthy, to get contacts, and the poor, so they have a social safety net, which in this case is provided by the church.

When I lived on a Kibbutz in Israel, we would have breakfast together in a large hall, we would travel together for work; my colleagues and I pollinated date palms. We would leave at dawn for work, but then congregate for a strong grainy coffee together around 8am. In the evening, although some families would eat in their own homes, it was common for most people to eat in a large communal hall. At Jewish festivals such as Passover, the whole community would celebrate together. Catholic festivities in much of Southern Europe still maintain regular communal festivities, with communal gatherings at Christmas, Easter, and celebration days for their town's saint, as well as other festivities particular to that area. Protestant countries such as the UK, USA, Germany, and Holland have lost many of the religious festivals, apart from maybe occasional carol singing or going to a pantomime. Communal festivities in the religious calendar may serve to increase the social bonds to ensure people are looking after each other and have human contact with their neighbors. Socialization is extremely important for most of us to lead a healthy life. It has been found that death rates in the UK (from any cause) are lowest for those that drink moderate levels of alcohol, but higher both for tee-teetotalers and those that drink double the recommended alcohol limit. This is thought to be due to the lower level of socialization in those that abstain from alcohol, resulting in negative health effects.

Having a good social network not only benefits your health, but can help in promoting your business, finding a job, solving a problem, or even finding a trades-person. As humans we work as groups, and we're more effective as groups, but with the increased complexity of modern lives, we can often find ourselves feeling isolated and alone. Smart phones and television can be entertaining, but they are not a substitute for socialization. And despite problems we get when interacting with others, and the frustrations of awkward or unthoughtful people, the psychological benefits we get from positive social interactions completely outweigh the negative. Church socialization also has some level of social regulation; with someone who steals or deceives you within the church losing the trust of the congregation.

Christianity, as a church movement, are often criticized in western society for stances against homosexual marriages and abortion rights, as well as sometimes having non-progressive views. However, Christianity has also been very important in political influence and social changes that most of us would accept as positive. The Christian Quaker movement (The Society of Friends) were the first religious movement to condemn slavery, and were instrumental in its abolition. Initially, in 1776 Quakers prohibited their members from owning slaves, then in 1790 they petitioned the US Congress for the abolition of slavery. Throughout the late 1700s and early 1800s the Quakers published adverts and papers in the UK condemning slavery and drawing attention to the terrible suffering caused by the slave trade. The Quakers urged their members to vote for William Wilberforce as a member of parliament for Yorkshire, as they knew he was a vocal abolitionist. To tender public support for abolition they also drew attention to the enslavement of white Christian European slaves who had been taken by the Muslim Ottomon Empire in North Africa since the 1500s, by publishing the "Account of the Slavery of Friends in the Barbary States". The UK finally abolished the slave trade in 1807, though slaves in the colonies of the British Empire were not freed until 1838. The North African Barbary trade in European slaves ended in 1830 when the French invaded Algiers. Quakers also campaigned for women's rights and for prison reform to improve prisoners rights.

The Baptist minister, Martin Luther King Junior, led the US civil rights movement (1954), campaigning for fair voting rights for black Americans, as well as for better conditions and salaries for poor working class people in general. When a military coup in Brazil installed a repressive military regime (1964), the Catholic Church was vocal and active in campaigning against human rights abuses by the military. In the civil war in El Salvador, Archbishop Romero campaigned against breaches of human rights by the authorities. In 1980 the Archbishop made a sermon pleading with the army and National Guard:

> "I want to make a special appeal to soldiers, national guardsmen, and policemen: each of you is one of us. The peasants you kill are your own brothers and sisters. When you hear a man telling you to kill, remember God's words, 'thou shalt not kill.' No soldier is obliged to obey a law contrary to the law of God. In the name of God, in the name of our tormented people, I beseech you, I implore you; in the name of God I command you to stop the repression."[27]

He was assassinated the day after this sermon.

But it's not just Christianity that has lead to positive political change. The support of Hindu groups was important in supporting Gandhi in the liberation of India from the British (1947). Along with

27. Walters, *Saint Oscar Romero*

the Dutch Reformed Church and Archbishop Desmond Tutu campaigning against Apartheid in South Africa, so did Muslim Mosques. Both Christian Churches and Jewish groups were the main supporters of the campaign to institute the 1948 "Convention on the Prevention and Punishment of the Crime of Genocide". Thus, while a religious institution and the body of members can be repressive, as the Catholic Church were during *The Spanish Inquisition*, a church can also act as a political force for good, speaking out against injustice even at the threat to the lives of their members. Through faith and conviction in what is right, people have been able to sacrifice their time, risk their families and their own life, to create a better, fairer, and more equitable society.

Despite my own personal problems with finding churches that don't hold prejudices or don't have a rent seeking pastor, I do respect what the larger Christian church does globally. There are numerous Christian charities, and they're not focusing on Christians, but on those in need, regardless of race, gender or religion. The ease in which Churches drift from their Christian mission and values is evident in the Bible, because much of Paul's Epistles are requests to various churches to reform themselves and come back to their Christian values:

> "The very fact that you have lawsuits among you means you have been completely defeated already. Why not rather be wronged? Why not rather be cheated? Instead, you yourselves cheat and do wrong, and you do this to your brothers and sisters."[28]

> "In the first place, I hear that when you come together as a church, there are divisions among you, and to some extent I believe it. No doubt there have to be differences among you to show which of you have God's approval. So then, when you come together, it is not the Lord's Supper you eat, for when you are eating, some of you go ahead with your own private suppers. As a result, one person remains hungry and another gets drunk. Don't you have homes to eat and drink in? Or do you despise the church of God by humiliating those who have nothing? What shall I say to you? Shall I praise you? Certainly not in this matter!"[29]

So we can see, churches stray, people get into their own power hierarchies, Christians compete and stop thinking of others and just of themselves; but also they can change, just as people can change, and they

---

28. 1 Cor 6:7–8
29. 1 Cor 11:18–22

can be reformed. Fundamentally, while the church can be an aid, your prime relationship is always directly with God, and not a human created institution, a pastor, nor a congregation. It's beautiful when a congregation or church can work for the betterment of society or others, but you must not let this congregation brain-wash you, force you to do that which you know is wrong, or remove you from your own Christian values.

10. Fasting

I DIDN'T WRITE THIS book to discuss what is written in the Bible, but to show how I came to Christianity due to the way it resonated with experiences and understanding I had gained independently of the Bible. However, now when I read the Bible many verses resonate with me because of my own personal experience. I believe that fasting is a fundamental practice in many spiritual practices and belief systems, and has real physical and psycho-spiritual effects. Importantly, an involuntary fast was the trigger of a religious experience for me. During an illness many years ago in Portugal, with a terrible stomach ache and vomiting, I was committed to drinking only boiled water (after cooling) for a period of more than 5 days. The religious experience following this will be described fully in the next chapter, but first let me discuss the importance of fasting.

Fasting is a major part of Christianity. It's not a common practice in Europe, but it is in Africa. When I was in hospital with Malaria and the doctors thought I was going to die, my wife and mother-in-law fasted as they prayed for me. Most churches here in Africa expect members of their congregation at some point to fast when they are asking something of God, and indeed during the year as part of general worship.

In the Bible fasting is mentioned more than 70 times, either explicitly or implicitly, either as directions to fast, or examples of people fasting. Saul, after the revelation from Jesus on the road to Damascus, did not eat or drink for 3 days[1]. Jesus fasted for 40 days and 40 nights in the desert[2] because he was "led by the Spirit into the wilderness to be tempted", and soon after Jesus states "It is written: Man shall not live on

---

1. Acts 9:9
2. Matt 4:2

bread alone, but on every word that comes from the mouth of God"[3]. Jesus also told his disciples the reason they couldn't drive out a particular demon was because both prayer and fasting were required[4]. It is clear that fasting is an important part of both Jewish and Christian belief, for various reasons including contrition, spiritual power, purification, connection with God, or asking favour from God.[5]

There are different methods of fasting, ranging from "avoiding wine, meat and pleasant bread" for three weeks[6], to Mosses not eating bread or water for 40 days in the presence of God when receiving the ten commandments on Mount Sinai.[7]

Most of us know that for the month of Ramadan Muslims do a *dry* fast i.e. no food or water, and also no sex. The dry fast only lasts during the day, and after dusk Muslims gather together to eat. The purpose is to remind Muslims of the less fortunate, to be thankful for what they have, and also to gain *Taqwa*, which means an increased awareness of Allah. The 9th month of the Islamic calendar is chosen as the time for fasting because that is when the Qur'an was revealed. Jews have seven different fasting periods, the best known being Yom Kippur (Day of Atonement), starting on the 10th day of the seventh month of the Jewish calendar. The ten days leading to Yom Kippur represent the last 10 days of Moses in the wilderness, before bringing back the ten commandments on the stone tablets. Fasting begins at sundown on the day of Yom Kippur and lasts until sundown the following day, though the next meal is usually a "break-fast" the following morning, with invited guests. During the fast Jews should abstain from food, drink, sex, bathing, wearing perfumes or lotions, and wearing leather shoes. Many Jews will be more flexible with these regulations and may just have a *wet* fast i.e. no eating, and maybe not even for the whole day.

Siddhartha Gautama Buddha, the founder of Buddhism, when as a prince he left the palace, he started an ascetic life, with regular extreme fasting. In India at the time fasting was considered an effective way to gain wisdom. Some stories tell that he went 6 years living on a grain of rice a day, as well as doing other ascetic practices such as

3. Matt 4:6
4. Matt 17:21
5. 2 Sam 12:15, 1 Kgs 21:27, Ezra 8:23, Neh 1:4, Ps 35:13, Dan 9:3, Joel 2:12, Luke 2:37, Luke 18:12, Acts 13:3
6. Dan 10:3
7. Exod 34:28

holding his breath for long periods of time. Zen tradition tells that he sat meditating under a type of fig tree (The Bodhi—or enlightenment tree, *Ficus religiosa*) and was determined not to break his meditation until he had gained understanding of the true path humans should take. After 7 weeks (49 days) he gained enlightenment, and rejected the strict adherence to asceticism. However, he developed the four noble truths about suffering and non-attachment. Thus, when you see Buddhist statues of Siddhartha Buddha, you may see a very deathly bony figure with sunken eyes, which is when he was an ascetic, or instead a fat smiling Buddha, which represents the time when he gave up his fasting. It's not that he became fat, but it symbolizes that he advised the *middle way* such as to not be overly attached to either greed, nor ascetic practices.

Fasting in Buddhism is considered a method of self-control. Thus there is sometimes restricted eating and drinking, but also this is a period of self control over our speech, thoughts and body. However, fasting is generally not a requirement in Buddhism. Some Buddhist monks observe uposatha (fasting), on the full moon, but in general there is only a call for *mindfulness* when eating food, so as not to over-indulge nor severely deny oneself. Where there is fasting in Buddhism it is short, from after the noon meal until the next morning: simply as a method of not over-indulging.

Hinduism uses fasting to purify the body and mind, to connect to God, as well as an act of devotion and sacrifice to God. Hindus have various fasting periods such as those of Vrat, Viradham and Upavasa, and these are based around the lunar calendar. The practices of fasting vary greatly during such holy periods, such as eating only one meal a day over a short period of time, only eating vegetarian food, or avoiding salt. Ekadashi is the most commonly observed fast, on the 11th day of each ascending and descending moon (about twice a month). Thus, while there are many days that fasting may occur, they tend not to be ascetic fasts. However, some Hindus may practice ascetic fasts for spiritual reasons, such as Mahatma Ghandi who fasted for 3 weeks for spiritual and political reasons.

Catholics have fasting on ash Wednesday and Good Friday, and often abstain from meat on Friday during lent or even all year round. The Church of Later Day Saints (Mormons) will fast on the first Sunday of each month. Baha'i have a 19 day wet fast (sunrise to sunset). Jains have an eight day wet fast, during *Ratri Bhojan Tyag*, with some only drinking boiled water. In these world religions the fasting is regularly associated with specific times of the year of religious significance. Though fasting necessarily incorporates aspects of sacrifice and bodily control and an attempt to bring ourselves closer to God, short fasts and simple short-term dietary restrictions are often more about drawing attention to the religious significance of the time of year and to socially recognize symbolic and cultural meaning. Actual spiritual connection or development of spiritual awareness I believe comes more strongly through complete wet fasting (just water) and through fasting for longer periods than in the typical ceremonial fasting.

The first time I heard about fasting for spiritual reasons was that of the Native Americans, at the Battle of Little Bighorn. The second treaty of Fort Laramie (1868) had guaranteed the Lakota, Sioux and Arapaho Indians exclusive possession of the Dakota territories west of the Missouri River. However, US settlers started mining on the Native American territories in their sacred lands, causing tension between both parties. Finally the US government sided with the American settlers and declared that Native Americans must return to their reservations or be considered hostile (31 Jan 1876). Thus, the Lakota, Cheyenne and Arapaho Indians banded together under the leadership of Sitting Bull and camped on a tributary of the Bighorn River, called Little Bighorn in Southern Montana. It was here at a religious *Sun Dance* ceremony that Sitting Bull had a prophetic vision of US soldiers toppling upside down within the camp. Sitting Bull considered this a sign there would be a great victory for the Native Americans. During this ceremony the Native Americans fasted for 3 days, in preparation for battle.

US soldiers under the leadership of General George Armstrong Custer were sent to find the Native Americans at the tributary where they were camping. Forward scouts reported that 800 poorly armed Native Americans were camped there. However, this was a huge underestimation because there were in fact around 2,000, and armed with modern repeating rifles. On their report, Custer split his troops into three companies, to block off escape routes. Dividing the troops ended in disaster. General Custer was defeated, and him and his men were all killed. Although the Native Americans found victory that day, later the US sent huge numbers of troops to the area to force a surrender.

Crazy Horse, a Lokota Native American, had been noted for his bravery in the battle of Little Bighorn. As with Sitting Bull, Crazy Horse had also had a vision following fasting, but much earlier in his life. Indeed, young Lakota men would normally be expected to do a vision quest and experience a *vision* as part of their normal life. This would be a guiding spiritual event, which would be necessary to have success in life, or to inform them on how to serve their community.

The Lokata vision quest comprises of a purification ceremony where the *seeker* would go to a secluded place for around four days and do dry fasting and prayer, often without sleep. This ceremony would be repeated at different times, until they have a vision. Crazy Horse received his vision as a teenager: he saw a man on a horse rising out of a lake and then changing colour. This man had one Eagle's feather in his hair, with a small stone tied behind an ear, and unusually, no war paint. The man talked, but without moving his lips, and he instructed Crazy Horse that before battle he was to rub dust on himself and never to wear a war head-dress or bind up his horses tail (a common practice), nor to take trophies in battle (such as enemy scalps). The man in his dream also told Crazy Horse that his death would not come in battle or at the hands of an enemy. From then onwards Crazy Horse followed the advice of the man in his dream. Instead of a head-dress, he just wore a single Eagle's feather, and copying the visage of the man in his dream he painted a lightening symbol on his face and carried a small stone tied to his upper body.

It is not just fasting that can induce altered psychological states or visions. Drugs, holding one's breath, sensory deprivation, illness and near death experience has also been linked with visions and spiritual experiences. It's likely that humans for hundreds of thousands of years have linked such visions to an alternative spiritual reality or spiritual connection. In Europe many of the cave paintings dating from the paleolithic era (2.5 million years ago to 10,000 BC) have been interpreted as representing shamanistic trance states and hallucinations. Indeed, shamanistic cultures have associated caves, natural high ledges and mountains, as entrances or connections to the spirit world. For example in France and Spain there are paintings dating between 40,000 and 14,000 years ago, daubed on the inside walls of remote caves situated high up in the mountains. It is believed the confined spaces and high altitude may have induced hypoxia due to the lack of oxygen. Hypoxia results in the release of dopamine, giving a natural "high" and inducing hallucinations. Sensory deprivation due to spending days in the absolute darkness of caves can also induce euphoria and hallucinations. Evidence that these caves had spiritual significance was that the deep cave systems, where the cave paintings were found, did not indicate habitation. Some of the images on such cave walls are also zig-zag or dot patterns, which are typical patterns seen during sensory deprivation. There are also paintings of the rarer large wild animals which were not part of their hunter-gatherer diet, such as lions. It is believed these powerful animals may have served as psychological representations of immense power to the paleolithic population.

Even in a church or a concert, a pastor or band is building the atmosphere up with repetition of words, quiet followed by a sudden roaring of noise, with rhythm and repetition, to a crescendo where people feel elated. A dance like gymnastic martial art game from Brazil called Capoeira, has a word for this elated energy and spiritual high; Axé. The two players engage in ritualized combat within a circle of loud singing and clapping people, moving to the rhythm which is dictated by percussion string instruments known as Berimbau, and a large resonating bass droning drum called an Atabaque. With the sound of the surrounding music and crowd, the rhythm, the hypnotic coordination with your partner, and the extreme exertion, you can feel this axé and get taken out of the moment; your tiredness wanes and you feel elated and not conscious of your own heavy breathing, with all the components of the event melding in to one. Capoeira has ties to the syncreatic religion Candomblé, with many of the songs being about Yemanjá, the Goddess of the Sea or have other African religious significance. In Candomblé some of that religious meaning has been covered up by Catholicism, using Saint Mary (Maria) as a pseudonym for Yemanjá, enabling the enslaved Africans in Brazil to continue practising their traditional religious beliefs in the guise of Catholicism. Indeed, Capoeira is listed as a UNESCO intangible heritage, in part because of the Capoeira songs and physical practice referencing some of the distant African spiritual beliefs.

Throughout much of our history we have been trying to reach these altered states, but why? It is clear that most humans believe there is more to reality than what we can see with our eyes, taste with our tongue, hear with our ears, and sense with our touch. After all, these senses evolved for our material needs in the *mundane* world. There are animals that don't have all the senses we have, such as without ears (crabs), or without eyes (some worms and cave or deep-sea invertebrates). Also, there are animals that can see things we don't: we cannot see ultra-violet light (whereas many insects can) nor infra-red light (but many reptiles can). No living organism (as far as we know) can sense radio-waves, but through special technology we know they exist. Radio waves don't just come from our own radio transmissions, but from the sun, nebulae, galaxies, and pulsing from neutron stars. Animals just haven't had the necessity to detect radio waves in order to survive, so there is no evolutionary reason to develop sense organs to detect them. Only recently have we discovered gravitational waves, that like radio waves, are passing through us all the time. We can be confident that our physical experience of reality as a human, with our limited senses and limited brains, is a minute part of what is the whole of reality. We can detect radio and gravitational waves now with scientific equipment, but how many other aspects of reality have we not discovered yet, or may never discover? However, it seems we have an instinctive understanding that what we experience with our senses in our *mundane* world is not a complete picture of the universe.

Maybe we seek to look beyond what we see day to day with our normal senses and experiences. Maybe this is why we pursue spiritual highs. Maybe this is why we want those highs from an exceptionally vigorous church service, a shaman, hallucinogenic drugs, sensory deprivation, or fasting. Whether the changed perception is really a deeper view of reality or just a psychological artifact, as humans we are certainly searching to reach beyond the material world. We desire the spiritual, we want to pull back the veil of reality created by our physical senses alone, and to connect with something that is beyond our bodily understanding.

What does fasting do to the body, physically and psychologically? As a Boy Scout and a keen survivalist in my early years, I had read that we could only survive 1 month without food, and a few days without water. After my religious experience, which had followed almost 6 days without food, I knew that I could safely and without too much suffering go without food for 6 days, probably much longer. Years after this event, after returning from Portugal to the UK, was when I once again fasted, but this time it was a voluntary fast, as part of protest against the British Government. You may remember that when I returned to the UK, the British government was not complying with my rights as a British and European citizen, and was denying my family entry to the UK. This was because then Prime Minister, Theresa May, had made a promise to reduce immigration from around 160,000 people a year, and to do that the Home Office had to break the law. During this 4 year legal battle with the Home Office, I had decided to go on hunger strike to draw attention to the injustice of being illegally separated from my family. Unfortunately British newspapers weren't interested in publicizing this:

the right wing publications were happy to have immigration reduced, even if illegally, and left wing papers were more interested in the plights of foreigners than British people; however I did get publicity in at least the Portuguese news. Looking back, the four years of legal struggle was enlightening in another, more intellectual way. As well as reading about others that had struggled against authority, such as Martin Luther King[8], and Henry Thoreau's[9], I also read up on the effects of fasting, including permanent effects, in-case my fast were to create permanent organ damage or death. The hunger strike lasted a measly 6 days, although unlike the first time when I was ill, this time I was also working throughout the fasting period, so I was burning far more calories. I didn't have any spiritual experience the second time, but I can use this experience to detail how fasting feels, as well as some background information I learned on the science of fasting.

When you stop eating completely your body is quite happy using the glucose sugar in your blood stream for around 12 hours, and releasing some stored glucose from your liver. Eating is a habit, so you will still feel hungry around your next meal time, though I am sure everyone reading this has skipped at least one meal before. You clearly won't feel hungry during your first night's sleep. After 12 hours without food, the high glucose level that our body is used to begins to drop. You'll feel calmer, and somehow more natural. Some people report headaches, which they attribute to toxins in our body fats being released, but I have not had those headaches and am not particularly convinced that it is the effect of toxin release. During those first 24 hours we develop a sense that we don't have to busy our minds with insignificant things: checking social media, being angry with the neighbour, or overthinking issues at work or home. Probably our body is helping us to start focusing on what is important for our immediate physical survival, food. You won't feel stressed, but indeed the opposite. I notice in myself that I'm not striving to get first in the queue, or competing to get something, or worrying about all the things I need to do. I'll be greeting people as friends, my mind starts reflecting on less competitive thoughts; on larger reflections of life and thoughts about the needs of others.

As you get toward completing 24 hours without food you'll really start to feel the hunger kick in; your body is simply telling you to eat

---

8. Clayborne, *Autobiography Martin Luther King*
9. Thoreau, *Civil Disobedience*

something. This hunger will increase even further over the next 24 hours, and this second day is the most difficult period as the hunger will be constantly distracting, and you'll feel tired and low on energy.

After two days, a change starts to occur, like your body waking up. Indeed physiologically, this is what is happening. Your body realizes there is no immediate food, and that to find food, you'll need to be able to move, think and act. Your body is hitting a stage called *Ketosis* whereby the glucose in your blood stream has decreased such that your body is now starting to metabolize stored fats. As the liver shifts from metabolizing glucose to metabolizing fats, ketone molecules also get released into the blood. While the liver cannot use these ketones to generate energy, other tissues can, such as the brain. A low carbohydrate diet known as the Atkins diet (or ketogenic diet) has the same effect: through limiting glucose in the blood, the body is instead metabolizing fats. A ketogenic diet is also known to be useful in reducing epilepsy incidences and in treating type 2 diabetes (the type commonly caused from excessive sugar intake).

Moving toward the third day of fasting, it seems you have plenty time since you're not having to cook, eat or wash dishes. You'll be surprised how much of your time in a day you spend cooking, eating and cleaning plates. With some renewed energy, it's an opportunity to do other things. If you are fasting for spiritual reasons you'll have plenty time to pray or meditate, otherwise you may want to write or paint with this extra time. However, you won't be able to do anything that is too taxing on the body, or the brain. The brain, while only being 2 percent of the mass of the body, uses 20 percent of the body's glucose derived energy. While feeling fine, and indeed very peaceful, your ability to do complex calculations or think deeply is limited. Also, though you won't feel weak, you'll tire much more quickly if you try to exercise.

After around 5 days you may once again start to feel a little light headed. You won't so much feel weak, but more peaceful and with your head in the clouds. Though you can move around normally, it does seem as if your joints are not quite as strong, and I expect any heavy lifting or plyometric (explosive) exercise may cause injury. You'll notice your thought processes are different. The peaceful mind, with a broad view of the world and focus on the more important things in life, deepens. However, your concentration will start to wane, as will your memory and fine-scale physical dexterity. What I found after five days that was particularly worrying, was I no longer felt hungry. Indeed, I really didn't want to eat. The first time fasting for 5 days you may even worry, as I did, that you'll never eat again. In terms of focus on your spiritual life, I am not sure how much additional benefit there is after 5 days. I can only say up to six days, but day six felt much like day five. Other than self-discipline I am not sure that there is a spiritual advantage of fasting more than 5 days. I suspect fasting doesn't get more difficult, apart from gradually decreasing physical and mental capacity. The most difficult period during fasting for me was between 24 and 48 hours, where my hunger was the greatest. Following this, the hunger drops. This is possibly why longer term fasting can be risky: your body is no longer telling you to eat.

While describing this I don't want to confuse voluntary fasting with imposed starvation. With non-voluntary fasting for prolonged periods (more than two days), which I experienced both in Portugal during the economic crisis, and in the UK when returning and finding myself homeless. At that point I would sleep in a forest or wasteland as nearby a job interview location as I could find, then in the morning would sneak in to the building's toilets and wash myself. I didn't have money for food, or to clean my teeth with toothpaste. However, at one university where I was going for an interview, two men promoting Islam had given me a Miswak. This is a small stick made from the *Salvadora persica tree* (native to India) with which you can use the tip to scrub your teeth. This tip gradually breaks down to assume a bristly paint-brush appearance and the wood has anti-bacterial chemicals. Though I didn't like the taste, and it didn't feel as fresh as cleaning with commercial toothpaste, it was much better than not cleaning my teeth, and the single stick lasted many weeks. Anyway, during the hunger of these periods, I didn't feel spiritually happy; I felt hungry and that I needed to find food. Worse than that, was also the fear that I might not find food. With voluntary fasting you don't fear that when you decide to stop you won't have food. When homeless my thoughts were occupied with: When will I eat next? How will I get food? Will finding food get more difficult as I get weaker? Will I have to eat out of bins? At what stage will I have to eat things that will repulse me? Thankfully though, this period of very sporadic eating lasted only around two weeks, and I didn't have to beg as people around me occasionally helped by providing some food. One extremely kind barman in Wales even allowed me to sleep for two weeks above the bar while it was being refurbished. So, I don't think there is a strong similarity between voluntary fasting and having a lack of food.

Through the experience of my voluntary fasts, and through my religious convictions, now each month I do a limited *wet* fast (water only) for 24 hours. It brings a sense of peace and greater purpose. Because I do it regularly, and am accustomed to it, I also see it as a form of discipline: you're saying to your body "My mind controls my body, and I am not subject to my bodily desires". That desire for food, sex, material gain, social standing and your emotional responses of jealousy or anger; it seems these can be tamed through a simple 24 hour fast. You feel more loving, more at peace, and more part of the universe. It's not only because it makes you feel more grounded and spiritual, but also the fast resets your appetite. When you start eating again you generally don't want a large meal, just something simple, and you fill up quickly. Much of our eating is habitual and social, and not an act to replenish the body. You'll probably notice that if you eat a large meal in the evening, then you wake up hungry because your stomach has expanded. Our bodies are quite efficient at utilizing or storing food that we eat. If you eat an excess of glucose it gets converted into glycogen in the liver or can be converted to adipose (fat) tissue. Eat too many complex carbohydrates or fats, and they'll get stored as fats. An excess of proteins doesn't get wasted, they get broken down or *deaminated*, whereby the amino acids are removed by the liver, and the remaining compounds are converted to stored fat; with the excess amino acids excreted in urine. One of the reasons intermittent (wet) fasting can be an effective way of dieting is because it reduces sugar levels, stops the accumulation of excess fat, and can help reset our desire for food to a more moderate level. It also helps with reducing insulin resistance, a condition that leads to type 2 diabetes.

A popular myth is that we die of starvation because of lack of calories. This is usually not the case. One of the most important studies in fasting is with Irish political hunger strikers in prison during *The Troubles* in Northern Ireland. Many of these strikers refused food to the point of death. On average it took 76 days for a hunger striker to die; many more than the 30 days I had been told in survival books. Of course these hunger strikers were in prison and not active. The main cause of death through starvation is the lack of vitamins to fight off illness. The body becomes extremely susceptible to flu or colds and the bodies defenses are heavily compromised. Also, though we may survive for around two months without any food, that doesn't mean we won't suffer permanent organ damage before this. Thus, I would consider 40 days an upper limit for safe fasting, but to be aware that people have died when fasting for as few as 30 days. I have never had such an extended fast, and though I know in Africa some people fast for 40 days, I certainly don't recommend it and would warn that it is a serious health risk. Four people in the Bible fasted for 40 days: Jesus[10], Moses[11], Joshua[12] and Elijah[13]. However, it's important to understand the number 40 in the Bible may not be literal, but symbolizes a period of trial or testing which one has to pass through. Recently in Malawi a pastor died after fasting for only 20 days, though I suspect he had underlying health issues. Agostino Barbieri is the record holder for the longest fast without solid food. Starting in June 1965 he lived on only vitamins, electrolytes, yeast (for essential amino acids) and sugarless tea, coffee and sparkling water—for 382 days. He did this to lose weight, starting off at a humongous 207 kg (456 pounds) and losing 125kg (276 pounds). Of course this is an exceptional case, and also using vitamin supplements and electrolytes.

My fasting always includes the consumption of water. While people do dry fasting, I don't recommend long periods (more than 2 days) without water. Our whole metabolism uses water as the medium for chemical reactions. After 3 days without water you will experience severe dehydration, and at 7 days it will become life threatening. It is not likely you'll last more than 12 days without water.

When Jesus was in the desert for 40 days without food or water, or Moses was on Mount Sinai for 40 days without food or water, though it may have been less and the number was symbolic, it is my belief that this was literally a period where they were entirely dependent on God and lived in the spirit, and really the period of time is less important than the inference that they were not experiencing life as a normal person during this period and were somehow spiritually connected. Whether this period is symbolic or real, or whether water may have been sucked off leaves, I clearly do not know. What is undeniable is that Christianity has a strong link with fasting as a practice for spiritual cleansing or getting closer to God, and that we have to understand our dependence on God comes before our dependence on food. Why do I personally feel that the practice of fasting is an essential spiritual practice? I guess because of my personal experience with fasting, where I do feel an increased spiritual connection, and because for me it's further evidence that Christianity as a religion isn't simply a tool for material benefit,

10. Matt 4:2
11. Deut 9:9
12. Exod 24:13–18
13. 1 Kgs 19:7–8

but goes beyond our personal desires to something that is spiritual and outside the mundane (material) existence.

11. A Religious Experience

MY MOTHER WENT TO a Catholic school and considered herself Catholic, though in my lifetime she never went to church. She had once said she would have liked to have been Jewish because of the nice festivals. In contrast, my father didn't speak much about religion but as I got older I realized he had a strong Christian faith. After my mother died, he went to church every week and became involved in helping the church and others in the community. He considered himself a protestant because he grew up in the Church of England. As a child I went to church every month because I was expected to, being a boy-scout (and my father was the scout leader), but I felt church was terribly boring.

From the age of around 15 I became very interested in philosophy. I'd taken a book out of the library describing 50 different philosophers and their philosophies, as well as counter arguments. What fascinated me was how convincing the philosophical argument could be, then how convincing the counter argument could be. I guess that was my first introduction to real critical thinking, as I tried to rationalize how both couldn't be true and to work out where the gaps in the contrasting logical positions were. Probably this is why I gravitated towards science: the working man's philosophical studies.

Because my parents didn't want to force a religious belief upon their children, I was never baptized. I did read much of the New Testament, and then around 18 I dipped in and out of many different churches. Whilst I felt there were some truths, it felt that these truths were used as a hook to pull you into the church, where you were then forced to concede to believing other aspects of the ideology which just didn't seem right. They were ultimately dissatisfying. I began to feel religion was a cultural phenomena and belief depended on your upbringing or cultural influence. Indeed I still feel for many people around the world it is sociocultural rather than a choice or belief based on experience. I later went through a period of trying to decondition my brain. I realized that many religious, social, ethical and even scientific beliefs were simply things I had been told or expected to believe because of the culture or people around me. At around this time, because I was also training in martial arts, I came across Zen Buddhism. It seemed to be the answer to what I was looking for: removing artificial logical constructs that are often based on human culture. I applied to join a local Zen Buddhist group, but because of little background in Buddhism, I was refused. I continued to read the excellent, informative and enjoyable books of D.T. Suzuki: three hefty volumes which for me at the time contained drastically novel thoughts. D.T. Suzuki was the authority in bringing Zen Buddhism to the western mind, without making it a *new-age* trend which some later writers on Zen seemed to do. I began to appreciate koans, and even started doing traditional Chinese painting. It did bring enormous peace to my heart and it radically changed my perspective of the world. I truly began to appreciate each moment in my life for what it was, in the here and now. In philosophical or religious discussions with work colleagues, it felt like I had the answers because I wasn't on any particular side and I had found the "pivot point" where I could see beyond the contrasts between right and wrong to some deeper yet simpler level of meaning.

Over those years I guess I considered myself a Zen Buddhist, though I felt no need to define myself. However, with time Zen Buddhism itself seemed to become a rigid structure. Monks sitting cross-legged in zazen for days on end, or living as hermits. I meditated, and it brought me enormous peace, but almost too much peace. Surely there was room in the world for fear, for excitement, for joy. Aren't these natural emotions, and there for a reason? The koans seemed to become more like word puzzles and less like the direct insight into reality I had first experienced. Maybe that insight was simply a mind game in itself whereby you can fool yourself into believing you had achieved enlightenment. Indeed, I started to believe that enlightenment i.e. a direct and complete understanding of the universe, was impossible for the human brain. Our brains think in a certain way because they have evolved to do so. Was religion simply a method of mediating stress? When we're in low stress situations or bored, it provides us with mental stimulation and some reason to exist? Conversely in high stress situations, when our life is under threat, we lose a job, or a loved one dies, it regulates the fear or suffering to a manageable level? Is religion simply a strategy we have developed to operate more effectively as an organism?

This put me on another path of exploration. Evangelical Christians throughout the world are called to proselytize; effectively to knock on doors and ask if you have discovered Jesus. While most people don't actually want to talk to these cold callers, for me I would be extremely interested to enquire about what they thought, and why they were Christian. Indeed, I wanted to understand if religion was a psychological aid for them, rather than a true belief. I would ask them "if you knew there was no God, would you still try to believe in God?" Their answer was mostly unsatisfying, usually responding that God was real or they didn't want to answer that, but the few that opened up to me responded "yes, I would still try and believe in God". For me that was good evidence to suggest that we utilize religion to help us psychologically. Given the long history of religion and that it has developed independently in so many different cultures, it's impossible to say religion is an anomaly, not natural, or not human. Richard Dawkins, the inventor of the term *meme* and a devout atheist, would no doubt say that it was an idea that had simply spread around like a mental virus. However, while an individual religion with its cultural background can spread as an idea, it seemed to me that religion itself undoubtedly develops in human beings regardless of their exposure to cultural religious ideas.

Let's think again of early religion, altered psychological experiences from sensory deprivation in caves, causing primitive humans doing cave paintings of swirls or zig-zags, or those large powerful rare animals. Maybe they feared or respected the power of such animals such that they considered them like Gods. Most early cultures develop a pantheistic religion, with spirits in stones, trees, and rivers. This may develop into a polytheistic religion, with a more abstract array of Gods that dominate certain aspects of human reality, such as a god of war, of harvest, and of the sea. Such religions merge and take ideas from other religions they encounter. Altered mental states seem to be a part of many religions, whether nibbling hallucinogenic bark in South America to get drug induced visions, or pastors in church speaking with extreme enthusiasm, repetition and range of volume, a call and response from the crowd, leading to a crescendo, speaking in tongues and writhing on the floor. We want an altered state of mind; a way of getting outside the *mundane* physical day to day reality to try to experience something deeper than we generally know or feel, to get behind that fabric of physical reality which we only experience with our eyes, ears and hands.

Religion may be there to enable us to operate efficiently at an optimum stress level, may be there to bring us out of the mundane reality, or may be a social construct of our society. Is it there to create deeper meaning, possibly even to provide some eternal meaning to our life, that is not affected by the wind and waves of year to year changes in job, family, friends, or country? Something that is stable and secure and isn't swayed by other confusing factors that can buffet around our thoughts and values daily? A rock we can rest on? And then there is the social and psychological benefit of being part of a church.

Maybe religion has an evolutionary benefit, bringing warring tribes together so they can fight against an even bigger enemy, by encouraging sharing within the *in-group* and uniting people in a single task, helping communities or societies fight for more resources and justifying the persecution and denial of resources to those in an *out-group*.

I guess I became more cynical of religion during this period of my life. I considered that while probably religion was useful, could I or should I really try to believe in something that was not real? At the back of my mind was always this philosophical and scientific conviction that the truth was important. So no matter how useful religion is, trying to convince myself or fool myself didn't change the fact I knew it was still not reality. Ultimately it would not help me live an appropriate life because my self-induced belief was a lie. Thus, fundamentally I became an atheist, or at least agnostic; I felt no need to really define what I was, to argue with religious people in trying to convince them of the error of their ways. I knew myself that even if others were just fooling themselves, I didn't know either, and I didn't even know if it was actually better to fool ourselves or whether knowledge itself was artificial. We just had our own internal models of reality which helped us live our lives. Some models were just more effective than others, but certainly I didn't know which.

Now I don't necessarily think it's good to have heroes in your life, and especially not to idolize people. Most people are very different from our image of them, and what we really admire is some aspect of what they have done in their life. However, the day I discovered the Chinese philosopher from 230 BC, Chuang Tzu, was a day that sticks out clearly in my memory as the first time I found what could best be described as a hero.

I was visiting my girlfriend at Nottingham University during the period of her exams, and though she appreciated the company, she was extremely busy, so I had plenty time on my own to wander around the campus. On one of these days I was strolling through the auburn and yellow leaves of autumn, casually kicking a few into the air, feeling somewhat melancholy and bored. It was then I came across the university library. I meandered in, and started looking at the ecology books to see if there was anything that wasn't in my university library back in London. Indeed I found some ecological modelling books, that seemed amazing, but I didn't really want to get my head around complex mathematics that day. Instead I decided to browse the religion section. As expected, there were heaps of books on Christianity, some on Judaism and Islam, and then a few on other fringe religions. I saw nothing on Zen, but there was a single dog-eared and well thumbed old paperback on Taoism. I knew a little about Taoism, in that it had been an influence on Zen Buddhism, but I had only ever read about it and never directly read a classical Taoist text. This book was an old and unwieldy translation of Chuang Tzu. At the time I didn't realize it was the core text of Taoism, but I was hooked. I spent the rest of the day reading Chuang Tzu from cover to cover. It was funny, it was insightful. It was like Zen Buddhism without the shackles of discipline, pretentious logic puzzles, and routine. It was a completely liberating text. It didn't really state anything, what it did was question everything. It was exactly what I needed at that time—criticizing all the preconceptions we have, but not in a serious way. It was playful and ridiculed the way we all think about reality, whilst recognizing the intrinsic beauty in every single aspect of the world. Of course I've referenced Chang Tzu's texts extensively here already, but let me just provide you another passage to illustrates the writing what excited and liberated me at that time:

> "Master Hui said to Master Chuang, 'I have a big tree people call Stinky Quassia. Its great trunk is so gnarled and knotted that it cannot be measured with an inked line. Its small branches are so twisted and turned that neither compass nor L-square can be applied to them. It stands next to the road, but carpenters pay no attention to it. Now, sir, your words are just like my tree— big, useless, and heeded by no one.'
>
> 'Sir,' said Master Chuang, 'are you the only one who hasn't observed a wild cat or a weasel? Crouching down, it lies in wait for its prey. It leaps about east and west, avoiding neither high, nor low, until it gets caught in a snare or dies in a net. Then there is the yak, big as the clouds suspended in the sky. It's big, all right,

but it can't catch mice. Now you, sir, have a big tree and are bothered by its uselessness. Why don't you plant it in Never-never Land with its wide, open spaces? There you can roam in non-action by its side and sleep care-freely beneath it. Your Stinky Quassia's life will not be cut short by axes, nor will anything else harm it. Being useless, how could it ever come to grief?"[1]

Thus, I become a Taoist, though as with Zen, I wasn't defining myself as a Taoist, I simply felt that what Chuang Tzu said was not only right, it just could not intellectually or intuitively be wrong. It made me feel good about my life, and it simplified my life. I didn't feel I had to strive for things, nor worry. When my bicycle was stolen by youths, I just reflected on the temporariness of the material things we own: indeed it wasn't gone, it was simply being used by someone else. I truly felt I had become one with the universe, and there was nothing I had to fear or worry about. Unlike Zen, it was something profound beyond sutras or religious writings, but was truly revealed in every action and process of the universe. The koans that I had previously tried to analyse, now seemed just simple expressions of nature and reality. We can read Wordsworth's daffodil poem "I wondered lonely as a cloud . . . " but we don't see the clouds, or feel and smell the daffodils. Similarly Zen koans were self expression of the writers, but our own experience was actually here in the world, not in someone else's koan; even in expressive koans such as this by Matsuo Basho (in Japanese, and translated onomatopoeically by Alan Watts):

Furu ike ya
kawaza tobikomu
mizu no oto

The old pond,
A frog jumps in:
Plop![2]

However, that satisfaction with life that I had gained from Chuang Tzu gradually started to open up a new unforeseen dilemma. Despite feeling much more content, and fully believing in what Chuang Tzu had shown me about oneness, simplicity and inherent obviousness of the operations of the universe, I felt something was missing. It felt passive. As had happened with Zen Buddhism, I felt at peace, but very much

1. Mair, *Wandering on the Way*, 8–9.
2. Ayaz, *One Haiku of Basho*, 45.

as a person simply reacting to the world: a passive recipient of what happened around me.

At this time the internet and social networking was in its infancy. This was a time before smartphones, Facebook and WhatsApp. I only remember there being MySpace and a networking site called "Where Are You Now". A Brazilian friend of mine had moved to Mozambique, and despite me not understanding these sites, the only way to communicate with my friend was on "Where Are You Now". After delaying for several months, I eventually set up an account and sent a message over the internet. Though it may seems strange now, I didn't realize at first that there were other people I could communicate to online. One person stuck out and seemed to keep coming up in my feed, a young South African woman who seemed to be interested in philosophy like me. Even though never having met we quickly began chatting and quickly became internet friends. For many years of our lives we chatted and it was bizarre because events in our completely separate lives seemed to coincide with each other. One such coincidence was that we both began dating Italians. After some time, I was going to Padova in Italy for a conference on exactly the same week that she was travelling from South Africa to meet her boyfriend in Padova. We had so many such coincidences that we called each other "twin pea". Interestingly, when we met up in person in Padova, though pleasant, we both recognized that our real friendship was based on internet chatting and philosophizing. Later my twin pea introduced me to the philosopher Søren Kierkegaard. A Christian philosopher and the first existentialist in western philosophical thought. Kierkegaard's writing went on to influence Jean Paul Sartre and later existentialists.

This book here details much of why I became a Christian, but to say that I gave up Taoism would not be completely true. Taoism doesn't explicitly talk about God, except in the familiar sense that most religions talk about a creator. Taoism doesn't really require a solid belief in God. In Malawi there are various different names in the Chichewa language for God, with slightly different meanings. While Mulungu is the common translation of the Christian God, *Namalenga*, which is equivalent to *creator*, may be more equivalent of what is sometimes referred to in the Taoist texts. However, Taoism suggests that we completely break down our artificial thoughts and arguments into a simple, beautiful, complete but often mysterious reality. The imperfections we see, in our existence are still intrinsic to the beautiful and unified whole. Core Taoist texts include the Tao te Ching, The Book of Chuang Tzu, and The Book of

Lieh Tzu. As with all religions, layers of belief can be incorporated inside, some of which even contradict core concepts. Indeed, later texts on Taoism drifted into mysticism and alchemic magical practices with a quest for eternal life, which is at conflict with the original Taoist philosophical principles which accepted death as a natural part of the progression of life. Thus while my interest led me to read more esoteric texts on Taoism, I realized it was just a distraction from the real truths at the centre of Taoism. This is similar to the magic and miracles of Christianity following on from Paul the Apostle, not only were they not necessary, they seemed to complicate and distract from the overridingly important and cohesive main message. Of course, as a religion passes through different ages, it gets shaped to appeal to certain groups and indeed different writers tend to emphasize different aspects to make specific points. Much more academically astute Christian historians can discuss such details, such as Bart Ehrman and Burton Mack, and such an analysis is not the intention of this book. However, the point I want to make is that the Bible was written by humans, even if inspired by God, and what we sometimes see as contradictions are neither because of a great mystery, nor because the Bible is blatantly wrong, but because there is a historic, social and personal context to how it was written. For example, in Matthew[3], Mark[4] and Luke[5] the last supper before Jesus' crucifixion is clearly the Passover meal, whereas as in John[6] he makes a point that it is before Passover: John had diverged from earlier texts because he wanted to associate Jesus' crucifixion with the sacrifice of a lamb at Passover, in a clear message that Jesus was the sacrifice.

Kierkegaard was very disenchanted with the church. He felt that it blindly followed varied sets of beliefs which diverged from the truth, and that the religious establishment argued over philosophical points for no real purpose, and without commitment to the beliefs they espoused. He was not formally trained as a philosopher, and felt many people would argue philosophical points without practicing their own philosophy in their daily lives. How can someone say they believe something, but then through their actions show that they don't really believe? In essence Kierkegaard's existentialism was this; rather than just arguing over

3. Matt 26:17–20
4. Mark 14:12–17
5. Luke 22:7–16
6. John 13:1

philosophy to win intellectual status, we need to show what our philosophy is by living it.

> "Life can only be understood backwards; but it must be lived forwards."[7]

This concept of living your philosophy rather than arguing intellectual points, is a prevalent concept in both Stoicism as well as throughout the New Testament:

> "Keep reminding God's people of these things. Warn them before God against quarreling about words; it is of no value, and only ruins those who listen."[8]

> "Watch out for false prophets. They come to you in sheep's clothing, but inwardly they are ferocious wolves. By their fruit you will recognize them. Do people pick grapes from thorn-bushes, or figs from thistles? Likewise, every good tree bears good fruit, but a bad tree bears bad fruit. A good tree cannot bear bad fruit, and a bad tree cannot bear good fruit. Every tree that does not bear good fruit is cut down and thrown into the fire. Thus, by their fruit you will recognize them."[9]

Not being tied down by semantic philosophical or religious arguments, but rather developing a practical way of living certainly appealed to me. While I am intensely analytical, my philosophizing was not for academic reasons, but for my personal reasons of finding a way to live with which I could feel satisfied and confident in my values, approach to life, and way of seeing reality. As a scientist and amateur philosopher I had spent too much of my life thinking, and too little doing and acting on what I had deeply reflected on. This direct and practical approach also built upon a similar feeling that was within Taoism, though often explained in more poetic language:

> "Master Chuang and Master Hui were strolling across the bridge over the River Hao. 'The minnows have come out and are swimming so leisurely,' said Master Chuang. 'This is the joy of fishes.'
> 'You're not a fish,' said Master Hui. 'How do you know what the joy of fishes is?'
> 'You're not me,' said Master Chuang, 'so how do you know that I don't know what the joy of fishes is?'

7. Kierkegaard, *Journalen*, 306.
8. 2 Tim 2:14
9. Matt 7:15–20

'I'm not you,' said Master Hui, 'so I certainly do not know what you know. But you're certainly not a fish, so it is irrefutable that you do not know what the joy of fishes is.'

'Let's go back to where we started,' said Master Chuang. 'When you said, 'How do you know what the joy of fishes is?' you asked me because you already knew that I knew. I know it by strolling over the River Hao.'[10]

Kierkegaard also said that we should live a life of passion. At the time that wasn't me.: Buddhism has it's four noble truths, paraphrased as: life is suffering; the cause of suffering is attachment; we can stop our suffering; we stop our suffering by letting go of attachment. This is undeniably an effective tool. Taoism, instead has the concept of *letting go* and seeing the universe as one naturally functioning process; a process we don't need to fight or feel overly emotional about, accepting change as it comes. When someone dies, which they inevitably will, or you lose a job, which sometimes happens, or someone you love leaves you, these changes are natural and have their own timing. What Kierkegaard was saying seemed contrary to the life of peace that I had been following through Zen and Taoism. Instead, he was saying we should suffer, we should be fighting for certain things, we should be striving to become closer to God, and it wasn't something that ended, we do it our whole life.

For several years the writing of Kierkegaard made me reflect. Should I give up peace of mind to return to suffering and struggle, and probably a completely subjective struggle, for no ultimate reason? We all die, everything we do, everything we create will also eventually finish. Death is the great leveller because for ourselves all the things we've created, all the money we have collected, the family we have made—all that is gone from us, and no longer has meaning. Yes, we can leave children, or our contribution to the world through books, cities we've helped build or others we have helped, but all that will also eventually be dead and gone. When we see animals, they are not at peace. Animals often struggle for their food, for their young. Surely humans have been biologically designed to want more, be more, do more. We live in constant dissatisfaction. Shouldn't we just accept this nature, and that we should live life with vigour and passion despite the suffering it causes us, and despite knowing that life will end? Surely this is better than a life where we passively accept the world as it is, despite being content? Is it better to strive and suffer, and to be an influence on the world, or is it better to be content and happy, but passive?

10. Mair, *Wandering on the Way*, 165

Given the way I saw how I was reacting passively to situations through my Taoism, I started to believe that maybe Kierkegaard was correct. Of course, Kierkegaard was not talking about Hedonism, but about a Christian approach to life, and living passionately such that we could fulfill God's plan and follow a Christian life passionately. He felt it was normal to constantly evaluate our relationship with God, as well as to question ourselves. Martin Luther King Junior also mentions this importance of having meaning and purpose in your heart, regardless of the suffering it causes or whether or not you achieve it. Kierkegaard's approach certainly sounds tiring, and indeed Kierkegaard made tough decisions in his life, such as leaving his fiance so that he could continue his philosophical quest. I didn't follow his extreme examples, nor did I become a Christian at that time, but I did want to be more directed in life, less passive, and to change the world around me, not just respond to it.

This question of what we do to alleviate our suffering in life is perennial. Everyone at some time feels pain or sadness, and we don't want to feel that, so what do we do? A Hedonist would suggest that to counteract the suffering of life, we simply find as much enjoyment as we can for our brief existence. A Buddhist may say to alleviate suffering we should have less attachment to our desires. Stoics, and to some extent Taoists, may say that suffering is partly because we are not seeing things as they truly are. An atheist may say that suffering is common in humans, and we need to learn logical strategies to avoid it. Many Jews believe that suffering cleanses us of evil and creates a path for us to enter heaven. Many Muslims believe that suffering is a test of faith, opening up the soul and revealing it to God. I could certainly agree with all of these, but rather than any passive acceptance of suffering, or separation between suffering and our direction or role in life, I would most tightly cling to the words of the great religious philosopher and pastor, Martin Luther King Jr. This is his last address, at Bishop Charles J. Mason Temple in Memphis, the day before his assassination (edited; and also repeated at the start of this book):

> "One of the great agonies of life is that we are constantly trying to finish that which is unfinishable. Like David, we find ourselves having to face the fact that our dreams are not fulfilled. Life is a continual story of shattered dreams.
>
> Mahatma Gandhi labored for years for the independence of his people. But Gandhi was assassinated, and died with a broken heart, because that nation that he wanted to unite ended

up being divided between India and Pakistan as a result of the conflict between the Hindus and the Muslims. Woodrow Wilson dreamed a dream of a League of Nations, but he died before the promise was delivered.

The Apostle Paul talked one day about wanting to go to Spain. It was Paul's greatest dream to go to Spain, to carry the gospel there. Paul never got to Spain. He ended up in a prison cell in Rome. This is the story of life.

Our forebears used to sing about freedom. They dreamed of the day that they would be able to get out of the bosom of slavery, the long night of injustice. They thought about a better day as they dreamed their dream. They would say,

'I'm so glad the trouble don't last always. By and by, by and by, I'm going to lay down my heavy load.' So many died without having the dream fulfilled.

Each of you in some way is building a kind of temple. The struggle is always there. It gets discouraging sometimes. Some of us are trying to build a temple of peace. We speak out against war, we protest, but it seems that your head is going against a concrete wall. It seems to mean nothing. And so often, as you set out to build the temple of peace, you are left lonesome; you are left discouraged; you are left bewildered. Well, that is the story of life.

The thing that makes me happy is that I can hear a voice crying through the vista of time, saying: 'It may not come today or it may not come tomorrow, but it is well that it is within thine heart. It's well that you are trying.' You may not see it. The dream may not be fulfilled, but it's good that you have a desire to bring it into reality. It's well that it's in your heart."[11]

I was in Northern Ireland when my mother was diagnosed with lung cancer, while I was completing my PhD. I never got to see her, flying over to England but arriving at the side of her hospital bed 10 minutes after her death. Shortly after, myself and my fiance separated and I didn't realize it at the time, but I was slowly sinking into depression. Some of my best friends had left Northern Ireland, and I was isolated and alone with my thoughts. I also began to physically isolate myself from the remaining friends around me. I wanted to die. Surfing kept me alive: I would surf the biggest craziest waves. One such wave resulted in a particularly heavy wipe-out, turning too sharply on the face of the wave, falling down its face, and then the whole weight of the wave crashing on top of me and

11. Clayborne, *Autobiography Martin Luther King*, 340–41

pulling me under the surface. When I clawed myself through the foam back to the surface, the sea currents were pulling me toward the beautiful sea cliffs of White Rocks. I was repeatedly battered against these cliffs, exhausted and unable to swim through the rows of breaking waves, or fight the currents. Finally, as I was raked down the coast, I found a space to climb shakily up the cliff wall with the remains of my broken board hanging below me on the black chord. Events such as this were an opportunity where I could still feel lucky to be alive. In the brief hours I was surfing, the beauty of the sea, the birds, the curling waves formed by the interaction between moon, sea and land, and the real fear of death: these moments gave me respite and made me glad to be alive.

I wasn't thinking much about religion at that time; my head was in the clouds and I just worked and surfed. Eventually an opportunity for work came up in Portugal, and being one of the best places in the world to surf, I jumped at it. I quickly developed a strong friend network in Lisbon. My life became filled with dancing, surfing and work. I guess I didn't realize that I still had depression, indeed I was mostly having fun, but occasionally I would cry for no reason. This was actually odd for me, because I wasn't really a person that cried, and mostly I was very logical. At this time I was not going to church or interested in any religion, and not really reflecting on religion at all. Probably if asked I would have considered myself agnostic. Once I realized that this irrational crying was probably a hangover of depression I started to see a pattern in what was happening: I would become inexplicably sad, and then this would intensify my negative thoughts about life, and over a few days I would become more and more irrationally unhappy. Depression is a problem with the brain. With depression the brain is releasing chemicals which are toxic and in turn damages itself. The further you sink into depression, the worse the depression gets. However, having realized this over time, I began to develop what I can only describe as a little conscious section of my brain that would observe my other thought processes. When that part of my brain could see me getting sad, rather than being dragged into that sucking black hole of depression, I would psychologically flip an emergency switch and turn off my brain. I was not able or possibly strong enough, simply to think good thoughts. Instead, the pact I had made with myself, was that when I saw this negativity creeping up on the horizon, before being hopelessly sucked in, for three whole days I would just operate like a robot: eating, sleeping, working, exercising. I would ignore all feelings. By blocking any emotional response for three days I could prevent myself being sucked in, and as the three days came to an end it would seem that the dawn would once again start to return, and I could be a normal person again. Repeating this time and time again, maybe every month or so, as it occurred, this depression avoidance response began to become second nature.

Depression is like having a scar on your brain. The saying "What doesn't kill you just makes you stronger" isn't really true. Some things can permanently damage and incapacitate you. Depression is like being physically disabled, but worse, because no one can see it. It is incapacitating, and life threatening. Thankfully, after maybe 6 years I had found a way to deal with it, and though it is like a deep scar, through this technique the depression gradually waned and the scar became less prominent. I had found a way to control it and allow my brain to start healing.

It was maybe a year after this that I fell ill with a stomach bug, causing me to vomit. Being quite a resolute person I had a simple way to deal with stomach bugs: 24 hours with only boiled water. So I was at home and, having reached 24 hours with only boiled water, I had stopped vomiting. I felt much better, but somewhat hungry. I heated half a bowl of mushroom soup and took a single spoon full, only to feel a wave of nausea hit me again. I vomited in the bathroom and my body began to feel shaky and feverish again. Ok, I thought to myself, another 24 hours without food. No harm at all. So I continued my rest at home. This 24 hours stretched to 48 hours as I felt I hadn't recovered and I didn't want to risk resetting this boiled water strategy. As I approached the end of the fourth day without food, I felt I should go back to work. I no longer felt hungry; indeed the thought of food repulsed me. I felt light headed, but fine. Going back to work was fine, and I just had a normal day, except that I didn't feel I could eat anything. On the second day at work, a friend invited me to the on-site cafe for a *bico*; a strong coffee that Portuguese, Spanish and Italians drink from a cup about four times the size of a thimble.

The cafe was crowded and we stood chatting together. I took a sip of coffee and quite suddenly felt transported to a completely different reality. My body was still there in the cafe, and indeed I was still talking, but my mind and spirit were elsewhere.

First, it was like everything had dropped away. Everything I logically thought was true, was superficial. All the critical analysis: the structures, logic and mathematics that we use to analyse and to discuss things, were clearly artificial, like pulling a table cloth off a beautiful table. Everything had dropped away because it didn't seem that I was interpreting reality through my senses. It wasn't seeing, not really feeling, not hearing, it was simply absolute and complete knowledge and understanding. I don't mean that I knew *extra* things—it was that conventional knowledge was just dust, and suddenly this had been blown away to instantly reveal a reality that was directly obvious and no longer clouded by preconceptions or thought processes.

What I knew completely, was that there was something sentient but also part of reality and the universe, probably what we call God. And it loved me absolutely and completely. When I say completely, I mean it was intrinsic to God and to me. I knew I had absolutely nothing to worry about. Everything would be as it should be, and it was beautiful. All was perfect in the way things work out and resolve. This understanding of being entirely loved gave me this huge sense of contentment and peace.

The other thing I realized, was that we have a destiny. Again, I was not told this, did not learn it, but simply saw that it was true because it was truer than any internalization or sense experience could be; it was fundamental. This destiny, was not my personal destiny as an individual, but me being part of a larger human destiny, for which we were all playing our part. It was like I had a specific natural path I had to follow, as do we all. We get the choice whether to follow it. Sometimes we don't know where we should be going, but we always get directed back to it. If we make poor choices, or suffer from sadness or confusion, we divert from this path, but we are always always able to get back to that path, no matter how long we have been diverted.

This whole experience lasted maybe 20 minutes, about as long as the conversation my body was still having in the cafe. It wasn't like I was spirited away somewhere. It was like there was a physical body and brain that was on auto-pilot, having a conversation, and part of me was experiencing this level of understanding completely above what we normally see as reality, but in fact is just a facade of reality; I was in reality. My friend was still conversing with me all this time, and I was responding. I didn't say anything about this experience to my friend during or following that event, but simply left when we had finished talking, and went back to my office. I was trembling slightly, and wrote down everything I had just experienced in an email, to send to myself, so in my normal life I would not forget it.

This event didn't change me immediately, nor for the next few years. It simply gave me something to reflect on. I asked myself, was it just a caffeine high following almost 6 days without food? Did it reflect my subconscious ideas of religion? Three things that really stuck out, and

I guess was the take home message for me, were: (i) all that we logically think with our brain is a type of illusion, built around the material world in which we live; (ii) God loves us absolutely completely and entirely, and is sentient—but not human or really a material being in any way we can understand, and also God is in some profound way part of, or linked with, the whole of creation while not being just creation itself; (iii) that as humans we have a destiny and each individual has their role to play in this destiny. It isn't that we don't have free choice. While the destiny as a whole is inevitable, in our lives we choose how closely we follow what is destined for us at any particular time. But also, that destiny is not a constraint. It is simply that deviating from that destiny may cause us to unnecessarily suffer, be uncomfortable, or feel lost.

Certainly immediately prior to this I did not believe in any form of destiny, as an individual, as a human species, or even as a planet. It simply made no logical sense to me and I don't think I had ever really believed in destiny. As explained before, I did believe that time was an illusion, and that potentially we could see the future, but I didn't think there was a reason or meaning behind life. For me, life was simply a process, and much of that was based around evolution and natural selection, as a process (though not specifically just a survival motivation). Although the feeling that we are all part of some larger functioning thing, such as the Tao, could have been influenced by my earlier strong influences from Taoism, this was different. Whereas in Taoism, the Tao is simply the natural functional process of the universe, the experience I had pointed to a specific human destiny for which we each had specific parts to play.

A major criticism of human destiny is the "how can a newborn baby that immediately dies have a destiny" form of argument. In a similar way that Jeremiah 29:11 says "'For I know the plans I have for you' declared the Lord, 'plans to prosper you and not to harm you, plans to give you a hope and a future'", was not about people as individuals, nor was that about their own individual lives, but was about them as humans. Similarly our destiny is not personal, but part of something larger. The death of the baby has an effect on the parents and processes, and is part of that family's life. It is inevitable and important, and despite all of our sufferings in life, even if this is throughout our whole life and terminates with a tragic end, it is part of the broader and much greater destiny. We very likely will have to suffer in our lives. Paul the Apostle died in prison; but he had a huge influence on the world. Many people, indeed all people, have effects from their life we cannot fully comprehend. The small gesture, such as the 10 year old German girl on the train that gave sandwiches to two hungry foreign travelers, can have a profound effect that echoes through time.

My religious experience also changed how I understood the Bible and certain passages that were previously interesting, but not profound, were given much greater significance. The following passage, repeating it once again, is not just about people cooperating to build a church in the name of God, but reflecting a much larger point about human duty and destiny, and the relationship of our actions to the power of God and the universes' destiny:

> "I planted the seed, Apollos watered it, but God has been making it grow. So neither the one who plants nor the one who waters is anything, but only God, who makes things grow. The one who plants and the one who waters have one purpose, and they will each be rewarded according to their own labor."[12]

Reflecting on the experience also changed the way that I viewed my own and other people's relationship to God. I stopped asking "what is God doing for me?", "Why is God allowing these bad things to happen?" and instead started to think, "how am I serving God?", "How are we, as the people that are being asked to plant the seed and water the plants, doing our job?" Wind and storms will come, people will be born and die, but ultimately we're part of generations of people in a single team working for God.

Following the experience I also felt some sense of kinship with Paul in the Bible. I could relate to his experience on the road to Damascus. I could see that his revelationary experience was from God, and just as with myself, the experience was contrary to existing thought processes and was transformative. Paul didn't eat or drink anything for three days after his encounter with God (Jesus) on the way to Damascus. It is now undeniable to me, from reading what and how he writes in the books of Galatians, Romans, Corinthians, Philemon, Philippians and Thessalonians 1, that he speaks with wisdom, love, simplicity and confidence that he gained from direct and profound revelationary experience. What occurred to me was also that no matter how much we try to explain these things with words, people will use logic and word-play to test the limits of what we say, to take it to extremes and to find loop-holes. However, the truth comes first and exists in its clear and undeniable entirety. Our logical analysis of this truth comes second, and tries to formulate word structures which

12. 1 Cor 3

inadequately communicate an approximation of the truth, or sometimes things that are nothing like the truth.

Now, for me, I can see that there are only two things we can definitively know are true; direct communication from God, and how we feel. Of course if someone says our child has just died in a horrific car accident, we would immediately feel deep sadness, even if it was just a terrible prank. But that sadness and emotional response is real, even if the event isn't. Regardless of the trigger for that emotion, the emotion itself is something we feel and know is true. Absolutely everything outside these two, are simply thought models of reality. "But what about mathematics?" I hear the more philosophically inclined reader ask. Well, yes. 2+2=4 because we defined it in the framework of mathematics. Similarly, if you drop an apple it will fall, but even me describing it to you is simply a model of reality in your brain. It isn't happening now, it is just what you expect given your experience. It's a scientific predictive structure—a model of how our material reality works. This logic is like a layer of thick dust on top of some beautiful perfect crystal-clear reality that lies at the heart of everything. Just as Einstein showed that Newton's equation of Force equals mass multiplied by acceleration, while being more or less correct at the scale of the Earth, it isn't accurate on larger scales. Einstein proved that mass changes with the velocity of the object, so how can Force equal mass times acceleration be accurate? Even now, we don't know why the arms of spiral galaxies rotate much faster than would be predicted under Einstein's laws. While science is a hugely useful tool, we must never forget that they are interpretative models.

We all live these material lives, in which we can have functioning models of what to do and how to be, but there is something much simpler, much more profound, from which all of this half-understanding comes from. This inability to use logic to describe spirituality is also why it is safer to take the major message of religion, about loving others, and not to argue too much over the fine details. Our human brains won't reach that ultimate truth through logical argument. This isn't to say we should reject logic. In our day to day lives we need logic; we utilize logic to make good decisions and science to develop technology and predict outcomes. We develop good functioning models of reality and we should not deny the power and predictive use of scientific studies; which are far more useful than myths about the physical world developed thousands of years ago. However, to find that fundamental understanding around which we as humans are entirely based; that understanding that gives meaning to everything, which is the real basis of all our actions and pursuits—this is not found in logic. Not because logic is not good enough to describe it, but because logic is a conceptual process outside direct reality.

I guess this is also why, in this book, I have described why I am a Christian. It wasn't upbringing and cultural indoctrination and it wasn't by faith in the church or by listening to pastors. Many readers may believe it was by logic—I was looking at what characteristics humans needed to live fulfilling lives: meaning, community, forgiveness, a passion for life, a sense of autonomy or free will. However, really it was none of these. What made me a Christian sprang from the seed that was planted in me from this religious experience. Without realizing, it grew roots in me, converting all these earlier concepts into something else, something that functions simply and profoundly in my life.

Would I have instead been a Muslim or Jew if I had never known Christianity? Would I even have continued to be a Taoist or Buddhist? Possibly, but just as I have done with my Christianity, I would have stripped it away to the fundamentals of the functional truth. Christian is simply a label, a name. I don't believe Jesus was the biological son of God, and I don't believe in an after-life. Many people don't even believe that Jesus existed and that there was a resurrection and virgin birth. None of this actually matters to me. I know God exists. I know our lives have meaning. I know we have a role, our job in the universe, to work at, even if we may not exactly know what it is all the time. I know that many characteristics of Christianity guide us and help us on our path. No matter what we label ourselves, we can move forward with faith, hope and joy in our hearts, but especially with love, and also by showing others that God's love is absolute and complete.

Bibliography

Ayaz1 Gohar and Khan Muhammad Ali. "One Haiku of Basho with many translations: An imperfect re-creation." *International Journal of English and Education.* Volume:7, Issue:1, January 2018.

Blume Fred, Bruce Frier, Krueger Paul, Connolly Serena, Corcoran Simon, Crawford Michael, Dillon John, Kehoe Dennis, Lenski Noel, McGinn Thomas, Pazdernick Charles, Salway Benet, Kearley Timothy, eds. *The Codex of Justinian : a new annotated translation, with parallel Latin and Greek text.* Translated by Blume Fred. Cambridge: Cambridge University Press, 2016.

Clayborne Carson, ed. *Autobiography of Martin Luther King Jr.* New York: Warner, 1998.

Constitutional Rights Foundation. *Religious Tolerance and Persecution in the Roman Empire.* 2023. url: https://www.crf-usa.org/bill-of-rights-in-action/bria-13-4-b-religious-tolerance-and-persecution-in-the-roman-empire

Darley J M and Latane B. "Bystander intervention in emergencies: Diffusion of responsibility." *Journal of Personality and Social Psychology*, 8: 4 part 1 (1968) 377–383.

Darwin Charles and Kebler Leonard. *On the origin of species by means of natural selection, or, The preservation of favoured races in the struggle for life.* London: J. Murray, 1859.

Dawkins Richard. *The Blind Watchmaker.* New York: Norton & Company, 1986.

———. *The Selfish Gene.* Oxford University Press, 1976.

Ehrman Bart D. How *Jesus Became God: The Exaltation of a Jewish Preacher from Galilee.* San Francisco: HarperOne, 2014

Engberg-Pedersen Troels. *Paul and the Stoics.* Louisville: Westminster John Knox, 2000.

Frankl Viktor E. *Man's Search for Meaning : an Introduction to Logotherapy.* Boston: Beacon, 1962.

Haney C, Banks C, Zimbardo P and Aronson E. "Study of prisoners and guards in a simulated prison." *Naval Research Reviews 9* (1973) 1–17.

Holsworth Larry. *Biblical Miracles that Appear in Multiple Cultures and Times.* August 16, 2019. url: https://historycollection.com/biblical-miracles-that-appear-in-multiple-cultures-and-times/

Kelly Russell. *Tithing is not a Christian doctrine; summary of PhD*, March 05, 2006. url: https://freebelievers.com/article/tithing-is-not-a-christian-doctrine

Kierkegaard Søren. *Fear and Trembling.* New York: Penguin, 1985.

———. *Journalen 167 (1843)*. Copenhagen: Kierkegaard Research Center. 1997, volume 18.

———. *Journals and Notebooks, Volume 4*. Edited by Cappelørn Niels, Söderquist Brian, Rumble Vanessa, Kirmmse Bruce and Rasmussen Joel. New Jersey: Princeton University Press, 2011.

Kubo Tsugunari and Yuyama Akira (translators). *The Lotus Sutra*. Taishō Volume 9, Number 262. California: Numata Center for Buddhist Translation and Research, 2007. url: file:///home/bob/Downloads/dBET_T0262_LotusSutra_2007.pdf

Mack Burton. *The Lost Gospel: The Book of Q and Christian Origins*. San Francisco: HarperOne, 1994.

Mair Victor. *Wandering on the Way. Early Taoist Tales and Parables of Chuang Tzu*. New York: Bantam, 1994.

Merton Thomas. *The Way of Chuang Tzu*. London, Burns & Oates, 1995.

Morgan Elaine. *The Aquatic Ape Hypothesis*. London: Souvenir, 1997.

Rakshit D. "Cavemen were probably hallucinating when they painted on walls, research says." *The Swaddle*. 21 April 2021. url: https://theswaddle.com/cavemen-were-probably-hallucinating-when-they-painted-on-walls-research-says/

Rasimus Tuomas, Engberg-Pedersen Troels, and Dunderberg Ismo, eds. *Stoicism in Early Christianity*. Michigan: Baker Academic, 2010.

Ridley Matt. *The Red Queen: Sex and the Evolution of Human Nature*. New York: Harper Perennial, 1993.

Suzman James. *Affluence Without Abundance: What We Can Learn from the World's Most Successful Civilisation*. New York: Bloomsbury USA, 2017.

Suzuki Daisetz Teitaro. *Essays in Zen Buddhism*. New York: Grove, 1994.

———. *An introduction to Zen Buddhism*. New York: Grove, 1994.

———. *Manual of Zen Buddhism*. New York: Grove, 1994.

Thoreau Henry David. *Civil Disobedience*. California: Empire, 2011 (originally published 1849).

Ward Benedicta. *Sayings of the Desert Fathers*. York, UK: Mowbray, 1975.

Walters Kerry. *Giving Up god . . . To Find God: Breaking Free of Idolatry*. New York: Orbis, 2013.

———. *Revolutionary Deists: Early America's Rational Infidels*. New York: Prometheus. 2010.

———. *Saint Oscar Romero: Pastor, Prophet, Martyr*. Cincinnati: Franciscan Media. 2018

Wong Eva. *Lieh Tzu: A Taoist Guide to Practical Living*. Boulder, Colorado: Shambala Publications, 2001.

www.ingramcontent.com/pod-product-compliance
Lightning Source LLC
Chambersburg PA
CBHW051925160426
43198CB00012B/2036